PIONEERS OF POPULAR EDUCATION
1760–1850

Pioneers of Popular Education
1760–1850

by

HUGH M. POLLARD

JOHN MURRAY

FIFTY ALBEMARLE STREET LONDON

First published 1956

Printed in Great Britain by
Butler & Tanner Ltd, Frome and London
and published by John Murray (Publishers) Ltd

TO MY MOTHER

TOTUM MUNERIS HOC TUI EST

PREFACE

IT is a common objection to histories of education that they tend so to emphasize teachers of great and enduring value that minor figures, sometimes minor figures of considerable interest, have to be overlooked. Thus, in treating of the evolution of educational consciousness in Western Europe between 1760 and 1850, the standard works of reference usually, and to some extent rightly, concentrate upon the prodigious contributions which were given to pedagogical progress by such outstanding figures as Rousseau, Pestalozzi, Froebel, Herbart and Fichte, whilst ignoring for the most part the less brilliant achievements of such men as Basedow, de Fellenberg, Wehrli, Father Girard and van den Ende. And this, of course, is a natural reaction in the twentieth century, for time alters many viewpoints and, after the passage of more than a hundred years, we feel ourselves more fitted not only to assess the worth of individual reformers of the past but also to decide which of them were of primary and which of secondary importance.

During the first half of the nineteenth century, however, the superiority of many of these reformers was not so evident as it is to-day and certainly by no means so in Great Britain. Indeed it can confidently be stated that, though Rousseau and Pestalozzi gradually gained recognition during this period for the boldness and originality of their educational ideas, Froebel, Fichte and Herbart, all of whom later exercised considerable influence in this country, were almost totally ignored by our early nineteenth-century forbears. For they, we must realize, when they thought about education, had other heroes and a vastly different set of opinions. And for this reason there is perhaps a particular interest in studying the Continental reformers who attracted attention in this country between 1800 and 1850. Certainly, by so doing, we obtain a different educational perspective and discover a number of individuals whose efforts are now almost totally ignored and whose opinions have long been neglected.

The present work is an attempt to obtain such a perspective. Thus, in the first eleven chapters, the emphasis is mainly on the Continent and, in particular, on the chief sources whence this country drew

educational inspiration during the first half of the nineteenth century
—sources, be it noted, as disparate as the Brothers of the Christian
Doctrine in France, the architects of the state systems of education
in Holland and Prussia, and the early disciples of Rousseau in Switzerland. To obtain some measure of continuity, however, it has been
necessary not merely to discuss the work of isolated individuals but
also to fit them into the background—intellectual, political or social
—which best helps to explain their significance.

In the last eleven chapters an account has been given of the
various means by which information concerning educational experiments abroad reached Great Britain, culminating in a detailed
examination of the career of Kay-Shuttleworth—the man who, more
than any other, may be said to have gathered together the threads of
foreign influence and woven them into the very fabric of English
primary education. In this section, moreover, only those reformers
who had personal knowledge of educational life on the Continent
between 1800 and 1850 have been included—with the solitary exception of Elizabeth Mayo. And she could scarcely be excluded for
she worked entirely under the direction of her brother, Charles, who,
in the early 1820's, was one of Pestalozzi's ablest assistants.

Yet the work should not be regarded as two totally unrelated
parts, for it is planned as a continuous whole and a knowledge of
the contents of the first half is assumed in the remainder. Indeed,
unless we know what such a man as Father Girard thought and
believed about schools and teaching, it is virtually impossible to
understand the impression which he made, for example, on Bell,
Owen or Kay-Shuttleworth. And that is why the careers of some
of the Continental reformers have been sketched in considerable
detail.

It is hoped, however, that few aspects of Continental educational
life have been discussed which do not serve ultimately to illuminate
educational thought and practice in this country. In fact the primary
object of the present study is to show how Great Britain, during the
first half of the nineteenth century, benefited from pedagogical ideas
imported from Europe and ultimately sought ways and means of
establishing herself, alongside Switzerland, Holland and Prussia, as
a champion of educational reform.

The writing of so comprehensive a book as well as the assembling
of so much detailed information has naturally made necessary the

advice and co-operation of a large number of people. By way of
concluding these prefatory remarks, therefore, I should like to pay
tribute to the following individuals: for criticism of the manuscript
as a whole—Professor A. J. D. Porteous and Professor G. H. Turnbull; for expert and patient guidance through the labyrinthine ways
of nineteenth-century education—Margaret Spence of the University of Liverpool; for assistance with regard to individual chapters—
Aage H. Pedersen of the University of Aarhus, Oddvar Vormeland
of the University of Oslo, Ferruccio Gelli of the University of Florence, Lily H. Gallois of the University of Leyden, and A. Bartels,
editor of the *Weekblad voor Middelbare Scholen en Lycea* in The Hague;
for permission to use the quotation on page 106—John Curwen
and Sons, Ltd.; for help in compiling the Index—Mr. S. Sagar; for
access to the private papers of Sir James Kay-Shuttleworth—Lord
Shuttleworth and the Hon. Rachel B. Kay-Shuttleworth; and for
constant aid and advice from the very inception of this work until its
completion—Winifred Daniel and Allan J. Artingstoll.

H. M. P.

Symonstone
  May 1956.

CONTENTS

Fix your eyes on nature, follow the path traced by her.

ROUSSEAU: *Emile*

For nature is but another page of revelation, and the training of the intellect is inseparable from the preparation of the immortal spirit for a more effectual worship.

KAY-SHUTTLEWORTH: *Public Education*

PART ONE

The Continent

1

THE STATE OF PRIMARY EDUCATION IN EUROPE PRIOR TO THE FRENCH REVOLUTION

> Si les écoles et les instituteurs paraissent avoir été plus nombreux dans l'ancienne France qu'on ne l'avait cru jusqu'à présent, il faut d'autre part, pour éviter de tomber dans une illusion que certains apologistes de l'ancien régime semblent vouloir entretenir, se rendre bien compte de ce qu'étaient en réalité ces écoles et ces maîtres. Dans les provinces les plus éclairées, les maisons d'école étaient souvent de pauvres cabanes couvertes en chaume; ailleurs, l'école n'avait même pas de local déterminé, ou bien se tenait dans une grange, dans un hangar, dans une cave, dans une écurie.'
>
> J. GAUTHIER—Article on *La France et l'Ancien Régime* 1887.

In the summer of 1788 a gentleman farmer from Suffolk, Arthur Young by name, was making a leisurely journey through France mounted on his old blind mare. As he jogged along, unconscious of the fact that he travelled in the eerie calm preceding a storm, he noticed along the roadside many peasant women without shoes and stockings who were gathering nettles and grasses with which to make soup. The spectacle struck him as somewhat remarkable, and he noted it in his diary. He was, in fact, amazed at the dire poverty which confronted him, but he need not have been. Had he journeyed in like manner through Poland, Austria, Hungary, Greece, Italy, Spain or Portugal, he would everywhere have encountered equally distressing examples of want. In many European countries the state of serfdom was taken for granted. In France, that evil at least had disappeared. In some ways, therefore, the lot of the French peasant was not so wretched as that of his counterpart in say Poland or Hungary. Even so, it struck Arthur Young as sufficiently painful to merit comment. He felt that France was heading for disaster because on every side he saw nothing but the sharp contrast of poverty and privilege.

That this sad situation should have immediately impressed itself upon a foreign visitor was interesting, for to the average Frenchman the fate of the peasants in 1788, though bad, was not markedly different from what it had been in previous years. There was perhaps less food than usual, but then conditions had always been painful, and those whose livelihood depended on the earth's produce had become hardened to the hazards of seed-time and harvest. The women whom Young saw by the roadside were the successors to countless generations of poor country folk who had grown up cultivating their miserable acres in ignorance and want. They pressed their grapes in the lord's wine press, ground their corn in his mill, baked their bread in his oven, and paid their feudal dues simply because their fathers and grandfathers had done so before them. Most of them were at best semi-literate and happy to remain so. If that were not the case, and if some peasant showed signs of independent thought, there was always the 'corvée' to bring him to heel. Among less enlightened noblemen there was a tacit assumption that the peasantry was easy to govern in proportion to its ignorance.

The reason why so large a percentage of France's population remained untutored and unlettered was owing to the fact that no funds were available for popular instruction. Education was not then, as it is to-day, the concern of the State, but of the Church, whose authorities, whether Catholic or Protestant, made themselves answerable for all instruction. The teaching of children, in consequence, often became the sole responsibility of the curé or pastor, who was himself dependent for his existence on what his parishioners provided. There can be little surprise, then, that in many areas, where a parish consisted of several widely separated villages, the education of the poor suffered neglect. As it was, the curé or pastor had too many demands on his services without the additional responsibility of equipping, staffing and supervising schools.

In the towns and cities the position was equally desperate. In Paris, for example, such schools as existed for the benefit of poor children seemed calculated rather to foster than to banish ignorance. The most prevalent and historically the oldest of them were the 'petites écoles' or 'écoles de grammaire', which dated from the Middle Ages. The first of their kind was said to have originated in the precincts of Notre-Dame, when a responsible person from the Cathedral Chapter was appointed to organize the instruction of young people. This dignitary, known as the 'Ecolâtre',[1] assumed more and more responsibilities as the years passed, and when, after several centuries, the 'petites écoles' had spread into every district of the larger towns, he held much the same position as a modern Director of Education. He determined, for instance, the number of schools that should be opened in a given parish, what pupils should be admitted to them, and what teaching staff should be employed there. The 'petites écoles' charged fees, but a small number of destitute children were admitted free of charge. These unfortunate infants, however, were not allowed to mix on equal terms with the other pupils. Even during lesson hours they sat apart and were thus constantly reminded of their shame. The classes were conducted for the most part in the rooms of private houses, and girls as well as boys were admitted to them, though the two sexes were never allowed to receive instruction together. If some enterprising teacher attempted to run a joint class, he or she was immediately excommunicated. The masters and mistresses, appointed and authorized to teach by the 'Ecolâtre' himself, had no special qualifications. They were usually tradespeople who, to eke out a living, imparted the bare rudiments of Reading, Writing and Singing. From a pamphlet, written in the seventeenth century, we learn that they were made up of 'sergeants, cooks, gardeners, cab-drivers, bricklayers, second-hand clothiers, wig-makers and tavern keepers'.[2] Even on the most favourable estimate they could hardly have proved inspiring teachers.

Since the number of indigent children attending the 'petites écoles' was strictly limited, many hundreds of boys and girls wandered the streets of Paris deprived of any form of instruction. They assumed such large proportions, moreover, that half-way through the seventeenth century several curés decided that it was their duty to improve the situation. In order to do so they founded Charity Schools where the young vagrants were taught to read and say their catechism, and so successful did these institutions prove that within a few years they spread to every district of the city and received the

---

[1] Other names were 'Grand Chantre', 'Préchantre' and 'Primicerius'

[2] See p. 2203 of *Dictionnaire de Pédagogie et d'Instruction Primaire*, Vol. II, Part 1. Article on Paris

official approbation of the 'Ecolâtre' himself. His recognition, however, was subject to one condition, namely that the new schools should not teach writing. At first the request was faithfully observed, but, after some time, the curés, tiring of so meagre a time-table, sought to introduce the forbidden subject into their schools—an apparently harmless innovation that immediately provoked violent discussion. Not only did it bring the Charity Schools into conflict with the 'petites écoles', but likewise with the 'Maîtres Ecrivains'—a guild of craftsmen, who had enjoyed the privilege of teaching handwriting for over two centuries. Their task originally had been to illuminate manuscripts, but at length they had set up their own fee-paying establishments in which calligraphy was taught according to the best French and Italian models. Their rights were guaranteed by letters patent issued by Charles IX in 1570 and, in consequence, they strongly opposed the teaching of handwriting by anyone save themselves. About the 'petites écoles' the 'Maîtres Ecrivains' could do little, since the former antedated them by several centuries, but on any new attempts to rob them of their privilege they waged vigorous warfare. The Charity Schools, therefore, had a troubled existence. They were poorly equipped, badly staffed and harried on all sides by their two adversaries, but they continued in existence in many French towns throughout the eighteenth century.

The state of primary education in France during the Ancien Régime would present a sorry scene if consideration were limited to the 'petites écoles' and the Charity Schools, but their largely abortive efforts were happily not typical of everything that was done to provide training for destitute children. There was, for instance, the estimable work of the Brothers of the Christian Schools, a society of religious teachers founded on 24th June, 1682, by St. Jean-Baptiste De La Salle (1651–1719) which has remained in existence until the present day. Its members, according to the statutes, may not aspire to the priesthood, but are bound by the vows of poverty, chastity and obedience to give children a Christian education free of charge.

In the first chapter of the Rules, which De La Salle formulated for the Brothers, we find their mission stated clearly and simply. 'The purpose of this Society is to give a Christian education to children. It is for this reason that schools are conducted so that children, being under the care of masters from morning until night, may learn from them to live uprightly, be instructed in the truths of their religion, be inspired by Christian maxims, and receive the education they require.' [3]

De La Salle and the Brothers of the Christian Schools were the first people to devote their energies exclusively to rescuing those children, already mentioned, who wandered the streets of French towns, subject to all the vices that ignorance and vagabondage engender. Their work, from modest beginnings in Rheims, soon spread to Paris and thence to many towns in France, Switzerland and Italy. Eventually it extended through most countries of Europe and finally reached the New World, and wherever the Society carried its message, it remained faithful to the wishes of De La Salle —the Christian education of youth, the cultivation of letters and the diffusion of knowledge.

We may form some idea of the earnestness with which the Brothers tackled their work amongst poverty-stricken children if we consider a typical day in their lives.

They were called at 4.30 a.m. and allowed fifteen minutes in which to dress. At 4.45 they washed. From 5.0 to 5.15 they said morning prayers. From 5.15 to 5.45 they had private meditation. At 5.45 they recited the 'Litanies of Divine Providence' and the 'Memorare', and at 6.0 they went to Mass. At 6.30 they repaired to the common room to prepare lessons, and at 7.15 had a frugal meal which was accompanied by public reading. After breaking their fast they recited the rosary. Then they donned their three-cornered hats and thick mantles and proceeded through the streets in order to reach their schools before 8.0. On arrival they expected to find the boys working silently at their lessons. Once the Brothers had entered the building, the school doors were locked against any pupils who might arrive late. The boys rose as the Brothers entered the classrooms and doffed their caps. At 8.0 the entire school recited prayers, after which the Brother in charge said grace and the boys' breakfast began. The pupils brought their own food to school and ate it in silence. Whilst partaking of it they learned the catechism. No one was allowed to waste so much as a crumb of bread, and a boy went round with a basket to collect any morsels of food that were not wanted. These were given to the poorest children who had brought nothing to eat. Once breakfast was over, usually

[3] See p. 89 of *De La Salle—A Pioneer of Modern Education* by W. J. Battersby, 1949

by 8.30, a Brother said a few words of encouragement called the morning reflection and announced that lessons were ready to start.

The boys were most carefully graded. In the first section they were taught to pronounce and spell simple words by means of a wall chart. In the second they learned to read from books, and in the third they were given considerable practice in handwriting. Throughout the time devoted to lessons, two boys knelt in the corner of the classroom saying the rosary and replacing each other at intervals of a few minutes. On the stroke of every hour the whole class said a prayer. Morning lessons ended at 10.0, when the boys were taken to Mass in a neighbouring Church. After the Service they went home for a mid-day meal, and the Brothers returned to their community house.

At 11.30 the Brothers went to the oratory for a short religious exercise known as the 'Particular Examen'. At 11.45 they had a meal, followed by a walk in the courtyard until 1.0 p.m. Then they proceeded once more to the oratory for the Litany of St. Joseph and afterwards returned to their schools.

Afternoon lessons lasted from 1.30 to 4.30. During the first two and a half hours the senior pupils practised writing in various hands —Italian, Roman, French, Secretary, etc.—and likewise did arithmetical problems. The last half-hour of every school day, however, was devoted to instruction in the catechism—a lesson to which the greatest attention was given. The teachers, by constant questioning, were expected to make their pupils aware of the supreme importance of the Christian message. Once this lesson was over the entire school sang a hymn, recited a short prayer and then left for home.

At 4.30 the Brothers returned to the community house. At 5.0 they said brief devotions in the oratory. At 5.30 a bell summoned them to reading in the common room. At 6.0 they recited further prayers. At 6.30 they partook of an evening meal which was eaten in silence, and at 6.45 they were free until 8.0. From 8.0 to 8.30 they had religious study, followed by evening prayers, and at 8.45 they retired to bed.[4]

Such was the daily routine of the Brothers of the Christian Schools, and one cannot praise too highly their fortitude, resolute endurance and deep sense of mission. With all humility they dedi-

---

[4] This day in the life of the Brothers has been admirably reconstructed by W. J. Battersby in *De La Salle—A Pioneer of Modern Education*. See pp. 69–75

cated their lives to the task of spreading popular enlightenment whenever and wherever they could. In addition to their day schools for poor boys, they ran boarding establishments for the sons of the bourgeoisie, houses of correction for juvenile delinquents and evening classes for apprentices and journeymen. Little wonder, then, that the 'Frères Ignorantins'[5] became so highly esteemed in many French towns. On the eve of the Revolution they had no less than 121 houses, 800 Brothers, 550 classes and 36,000 pupils. And what was almost as important as the help they afforded vast numbers of downtrodden people, was their significant contribution to educational theory. By their untiring efforts to diffuse learning, they upheld the conception that even the children of common people were entitled to some form of instruction. By the mere fact that they themselves were trained teachers, they raised to a respectable position the hitherto despised position of schoolmaster ; and by their insistence on the use of the vernacular instead of Latin, they paved the way for greatly improved methods of teaching. If we feel inclined to see their schools as rather grim institutions, completely lacking in warmth, we do well to compare them with other existing means of education such as the 'petites écoles' and the Charity Schools. Against such a background the schools of the Brothers stand out as most praiseworthy efforts to banish the curse of ignorance.

It was unfortunate for France that the Brothers confined their activities for the most part to urban districts. Had they been sufficiently strong in numbers to extend their influence to many of the rural areas as well, then the history of French primary education might have been a different story. As it was, the state of learning in the country districts varied considerably. In provinces such as Artois, Flanders and Picardy, somewhere about fifty per cent of the males were able to sign their names. In others, such as Auvergne, Languedoc and Provence, the percentage fell to about thirteen.[6] The number of women who could write their signature was, of course, much smaller. The disparity between the different provinces probably did not mean that the schools were better in the North than in the South. It simply indicated that there were more of them

[5] 'Frères Ignorantins' was a popular name for the Brothers during the eighteenth and nineteenth centuries, owing to the fact that they did not teach Latin in their schools

[6] See p. 1054 of Vol. I, Part 1 of *Dictionnaire de Pédagogie et d'Instruction Primaire*. Article on France

per head of the population. In any case there is no evidence to suggest that the rural school, be it in Picardy or Provence, was ever an enlightened institution. Indeed, viewing primary instruction as a whole, it is safe to say that, with the exception of the Brothers' schools, such provisions as did exist for educating poor children during the Ancien Régime were woefully deficient. In this respect, however, France was no whit different from other European countries. If we examine the state of elementary schools in Holland, Denmark, Germany, Italy and Switzerland, we find the same distressing spectacle of young people growing up in ignorance and misery. For the most part these boys and girls were either left to fend for themselves or crowded, like cattle, into miserable hovels where some unfortunate herdsman or invalided soldier endeavoured to pass on to them whatever scraps of information he possessed. In Canton Zurich, for example, there were, in 1778, some 350 country schools of which less than a hundred had their own buildings. Most of the teaching, in consequence, had to be carried out in cottages—often under conditions of appalling squalor, as the following piece of contemporary evidence attests: 'When I opened the door, I became conscious straightaway of an oppressive feeling of dampness. There before me, packed in a dark corner, was our nation's most valuable possession—its youth—breathing the hot and fetid atmosphere. The windows had never been cleaned, nor had the room been aired. The children were so closely heaped together that it was impossible for them to get up and leave without climbing over seats and tables.'[7] Little wonder, then, that the pupils were shamefully neglected, and that the schools became breeding grounds not only of ignorance and prejudice, but also of depravity and disease.

What was even worse than the cottage classrooms, however, was the type of teacher to be found in them. The point is illustrated by the following description of a typical schoolmaster in a remote district of France. In 1750 Pastor Stuber left Strasbourg to work in Waldbach, an isolated village in the Vosges mountains. After viewing the primitive dwellings of his parishioners, he asked to be shown the school. 'He was then conducted', we are told,[8] 'into a miserable cottage, where a number of children were crowded together without

---

[7] See Morf, *Zur Biographie Pestalozzis*, Vol. I, p. 18

[8] See pp. 8 and 9 of *Memoirs of Jean Frederic Oberlin* by Mrs. Francis Cunningham. London: Holdsworth and Ball, 1831

any occupation, and in so wild and noisy a state that it was with some difficulty that he could gain any reply to his enquiries for the master.

' "There he is," said one of them, as soon as silence could be obtained, pointing to a withered old man, who lay on a little bed in one corner of the apartment.

' "Are you the schoolmaster, my good friend ? " enquired Stuber.

' "Yes, Sir."

' "And what do you teach the children ?"

' "Nothing, Sir."

' "Nothing!—how is that?"

' "Because," replied the old man, with characteristic simplicity, "I know nothing myself."

' "Why then were you instituted schoolmaster?"

' "Why, Sir, I had been taking care of the Waldbach pigs for a great number of years, and when I got too old and infirm for that employment, they sent me here to take care of the children." '

Cases of this kind were not confined to one school or one locality. The Waldbach schoolmaster was typical of hundreds of teachers throughout the length and breadth of Europe. In Prussia, the sacred task of training youth was committed to war veterans; in Holland, to aged servants and unemployed cabmen; in Switzerland, to ignorant artisans, discharged soldiers and uneducated youths.

Such was the appalling state of primary instruction in Europe towards the end of the eighteenth century. It was, for the most part, a sad story of sordidness, suffocation, fetor and gloom. Yet not everyone agreed that it was either necessary or inescapable. Already, in several countries, there were men at work who, believing the evils to be remediable, were striving to benefit mankind by a more enlightened conception of education. Before their ideas could be accepted, however, many countries were to be shaken severely by one of the most tremendous political and social upheavals that Europe had so far encountered.

2

THE ORIGIN OF THE NATURE SCHOOL AND ITS INFLUENCE ON GERMANY— ROUSSEAU, BASEDOW, SALZMANN, VON ROCHOW AND RICHTER

'Rousseau, avec le eu de génie, fut un météore éclatant, qui pouvait éblouir et égarer, mais aussi éclairer des régions obscures où l'œil ordinaire ne pénètre jamais. L'auteur avait debuté dans la carrière littéraire par un paradoxe. Il les accumula dans son "Emile"; mais ces erreurs mêmes rendirent l'ouvrage plus piquant, et les contra-dictions publiques, comme il arrive, ne firent que redoubler l'atten-tion et la curiosité. Tout le monde voulut voir cette production originale, et tandis que les esprits faibles ou corrompus se disputaient le venin, les sages vinrent sucer ce qu'il y avait de salutaire dans le mélange.'

FATHER GIRARD—*Rapport sur l'institut de Pestalozzi.* 1810

THE dividing line which separated the old order of things from the new was first drawn in France in 1789. Before that date the authoritarian world of the Middle Ages and feudalism was still all-powerful and triumphant if somewhat unsteady and apprehensive. In that year, however, the Ancien Régime received a blow from which it never recovered. The Revolution, once it arrived, was sudden, but it was not, as it appeared to be, a minor revolt which, in the space of a few weeks, spread rapidly throughout the country. It came as the climax to many years of preparation by philosophers as well as politicians, and its origins lay hidden in that peculiarly fertile period some thirty or forty years previously when Diderot, d'Alembert, Montesquieu and Voltaire were busy enunciating their views. It owed much, also, to the philosophy and writings of Jean-Jacques Rousseau, that erratic genius who voiced so clearly the change of mood that was to sweep through France during the second half of the eighteenth century, and whose radical ideas were primarily responsible for transforming a passive acceptance of bondage into an active desire for freedom.

In the years 1761 and 1762 Rousseau published three works, all of which were to exercise a profound influence on contemporary thought and action. First there was *Julie or the New Heloise* (1761), a novel of sentiment, full of the drama of love and conflict, which not only thrilled its readers but likewise answered a peculiar need of the times. Writers had grown weary of the formality of Classicism and were searching for wider horizons and different techniques. In *The New Heloise* they found the answer to their quest and hailed it as an important work which would mark a reawakening of literature. In this they were correct. Rousseau, apparently by accident, had written a novel which was to herald the whole Romantic movement in Western Europe. In France he was followed by Bernardin de Saint-Pierre and Chateaubriand, in Germany by Schiller and Goethe, and in England by Wordsworth and Shelley. Secondly there was *The Social Contract* (1762), a book of great moment in the history of social philosophy whose influence soon spread throughout Europe and the New World. To many it came as a message of hope to read that man was born free but was everywhere to be found in chains, and that the abandonment of liberty meant the renunciation of manhood. Such challenging declarations had a powerful effect on the long-suppressed desire for liberation that showed itself soon afterwards in the American and French Revolutions and in the whole democratic movement of the nineteenth century. Thus, once again, on this occasion as the unexpected champion of political freedom, Rousseau became both the prophet and interpreter of his age. Thirdly there was *Emile*, a curious work which purported to be a novel. So slight was the fictional element, however, and so hard did the author strive to instruct those who read it, that it may more properly be described as a protracted philosophical essay. The purpose of *Emile* was to point out many lessons of value that man so far had failed to learn from Nature, and to stress the necessity of viewing the acquisition of knowledge from the child's point of view. It was in many ways a difficult work, teeming with new ideas which were either full of meaning or highly fanciful, but it so fascinated its readers that it gave a wholly new direction to educational thought. For the third time, therefore, Rousseau revealed himself as the initiator of a powerful revolutionary trend.

The essential idea underlying *Emile* was that society was corrupt and that only a sound education based upon freedom could transform it. Yet Rousseau did not envisage any widespread system of education in his novel. He was not thinking primarily of schools nor did he address himself to the public. Instead he pictured a woodland château in France where Emile, a rich orphan of noble parentage, was entrusted for his upbringing to the care of a wise tutor. By creating such an artificial situation, corresponding roughly to the life led by Robinson Crusoe on his island home, Rousseau provided himself with a vantage point from which he could attack the educational aims of a thoroughly decadent civilization.

His chief argument was that the current method of teaching children by commands and stern discipline was basically wrong in so far as it produced nothing but slaves and tyrants. The correct way was to give the young boy freedom from his earliest years in order that he might learn by experience. He contended that since Nature intended the child to be a child before he became a man, the tutor's duty was to await development from within rather than force entry from without.

Accordingly Rousseau divided the space of time which separated early infancy from manhood into three distinct periods.

In the first he concerned himself with the malpractices common at the time which ensured improper treatment for the child from his very birth. Rousseau began by offering his advice to the mother. Instead of calling in a nurse to suckle her child for her, she should nourish her own offspring. Such a way of feeding was correct because it was natural. In addition she should beware of wrapping her child in swaddling clothes, which restricted the movement of his limbs, since freedom, even at so tender an age, was a vital necessity. Nothing connected with the newborn infant escaped Rousseau's notice, and he pursued his enquiries into such subjects as breast feeding, the weaning of the child and the cutting of the first teeth, simply because he felt that ills occurring later in life could frequently be traced to wrong treatment in the early days of childhood when Nature had been not only disregarded but thwarted.

Once babyhood and dependence upon others had passed, the child entered on the second stage of development, which lasted until he was twelve or thirteen. During that period it was only too easy for the seeds of error to be sown in his mind, and consequently great care had to be exercised. Rousseau, delighting in his love of paradox, suggested that the most important rule for the tutor to follow was not to save time but to waste it. All education, in other words, should be negative. It was more important to prevent the growth of bad habits than to foster the development of good ones. If the tutor directed his energy towards producing a healthy constitution in his young charge by means of precepts, he would probably have to resort to coercion. But compulsion of any kind was wrong and in opposition to Nature's method of teaching. In consequence formal instruction was discouraged. It mattered little whether the boy reached the age of twelve without being able to read or to distinguish his right hand from his left. What was of importance was the strengthening of his body and the training of his senses. Great attention had to be paid to sight, hearing, smell and touch, therefore, because observation through the senses was the only way of discovering the workings of Nature. Indeed an essential part of the art of instruction lay in surrounding the boy with objects which would stimulate his curiosity and lead him to discover more and more about natural phenomena. If, for instance, he showed an interest in the sun, he should be taken to a neighbouring hill whence he could see it rise and set. No indication, however, should be afforded him that it first appeared in the East and later declined in the West. If he were allowed to observe such facts for himself, he would begin to think about them. That was the correct way of introducing new subject matter to a pupil. Information should be provided as it were accidentally, and then the mind would be encouraged to make further discoveries for itself.

The third period, which began at thirteen, did not occasion any basic alteration in the method of teaching. Up to that age the boy had been hampered by physical limitations, but suddenly he began to outgrow them. Greater attention, therefore, had to be paid to gymnastics and the fostering of special interests. The boy's eagerness to enquire into causes and effects, already manifest in the second stage of his development, should likewise be encouraged. When stimulating a pupil's curiosity, however, it had constantly to be remembered that questions could be prompted but never answered, for, if once authority were substituted for reason, the whole process of self-realization by interrogation would be nullified. The tutor should reduce to a minimum the use of aids to study such as globes, compasses and balances, for it was more important for a boy to devise his own ways of solving problems than to rely on short cuts. The purpose of his education so far had been not to fill his head with a mass of facts, but to render him capable of finding things out for himself. Once he evinced a well-marked predisposition to discover more and more facts on his own initiative, he could be entrusted with books. The reading of carefully selected texts would stimulate his reasoning powers and help to develop his individuality. Later still, when reason and conscience were sufficiently strong to guide his actions and when the mind had been sent voyaging by means of study, he could be introduced to religion. The teaching of that subject, however, should have nothing to do with catechisms and formal dogmas. It should show how the beauty, power and majesty of Nature, first recognized by the five senses, eventually sank through them to touch man's spirit.

Those were the ideas which Rousseau preached so passionately in *Emile*. He wished above all to demonstrate to his contemporaries how effectively the capacities of the individual could be developed if only he would keep close to Nature and listen to her voice.

Yet, if any real conception is to be formed of what Rousseau intended, it is important to examine his use of the ambiguous word 'Nature'. By suggesting that we should make our lives conform to a natural pattern, he never meant that we should return to a primitive state of existence. He was aware how thoroughly undesirable such a retrogression would be, but he was also cognizant of the fact that civilization had tended to destroy something of value in man himself and something which could not be flouted without resultant injury. The portion of man which was thus maimed belonged to Nature. It became warped and twisted in the same way as a tree would become warped and twisted if it were not allowed to grow naturally and were clipped into strange and fanciful shapes. Perhaps, indeed, we come nearest to understanding what Rousseau meant by Nature if we consider his symbol of the tree—a symbol he was careful to establish in the opening words of the novel: 'Tout est bien, sortant des mains de l'auteur des choses; tout dégénère entre les mains de l'homme. Il aime la difformité, les monstres; il ne veut rien tel que l'a fait la nature, pas même l'homme. Il le faut contourner à sa mode, comme un arbre de son jardin.' [1]

[1] This point is emphasized by Jacques Barzun, in *Romanticism and the Modern Ego*,

The discovery of Nature as a new force in education soon excited the liveliest interest, for it was given to the world at a time when French had replaced Latin as the general medium of thought and when educated men everywhere in Europe responded promptly to anything new in the way of philosophy. Thus a discovery by d'Alembert, Voltaire or Rousseau had often barely been announced in Paris before it was travelling with rapidity from the Seine to the Danube, and from the Spree to the Neva. Even Kant, therefore, in his home at Königsberg, having heard of the importance of *Emile*, decided to break his day's routine, more regular than that of the town clock, to study the burthen of its message. It was strange indeed that a book, in many ways so fantastic, should have had so marked an effect, but that was precisely the case, and within a few years several reformers appeared in Germany who were anxious to give practical demonstration to its ideas.

Chief among these was Basedow (1723–90), the friend of Goethe, who may claim the distinction of being the first person to apply the new theories in a school. He it was who, in 1774, initiated his Philanthropinum at Dessau, an institute combining a seminary for training schoolmasters with a boarding school for boys between the ages of six and eighteen. So successful was this venture, moreover, that it soon attracted pupils from all parts of Germany and Switzerland. Indeed education enthusiasts, quickly realizing that something completely novel was taking place at Dessau, sought opportunities of visiting the school. Additional publicity came by way of a newspaper, started by Basedow and three associates in 1776, which stressed the central theme of their feeling for Nature and emphasized the wisdom of Rousseau's principle of teaching by means of objects. Finally the masters themselves achieved great renown for the institute through a public examination of their pupils, held on the 13th, 14th and 15th May, 1776, in the presence of a large number of people from different parts of Germany, which was expressly intended to demonstrate the effectiveness of their teaching methods. The doctrines that emerged from it were basically those of *Emile*. They included the teaching of natural religion as a substitute for the catechism, and the necessity of an appeal to reason rather than

who points out that Rousseau's idea of Nature 'is the given norm that we can discover under any deformation, like the eighteenth-century gentleman's hair under his wig' (p. 33)

memory in all forms of instruction. The pupils were seen following their normal routine, and it was evident that school appeared attractive to them. Discipline, for instance, was not maintained through fear, but by a system of marks which brought privileges to those who won them. And physical fitness was clearly a matter of great concern to the pupils. They could be observed bathing and fencing, playing games and riding horseback, doing gymnastic exercises and taking recreational trips into the neighbouring woods. Bodily health, it appeared, was as important as moral training. Indeed it was quickly obvious to all visitors that they were witnessing something new to them in educational theory and practice, and something as far removed from the existing methods of routine instruction as was well-nigh conceivable. Little wonder, then, that those who were interested in Basedow's methods flocked to Dessau. It was between 1781 and 1784 that the Philanthropinum enjoyed its greatest fame when it numbered some fifty-three boarders from all over Europe.

Another labourer in the same field, who was likewise influenced by the doctrines of *Emile*, was Salzmann (1744–1811). He began his career as a village pastor in a country district of Thuringia and first became aware of the grave deficiencies apparent in the existing means of instruction when he was called upon to reorganize the schools in his parish. Thus it was that questions concerning education came to hold a particular fascination for him and that he developed a keen interest in the pedagogical theory of Rousseau. Indeed so greatly did *Emile* impress him that in 1780 he attempted, in a long philosophical thesis, to reconcile the basic tenets of its prevailing philosophy with those of Christianity—a thesis which he subsequently published under the title of *Concerning the best means of teaching religion to children*,[2] and which aroused immense hostility among the more orthodox theologians of the day. In reply to their censures Salzmann wrote *The Book of the Crab or the method of giving an irrational education to children* (1780)[3]—a fine example of serio-comic art. The author's keen sense of irony was apparent throughout and nowhere more so than in the chapter headings: 'Means of making oneself detested by children; means of inspiring distrust in children; means of teaching children to be cruel; means of rendering

---

[2] *Ueber die besten Mittel Kindern Religion beizubringen*
[3] *Krebsbüchlein, oder Anweisung zu einer unvernünftigen Erziehung der Kinder*

children vindictive; means of inspiring in children a distaste of religion; means of rendering children insensible to the beauties of Nature; means of teaching children to lie.' And these mocking reminders to his critics of the unhealthy state of education were further elaborated in a series of inverted moral principles for the benefit of the teacher: 'Mislead children often. Punish them when they speak the truth. Accustom them to take pleasure in the sufferings of innocent creatures. Instruct them that God hates all those who are not of their religion.'

So lively a book, teeming with barbed raillery, not only provoked animated discussion in intellectual circles but soon attracted the attention of those who were dissatisfied with the traditional methods of teaching. Among the latter were Basedow and his fellow workers who, in 1780, made an offer to Salzmann that he should enter their institute as a master. Accordingly he quitted his parish and took up residence at the Philanthropinum where he was given charge of the religious instruction—a task greatly to his taste and one that left him leisure for private study.

During the first months of his stay at Dessau, Salzmann preserved complete faith in the worthwhileness of the enterprise. Gradually, however, his trust was destroyed because of Basedow's irascibility, and so he conceived the idea of founding a boarding school of his own, not near a town but as far in the country as practicable. To this end he acquired a small property at Schnepfenthal in Thuringia, thanks to the patronage of Duke Ernest II of Saxe-Gotha, and, in March 1784, left the Philanthropinum to embark on several years' hard toil. For eighteen months he had no other pupils save his own children and an adopted son, but slowly the school gained in recognition among the wealthier classes and the number of pupils increased. In 1788 there were sixteen; in 1789 twenty-two; and in 1790 twenty-nine. Then, for eighteen years, from 1790 to 1808, the school flourished and never held less than fifty pupils.

The fundamental educational concepts of the Schnepfenthal school did not differ greatly from those of the Philanthropinum. All teaching was first intended to create an awareness of the beauties and influence of Nature. Secondly it sought to promote sentiments of happiness and trust between the headmaster, the staff and the pupils. And thirdly it strove to impart a deep feeling of mutual regard among the boys themselves, for, as no branch of the physical universe remained independent of another, so it was not possible for one pupil to suffer or be glad without his friends likewise being affected. In consequence, from the very inception of the school in 1784, Salzmann strove ardently to maintain an intimate family atmosphere—a point of educational doctrine which was later emphasized by Pestalozzi. Thus yet another important teacher was inspired to turn his attention to educational reform and to Nature as the first and most important of all preceptors.

A further extension of Rousseau's principles was given by von Rochow (1734–1805), who became known to subsequent genera-tions of Prussians as 'the Pestalozzi of Brandenburg'. He it was who, on his estate at Reckahn, near Berlin, devoted much of his time to agricultural and educational improvements in order to ameliorate the situation of the peasants on his land. And it was he who, in 1772, wrote *An attempt at a school book for the children of peasants* [4] where, in a lengthy preface, he spoke feelingly of the sad situation of the rural schoolmaster, of the hardness of his life, and of the worry which was his constant lot because of financial insecurity. Furthermore, in 1776, he was one of those who were present at Dessau to hear the celebrated examination of the pupils of the Philanthropinum, and it was thus that he became friendly with Basedow, the two remain-ing in close contact until the latter's death in 1790.

It would be unwise, however, to see von Rochow merely as a disciple of Basedow, for the great merit of his work was that it arose out of his own experience. Indeed he understood the problems of his workpeople because he actually lived among them on his estate and knew, none better, the poverty, misery and ignorance which were their constant lot. It was for this reason that he founded schools, encouraged teachers, wrote text-books and strove un-mitigatedly to improve the physical, mental and spiritual lot of the poor. Thus the experiment at Reckahn had great educational significance, since by him, for the first time, the doctrines of Rous-seau were enlarged to embrace some form of schooling for the poor.

And the last of the four German teachers who owed a debt of gratitude to Rousseau was 'Jean-Paul' Richter—the very choice of whose sobriquet was unquestionably an expression of his desire to be to the German nation what 'Jean-Jacques' had been to the

---

[4] *Versuch eines Schulbuchs für Kinder der Landleute oder zum Gebrauch in Dorfschulen*

French. Yet his native countrymen acknowledged no resemblance on his part to anyone living or dead. To them he was quite simply 'the one and only Jean-Paul'.[5]

The mark of originality which his compatriots detected in him, however, was not confined to his behaviour and literary efforts. It showed itself, for example, in the school which he founded in 1789 in the little town of Schwarzenbach. His pupils, who varied in age from seven to fifteen, numbered only seven and were most of them the sons of friends. Indeed, as he himself asserted, the miniature establishment was decidedly 'baroque' with a headmaster who could be compared with Saturn and the pupils with the planet's satellites. Yet it was there that Richter made a bold attempt to translate into action the educational principles of *Emile*. Thus he early determined that, since he was totally unable to apply the same kind of instruction to all his pupils, he would abolish formal teaching altogether and content himself with stimulating personal interests. But, at the beginning, we discover, he was beset with doubts as to the wisdom of this procedure, expressing apprehension lest his charges, on leaving him, should find themselves less well educated than on the day when first he had begun to teach them. Gradually, however, his fears were dispelled as he became aware of his pupils' progress, and he rejoiced to think that his rather informal way of teaching had proved so successful a means of helping them.

Richter kept his pupils five years and, during that period, collected the ideas which he published later in *Levana* (1807)—a book which, despite its strange reminiscences and abstruse allusions, presented an interesting point of view. In the passages where he dwelt on the necessity of training the body as well as the mind, and where he considered the importance of the mother's rôle in the home, Richter was clearly continuing for his generation the thought of Rousseau. He argued, for instance, that the innate cheerfulness of the child disposition should at all times be respected, and insisted that games, singing and music were all of the greatest importance. He was convinced, too, that education should, above all else, conform to the order of Nature. By means of intercourse with the natural world, he said, the senses, emotions and thoughts were quickened, and the very being of the child, thus awakened, was brought into contact with the inner life of things. But he disagreed

[5] Jean-Paul der Einzige

with Rousseau on the subject of punishment. To him punishment, even corporal punishment, was right in certain circumstances, for life was too short for every teacher to wait until each of his pupils had tested by his own experience the consequences of his mistakes. Again he differed from Rousseau about religious education. He considered that one should speak to a child about God and give him some idea of the supernatural forces in the world without waiting until he was fifteen years of age. He disapproved of pupils being isolated in order to achieve 'a fugitive and cloistered virtue'. He preferred to let them loose in the world and to correct warping influences as and when they occurred.

As may be appreciated, then, Rousseau's impact on German educational thought and practice was by no means negligible. Indeed the experiments of Basedow, Salzmann, von Rochow and Richter have great historical significance for they were early examples of a wholly new direction in the principles and practice of teaching and learning, conducted during a period of peculiar interest in human culture when many men—poets and philosophers as well as teachers—were striving to interpret Nature's message. But there was more to them even than that. They helped by the dissemination of their doctrines to prepare the ground in Prussia for an almost universal acceptance of the new trend in educational theory when that country decided to overhaul her school system following the disasters of Jena. Furthermore, the ideas of Basedow, in particular, did not go unnoticed by a few teachers in Switzerland, who had great sympathy for the new school of thought and who strove to interpret it for the benefit of poor children. It was, then, by the practice and precept of such men as Pestalozzi, de Fellenberg and Wehrli that the Nature School was next enriched and developed.

3

THE NATURE SCHOOL IN
SWITZERLAND—PESTALOZZI

'The welfare of the people was Pestalozzi's aim—the welfare of the
common, crude population. He desired to take care of those of
whom fewest do take care. He did not seek the crown of glory in
mansions, but in hovels.'

HERBART—*Pestalozzis Idee eines ABC der Anschauung.* 1802

THE second half of the eighteenth century, which saw the birth of
the Nature School in France and the first attempts to apply its
theories in Germany, finally witnessed an even greater achievement
—the triumph of its ideals in Switzerland. So avidly, indeed, did
that country seize upon Rousseau's gospel and so effectively did she
interpret it that Jullien de Paris, the French educationist, was
prompted to remark:

'Aux autres nations offrant un grand exemple
De l'éducation, l'Helvétie est le temple.' [1]

That Switzerland should thus leap to the forefront in the battle
against ignorance was principally owing to the efforts of one man—
Johann Heinrich Pestalozzi (1745–1827), a teacher of remarkable
genius, who far outdistanced any other educational thinker of his
generation. He it was who attempted to ascertain what scheme of
natural development lay concealed in the way a peasant woman
instructed her children and to systematize educational theory in the
light of his discoveries. Such a formidable undertaking, as might be
expected, necessitated many years of patient investigation and had
perforce to take into account the researches of his immediate predecessors who had already discovered something of Nature's educative
powers. To see Pestalozzi in his true historical setting, therefore, it

[1] See *Notice Biographique sur le Père Girard de Fribourg* (1850), p. 20

23

is important to recall those early teachers in Germany who first demonstrated with what remarkable success the principles of *Emile* could be applied in schools. In one sense he may be regarded as their heir, in so far as his work was the logical outcome of ideas initially propounded by Rousseau and developed by the Philanthropinists. But it has also to be remembered that he began where they left off, and that his subsequent enquiries led him into many strange regions of thought with which they would have been totally unfamiliar. Indeed Pestalozzi, himself, was all too often beset with doubts as to what he was trying to discover, yet he persevered so painstakingly with his investigations that he not only gave the most complete exposition to date of the theory of education by Nature, but advanced that theory to the point where it joined forces with psychology. In order to realize the magnitude of such an achievement, however, and to see the amazing way in which he enriched the educational life of the late eighteenth and early nineteenth centuries, it is necessary, as nearly as one can, to follow the gradual evolution of his ideas.

It was during his period of study at the Collegium Carolinum in Zurich, where he went when he was nineteen, that Pestalozzi first demonstrated any enthusiasm for the many arresting ideas which were then emanating from French philosophers and writers. There he came under the influence of two great humanitarian teachers, Bodmer and Breitinger, who took pains to point out to him the necessity of a fundamental reform in the structure of society if justice and freedom were to survive.   There, too, he was introduced to the *Emile* and *Social Contract* of Rousseau—two books which made a deep impression on him. 'The principles of liberty,' he wrote in *Swansong*, 'revived by Rousseau and presented under an ideal form, fortified the desire in my heart to find a larger field of action in which I should be able to be of use to the people.' [2]

At first he thought that 'the larger field of action' might be found in the pastorate of the Protestant Church but, in 1767, apparently convinced that agriculture alone could provide an answer to the manifold social problems that beset his native land, he decided instead to study rural economy. Accordingly, in 1768, he went to live for twelve months with Tschiffeli, the celebrated agronomist, who had recently introduced the growing of madder into Switzer-

[2] See *J. H. Pestalozzis Ausgewählte Werke* edited by F. Mann, Vol. II, p. 322

land—a period of training that greatly interested him and prompted him to start a similar experiment. As soon as he could command the necessary capital, therefore, which he did by reason of his marriage the next year, he purchased an estate at Neuhof where he attempted to put into practice many of Tschiffeli's ideas. But the results were disastrous. Pestalozzi was completely lacking in any business sense and knew little of the hazards of hill farming. It is significant, however, that he first attempted to earn a living by the cultivation of the soil, and that, when the venture ended in ruin and his financial state became so perilous that he decided to found a school for poor children, he again turned to agriculture to solve his problems. Yet his first tentative efforts to deal with children were not crowned with success. We hear nothing of the deep affection which, at a later date, he was to inspire in his pupils. Pestalozzi was at the outset of his career and had as yet no clear-cut teaching principles.

The end of the Neuhof Institute came in 1779, owing primarily to the fact that there was no one at hand to manage the business side of the undertaking. The children had to be sent away and the estate sold to satisfy creditors. Pestalozzi was reduced to a state of extreme poverty and suffered untold mental agony. He was disliked, suspected and often openly reviled by the neighbouring peasants, and it says much for his inherent nobility of character that he bore no trace of malice in later years for the treatment he received at that time. Indeed his suffering served only to increase his awareness of the ignorance of so many of his compatriots and to convince him that formal instruction alone could supply the answer to their needs. The Neuhof disaster was thus an important step in his career as it drove him to consider and try to clarify his own educational ideas.

Soon after this, at the suggestion of one of his friends, Iselin, Pestalozzi attempted to express the results of his deliberations in writing. His first book, published in 1780, was a series of detached thoughts on education, morals and religion, which he called *Evening Hours of a Hermit*.[3] But there was nothing particularly noteworthy about the work save that it clearly demonstrated how much he owed to Rousseau.

At the beginning of 1781, however, the first part of *Leonard and Gertrude* [4] appeared, which immediately revealed Pestalozzi to an astonished public as an author of originality and merit. In its bare

[3] *Die Abendstunde eines Einsiedlers*   [4] *Lienhard und Gertrud*

outline the work was a simple account of a village community, which showed how ultimately all the good peasants prospered and the wicked ones were punished—a highly ingenuous theme which might easily have descended to the banal. So sensitively was the novel written, however, and so charmingly did it portray the atmosphere of rustic life, that it immediately achieved great popularity in Switzerland and Germany. The critics lavished praise upon it and, in particular, commended the detailed descriptions it contained of the conditions under which so many poor people lived during the latter half of the eighteenth century. But, on reading the work today, we are perhaps less conscious of that virtue than of others. What immediately strikes the imagination now is the fact that, in the first volume of *Leonard and Gertrude*, Pestalozzi stressed two points which were later to become fundamental in his educational philosophy. The first was the necessity of extending sympathy towards the poor and suffering members of society, and the second the importance of a mother's love, splendidly portrayed in every act of Gertrude, the deeply religious wife of the stone mason, Leonard.

The same points were emphasized somewhat less effectively in *Christopher and Alice*,[5] which appeared in 1782. In this book the author pictured a peasant family which passed the long winter evenings reading *Leonard and Gertrude*, chapter by chapter. He divided it into thirty sections and took care, in each of them, to point out some lesson of value that might otherwise have escaped detection. Meekness, honesty, kindness and courage were all extolled, but the greatest virtue of all was shown to be that of honouring one's mother. An insistence upon that particular duty was perhaps to be expected, since Pestalozzi, from the age of five, had been dependent on his own mother for everything. The debt he owed her, therefore, was enormous and he rarely lost sight of it. Indeed, throughout his long career, he never tired of repeating that the two most important factors in the training of youth were a serene family life and the influence of a good mother.

After the appearance of these two 'Volksbücher', Pestalozzi undertook the publication of a weekly newspaper called *Schweizer-Blatt*. It appeared every Thursday, from 3rd January to 26th December, 1782, and his own contributions were mostly articles connected with morals, politics and education. In them he stressed repeatedly that

[5] *Christoph und Else*

the great humanitarian work that faced all liberal-minded individuals was that of lifting the peasant from his ignorance and misery—a task that could only be fulfilled, as far as he could see, by the discipline of the mind through instruction. Occasionally, at this time, he seemed openly to question the wisdom of Rousseau, speculating, for instance, whether industry would answer the problem of the ignorant peasant boy by providing him with work and sufficient funds to continue his education in his spare time. The same ideas were expounded more fully in *Letters on the education of the poor youth in country districts*,[6] but whenever Pestalozzi wandered from the theory of education by Nature, it was not long before he sensed that he had taken a wrong turning and sought to retrace his steps—a point admirably illustrated by the education of his own child.

A part of a manuscript exists in the Pestalozzi Museum in Zurich, written by the famous educationist at the beginning of 1774, in which he noted the progress of his son, Jakob, who was then three and a half years old. The boy was exercised in drawing and forming his letters. The names of objects were taught to him in Greek and Latin, and, when his attention wandered, his father was severe with him. He was kept fully occupied for a certain amount of time each day and left no alternative save to work or be shut up in solitary confinement. At first the treatment was successful, and Pestalozzi, proud of his son, asked one of the peasants if he did not consider that Jakob had a good memory. The man agreed but affirmed that Pestalozzi was forcing the boy too much. The words must have impressed themselves on the father's mind for a reversal of procedure was adopted. Rousseau, reinstated as the rightful thinker on such subjects, was wholly accepted as correct, and young Jakob was allowed no other instructor save Nature. At the age of twelve he could neither read nor write, and Madame Pestalozzi, who was less enthusiastic than her husband about this kind of negative education in the manner of Emile, felt it her duty to supply the deficiency. Accordingly she taught her son to read and write, but in secret and unknown to her husband.

Such incidents are important in tracing the development of Pestalozzi's ideas, for they show that his was no passive acceptance of previously thought-out opinions. If, as was later the case, he came to search in Nature for all that was of value in education it was not

[6] *Briefe über die Erziehung der armen Landjugend*

simply because of a blind adherence to Rousseau. His opinions were his own and the result of most careful speculation.

From 1783 onwards, therefore, Pestalozzi would seem to have had a clearer idea as to what he hoped to achieve. He knew, for instance, that he wished to promote the welfare of the common people and that he intended to do so by means of systematic instruction. He realized that, if he himself were to devise a new method of teaching, it would have to be based, in some way not yet clear to him, on the manner in which a peasant woman trained her children. And finally, after further deliberation, he had become convinced of the validity of Rousseau's theories. Having thus clarified his ideas he set to work with renewed vigour to define and analyse the ways in which Nature could promote intellectual growth. From this time forward, then, it would seem that two questions in particular occupied his thoughts: 'How does Nature educate?' and 'What is her method, curriculum and final objective?' The answers to these queries, often arrived at after months of patient investigation, were embodied in his further writings.

In 1785 he published the second and third parts of *Leonard and Gertrude* and it was immediately apparent that he had considerably widened the scope of the work. In the second part, for instance, he drew up a list of the various kinds of injustice and tyranny that afflicted so many of his fellow-countrymen—a list which, once it was completed, obviously helped him to a better understanding of his mission. And, in the third part, he pointed out the remedies that should be put into force to alleviate the sad condition of those who dwelt in Bonnal. The first reform should begin with the schoolmaster, the second with the school. Both these reforms were advocated in the book by the industrialist Meyer. He condemned the old-fashioned teacher, who could neither read nor write, and severely criticized the condition of the village school whose stench was worse than that of a cow-shed. The old schoolmaster at Bonnal was replaced by the young Lieutenant Glüphi, an invalid of the wars. With a girl named Mareili and a peasant boy, Renold, he began his crusade against filth, laziness and disorder. Gertrude helped them and encouraged the project by her insistence that what she had done with ten children they could do with forty. Then, after some weeks, the school began. Glüphi directed all the teaching and maintained a wise discipline. The children did a great deal of manual work and were instructed in Reading, Writing and Arithmetic. There was, at that stage of the novel, an almost imperceptible merging of the author's ideal self with the character of Glüphi, and Pestalozzi obviously drew on his experience at Neuhof for the material. Several chapters, for instance, were devoted to describing the means used by Glüphi to maintain order, to foster good habits among his children and to instruct them in elementary knowledge. In such passages one may trace the beginning of education through close observation which was to be so marked a characteristic of the Pestalozzian method at a later date. In his school at Bonnal, Glüphi insisted that the children be taught to pay particular attention to what they saw and heard because accurate observation through the senses was the first step towards real knowledge.

The third volume of the novel was intended to demonstrate how the same beauty and strength that characterized Nature could like-wise be found in Man, yet it gave little pleasure to the public. And the fourth part, which appeared in 1787, afforded even less. In it the author was concerned with the inadequacies of the existing legal system and drew up long lists of suggested reforms. The young schoolmaster was shown to be the only person who could effect any great improvement in the laws that governed society, and his re-forms, as practised at Bonnal, inspired a neighbouring Prince to ensure adequate protection for his subjects against corruption, abuse and the miscarriage of justice.

Pestalozzi, at that stage in his investigations, was undoubtedly beset with many misgivings as to what the exact functions of a schoolmaster were. But he had succeeded in clarifying his ideas on education in at least one further direction. He realized that, if he were to devise a satisfactory method of teaching children, he would have perforce to pay much stricter attention to cultivating the hear-ing and sight of his pupils.   Nature, he was convinced, began her educative process by quickening the senses.

After completing the four parts of *Leonard and Gertrude*, in which he temporarily gave expression to whatever thoughts he possessed on education and social reform, Pestalozzi's chief desire was to put down his pen and pass from theory to action, but his hopes of doing something to improve the lot of the Swiss peasants were not realized. He had, in fact, to wait many years before such an opportunity presented itself and, in the meantime, to continue his studies and literary work.

In 1789, however, his old friend Stapfer, who had been created Minister of Arts and Sciences in the new Swiss Republic, made an earnest request to Pestalozzi that he proceed without delay to the little canton of Nidwalden, at the southernmost tip of Lake Lucerne, in order to assemble and instruct a number of children who had been rendered homeless by the recent revolution. This offer was immediately accepted, and it was thus that Pestalozzi came to Stanz—the place which will ever be associated with his heroic efforts to alleviate the misery of afflicted war orphans.

It was on the 14th January, 1799, that a small group of these first entered the Ursuline convent at Stanz which had been secured for their reception. Throughout four months they had lived as beggars, without parents, home or shelter. Their misery was intense, their behaviour brutish and their condition pitiable. In fact the majority were scarcely distinguishable from animals. Yet Pestalozzi allowed nothing to deflect him from his mission or to daunt his conviction that each of them was capable of being redeemed. 'I was', he wrote to a friend, 'from morning till evening almost alone in their midst. Everything that was done for their body and soul proceeded from my hand. Every assistance, every help in time of need, every bit of teaching that they received came from me. My hand was in their hand, my eye rested on their eye, my tears flowed with their tears and my laughter accompanied their laughter. They were out of their surroundings and out of Stanz. They were with me and I was with them. Their soup was mine, their drink was mine. I had nothing. . . . I had them alone. If they were well I stood in their midst. If they were ill I was at their side. I slept in the midst of them. I was the last to go to bed at night and the first to rise in the morning. Even in bed I prayed with them and taught them until they were asleep. They wished it to be so.' [7] Thus he passed the winter. Pestalozzi's exertions were almost superhuman. The French invasion of Switzerland brought into relief his truly heroic character. He tried to do in the orphanage at Stanz what Glüphi had done in the school at Bonnal. Even his lessons and pedagogical aims were similar. We may note how he caused manual work to be alternated with elementary lessons in Reading, Writing and Arithmetic, and how he strove to win the hearts of his pupils by kindness and under-

---

[7] See Seyffarth's edition of Pestalozzi's works—Vol. VIII, pp. 404 and 405—*Ueber den Aufenthalt in Stanz*

standing in order to create a family atmosphere with mutual feelings of love, gratitude and unselfish regard for others. These important reforms had likewise been attempted by Glüphi.

As Pestalozzi's concept of teaching broadened in accordance with the theories he had thought out in *Leonard and Gertrude*, he sought, in particular, to cultivate the powers of attention, observation and memory of his pupils. At first he was unable to discern how such a procedure benefited him, but, after some weeks, became conscious that it was leading to a discovery of importance. It was there at Stanz that he conceived the idea that a simple method of teaching existed, different from anything he had so far ascertained, by means of which almost anyone, even a servant girl, would be able to instruct children. In consequence he worked incredibly hard for, deep inside himself, he knew there was an answer to the riddle of education, not far off in a problematical heaven, but there and then.

Unfortunately he was not allowed to pursue his investigations for long. In June 1799 the Russians and Austrians forced back the French as far as Stanz and the orphanage was required as a hospital. Pestalozzi, therefore, was forced to abandon his post and himself to seek refuge in Gurnigel in the Bernese mountains. He stayed there several weeks to regain his health, which had been undermined by excessive fatigue and worry, yet despite the beauty of the scenery he was unable to think of anything save the wretched orphans he had been forced to abandon. It was not long, however, before he was able to resume his work. In September 1799, again with the help of Stapfer, Pestalozzi succeeded in obtaining authority to work in the elementary schools of Burgdorf. Free lodging was given him in the castle of the town, and he took charge of twenty-five pupils, between the ages of five and eight, in an infant school run by one Fräulein Stähli. The work suited him admirably and, as he was given complete freedom to conduct whatever experiments he wished, he decided to concentrate more particularly on the teaching of Reading in the hope that he might discover more about the simple method of instruction he had so far failed to detect. Accordingly he worked for hours collecting combinations of syllables from the dictionary, which he made the children repeat aloud. At the end of eight months a public examination of all the children in Fräulein Stähli's school was held, and the results, in Pestalozzi's case, were highly gratifying. It was found that his pupils were at least three years in advance of those who had been taught to read according to the old method. Naturally he was delighted. He felt that he had managed to prove to his compatriots, at the age of forty-four, that there really was some sense in what he had been striving to accomplish throughout the years. Yet behind his mind there still lurked an immense difficulty. In trying to follow the educative process of Nature he had made two further discoveries—that all matter should be reduced to the simplest elements before being presented to the child mind, and that all teaching should proceed in easy steps from the more elementary stages of a subject to the more difficult. One vital problem, however, still defied solution. He had somehow to discover what he described as 'the connecting link between all the first elements of knowledge'.

When Pestalozzi began his second year in the Burgdorf municipal school he decided to take charge of a more advanced group of boys, doubtless because he was anxious to see if his methods would work equally well with them. Once again he directed his attention to the teaching of Reading and Language, and once again he would seem to have achieved unusually good results, as the following piece of evidence attests. A document is still to be seen in the Pestalozzi Museum in Zurich, written by a former pupil of the school named Ramsauer. He was only ten when first he met Pestalozzi and did not write his impressions until thirty-eight years later, so many authorities have doubted the accuracy of his testimony. But there would seem to be little point in questioning the obvious delight he took in Pestalozzi's teaching of Language for the memory of it was still green when he wrote his reminiscences. Ramsauer told how the lessons were conducted by means of holes in two old curtains which hung across one corner of the classroom and emphasized the fact that sometimes three hours would slip by unnoticed, so absorbed were the pupils in what they were doing. Pestalozzi would ask, 'Boys, what do you see?', and the reply would be, 'A hole in the curtain.' Then the pupils would repeat after him:

I see a hole in the curtain.

I see a long hole in the curtain.

Through the hole I see the wall.

Through the long, narrow hole I see the wall.

The second repetition might be as follows:

I see figures on the curtain.

I see black figures on the curtain.

I see black, round figures on the curtain.

I see a yellow, square figure on the curtain.

Near the yellow, square figure I see a black, round figure.

The square figure is joined to the black figure by a wide, black line.

Thus the lessons proceeded, their chief object being to make the children observe with unusual care.[8]

It is well we have Ramsauer's evidence, for we can thereby see, even if somewhat dimly, what Pestalozzi was trying to do. From immense concentration on the elementary stages of a subject he hoped to detect the elusive connecting link between all the first elements of knowledge. Up to beginning his work with the class of boys, however, he had repeatedly failed to do so, but suddenly, after he had been with them only a short time, he became conscious of a solution to his difficulties. The discovery was prompted by a chance remark of a man named Glayre, a member of the Executive Council of the canton of Vaud, to whom Pestalozzi was trying to explain his method of procedure, and who hazarded the suggestion 'Vous voulez mécaniser l'éducation.' [9]

The first explanation of his theories, in the light of the new discovery, came in an account of his work called *Report of the Method*,[10] which he wrote on 27th June, 1800, at the express wish of Stapfer, who wished to send a commission to Burgdorf to study his teaching methods. In it Pestalozzi developed the formula which Glayre had suggested, but substituted the word 'psychologize' for 'mechanize'.

'I am trying', he said in the *Report*, 'to psychologize the instruction of mankind; I am trying to bring it into harmony with the nature of my mind, with that of my circumstances and my relations to others. I start from no positive form of teaching as such, but simply ask myself: "What would you do, if you wished to give a single child all the knowledge and practical skill he needs, so that by wise care of his best opportunities, he may reach inner content?" '

Pestalozzi answered his own query in the following words:

'This can never be done without subordinating all forms of instruction to those eternal laws, by which the human mind is raised from physical impressions on the senses to clear ideas.

[8] See *Pestalozzi—His Life and Work* by Roger de Guimps, chapter IX

[9] See *Wie Gertrud Ihre Kinder Lehrt*, chapter I

[10] *Die Methode, eine Denkschrift Pestalozzis*

'I have tried to simplify the elements of all human experience according to these laws, and to put them into a series of typical examples that shall result in spreading a wide knowledge of Nature, general clearness of the most important ideas in the mind, and vigorous exercises of the chief bodily powers, even among the lowest classes.

'That which Nature puts before us, scattered and over a wide area, the Art (i.e. the Art of Teaching) puts together in narrower bounds and brings nearer to our five senses, by associations which facilitate the power of memory and strengthen the susceptibility of our senses, and make it easier for them, by daily practice, to present to us the objects for a longer time and in a more precise way.' [11]

The commissioners, for whom Pestalozzi wrote his exposition, visited the Burgdorf School in August and September 1800. In their report, dated 1st October, they noted that the children had been taught to read, write and add in an incredibly short period of time. In the first class they found the pupils learning to spell successfully by means of movable letters; and, in the second, they heard a more advanced group reading with accuracy and speed. Such results, the commissioners pointed out, were remarkable, especially as many of the boys had been with Pestalozzi only a matter of weeks.

Encouraged by their favourable views, Pestalozzi took a decisive course of action. He resigned from his teaching post in Burgdorf and, on 24th October, 1800, announced through the press that he was about to open an Institute of Education.

Thanks to the generosity of Stapfer, the new establishment was under way by the end of 1800, and Pestalozzi had at last achieved the great ambition of his life—an Institute in which he could perfect his method of teaching and a Normal School in which he could train the masters to apply it. One thing remained for him to do, and that was to give an account of the principles he sought to perpetuate. He did so in *How Gertrude Teaches Her Children*, which was published in October 1801.

It would be a mistake to connect the book with the earlier *Leonard and Gertrude* for it was not a work of fiction and the character of Gertrude played no part in it. It was a series of fourteen letters addressed by Pestalozzi to the librarian Gessner, in which the author attempted to clarify his views on teaching.

[11] See Appendix (pp. 199, 200 and 201) to *How Gertrude Teaches Her Children*. Swan Sonnenschein edition, 1907

In the first three letters Pestalozzi gave short accounts of his own life and those of his assistants, Krüsi and Tobler, up to the time of beginning the book. Then, in the fourth, fifth and sixth he described the laws governing the intellectual development of man, as he conceived of them. He reaffirmed the two chief hypotheses of his earlier *Report of the Method*: first that 'Anschauung' [12] was the basis of our knowledge, and secondly that it was possible to establish a natural method of classification for sense impressions.

Pestalozzi's great aim was to discover the method by which sense impressions might be arranged in sequence before being presented to the child mind, and thus to transform education into an 'Art' obeying definite laws. At first he was unable clearly to discern the primary data from which the 'Art' proceeded, but gradually became aware of certain truths connected with them. All knowledge was derived from sense impressions and was developed and clarified by means of the three concepts: Number, Form and Language. He therefore set himself to study the method by which an educated man strove to make clear to himself a situation distinguished by confused and wholly new impressions. Pestalozzi noted that, in a set of unfamiliar circumstances, the man observed: first, how many objects were displayed before him (i.e. Number); secondly, their appearance and outline (i.e. Form); and thirdly, how best he could describe each one of them by a particular sound or word (i.e. Language).

Pestalozzi concluded, therefore, that Number, Form and Language were the three pillars on which the educational edifice rested and, in the light of his conclusion, decided that children should be taught:

(1) to consider each object that was brought before them both as a separate unit in itself and as a member of a family of related objects;
(2) the size and proportions of the object;
(3) the words which applied to or described the said object.

In other words, children should be instructed on the threefold principle of counting, measuring and naming. This threefold

---

[12] 'Anschauung' is an almost untranslatable term which may roughly be paraphrased as 'first impressions of objects' or 'intuition'. It must be remembered that both Rousseau and Pestalozzi were empiricists and that they conceived of the mind at birth as a 'tabula rasa'. In consequence they believed that the whole of our knowledge came from sense experience

activity formed the basis of all knowledge, and the chief purpose of education lay in cultivating and strengthening the growth and union of its three component parts.

In his observation of the cultivated man placed in a strange environment and groping to orientate himself Pestalozzi noted that knowledge acquired through Number, Form and Language went through three stages of development. First it was certain knowledge (bestimmte Erkenntniss); later clear knowledge (klare Erkenntniss); and finally wholly distinct knowledge (deutliche Erkenntniss).[13]

The practical application of his method to the 'Art' of teaching was indicated in detail by Pestalozzi in the seventh and eighth letters, but, for some reason known only to himself, he chose to deal with the three concepts in the reverse order.

Elementary instruction in Language comprised the study of sounds and words. Pestalozzi affirmed that the mother should first familiarize the small child with such words as ba ba ba; da da da; ma ma ma; la la la, etc. in order to accustom his ear to her simple utterances. Next she should put a vowel in front of the consonants and make the child repeat the sounds aloud: ab ba; am ma; al la, etc. Later she should combine a vowel with two consonants: bud dub; bic cib; fag gaf, etc., and finally she should cause long and difficult words to be said aloud, beginning with the first syllable and adding thereto in succession the other elements of the word: apho, aphoris, aphorism; mu, muni, municip, municipal, municipality, etc. Such a system of learning Pestalozzi called his 'ABC of Method'. Whilst it was in progress the child should begin to learn names. It was important for him to increase his vocabulary in as many ways as he could in order to designate things exactly, and to ensure that this should happen Pestalozzi stressed the mother's duty to show her child pictures which would extend his familiarity with words. Such knowledge would soon embrace the names of all important things connected with the child's environment and afterwards be extended to include words about Nature, History and Geography. 'Experience has taught me,' wrote the author, 'that it is possible to bring children to learn lists of names perfectly by heart, in the time which is given to complete their power of reading. The gain to the children at this time, of so wide and complete a knowledge of so many and such comprehensive lists of names, is immense for making later in-

[13] See *How Gertrude Teaches Her Children*, pp. 86–89

struction easier (and is only to be regarded as the chaotic collection
of materials for a house that will be built later).' [14]

The study of Drawing and Handwriting began with an 'ABC of
Form', described by Pestalozzi as 'the art of simplifying and defining
the principles of measurement by exact separation of all inequalities
apparent to the observer'. The basis of the 'ABC of Form' was the
square—the elementary figure from which all others traced their
origin. Within the framework of a square, then, Pestalozzi devised
a series of exercises based on horizontal and vertical lines by means
of which all angles could be measured. From constantly performing
these exercises the child was enabled 'to judge rightly and express
himself clearly about every object in Nature, according to its external
proportions and its relations to others'. He was thus able, whenever
he looked at an object, 'to describe and name, not only the proportion of height to breadth, but the proportion of every single
deviation of its form from the square'.[15] Once all the exercises had
been thoroughly completed, then drawing presented no further
difficulties and could be taught with ease.

The 'Art of Drawing' was 'the power of representing to oneself
the sense impression made by any object, its outline and the characteristics contained within the outline, by means of similar lines, and
of being able to imitate the lines accurately'.[16] In other words, once
the child acquired 'the properties of the compass in his eye', he had
gained the capacity to measure. If, afterwards, he learnt accurately
to transfer to paper what his eye observed, he knew how to draw.
Pestalozzi began his teaching of Drawing with a series of exercises
based on the horizontal line. He next proceeded to the vertical line
and finally to the right angle. Handwriting became a kind of linear
drawing which was nothing more than a game when once the child
possessed a trained eye and a steady hand. Pestalozzi insisted that,
in the initial stages of Drawing and Handwriting, the pupil should
use a slate and chalk.

The 'Elementary Art of Number' had as its fundamental principle
the formula 'one and one makes two; one from two leaves one'.
Pestalozzi began his teaching of Arithmetic by presenting the child
with small pieces of cardboard with letters inscribed on them, by
means of which the pupil learnt not only to recognize the letters of

[14] *How Gertrude Teaches Her Children*, p. 112
[15] *Ibid.* p. 197   [16] *Ibid.* p. 112

the alphabet, but also to count, add and subtract. The pieces of cardboard were later replaced by pictures on which were large squares divided by horizontal lines in such a way as to constitute several rectangles of equal dimension. The topmost rectangle might be divided by vertical lines into ten small squares, the second rectangle into twenty, the third into thirty and so on. It would soon become obvious to any child that the second rectangle had twice the number of squares as the first, the third three times as many, etc. Thus the principle of fractions could easily be mastered because, with a little explanation from the teacher, it could be seen.

And the final question with which Pestalozzi dealt in *How Gertrude Teaches Her Children* was that of moral and religious education. He wondered how the sentiments of love, trust, gratitude and obedience were developed in the human heart, and found that they had their origin in the relationship that existed between the mother and her young child. The feelings first awakened by maternal tenderness in the heart of the infant were later transformed into moral and religious sentiments. It was through the idea of what his mother was to him that the child later became aware of God. 'The feelings of love, gratitude and trust that are developed at her bosom, extend and embrace God as father, God as mother.' [17] As Pestalozzi repeatedly stressed, it was on the natural feelings existing between a mother and her child that he based his entire educational philosophy.

How Gertrude Teaches Her Children was the most complete exposition of his pedagogical theories that Pestalozzi ever wrote and soon became the subject of animated discussion among those who sought to promote the welfare of the masses by means of systematic instruction. We cannot, however, appreciate the tremendous impact it made on current educational thought unless we recall those dismal institutions and squalid cottages where, for the most part, primary teaching was given. In schools of this kind, where the joy of human life was well-nigh stamped out, countless generations of poor children received their first introduction to letters and came to identify learning with nothing save constant floggings and a hatred of their teachers. Little wonder that they believed that no kind of training could be effective unless it was distasteful and that no subject could be taught in schools unless it was difficult and uninteresting. So

[17] *How Gertrude Teaches Her Children*, p. 197

much trouble was taken to make their studies unpleasant that they could hardly have believed otherwise. Yet those were the very idols of false education that Pestalozzi set out to destroy. In his book he clearly demonstrated that there was a new method of teaching which, if it were adopted, would interest and stimulate both teachers and taught. Through painstaking enquiry he showed that, if only masters would follow Nature instead of forcing it against its bent, ignorance and prejudice could be combated. That was why his revelation was so tremendously important and why his reflections on the acquisition of knowledge, despite their difficulty, continued to stimulate interest and discussion not only during his lifetime but long after his death. He had somehow managed, in the fourteen letters which together comprised *How Gertrude Teaches Her Children*, to summarize a portion of educational truth to which every age could give its own interpretation.

Once he had clarified his ideas on teaching, as far as he was ever able to do so, Pestalozzi devoted his time more to practice than to theory. The year 1801, therefore, was a turning point in his career. From that date he became more and more absorbed with training teachers to follow the new method of instruction he had devised. In endeavouring to trace the development of Pestalozzi's ideas, therefore, it would seem wise not to proceed beyond 1801 for two reasons —first because by that date he had said everything he had to say concerning educational theory, and secondly because, thenceforward, he fell more and more under the power of his various collaborators. So powerful indeed was the influence exercised upon him by such men as Niederer and Schmid that the practical schemes of work carried out in his name were frequently more theirs than his. The older Pestalozzi grew, the less capable he became of exercising any control over his Institute and the more prone was he to quarrel with his associates.

Yet, despite the troubles which seemed to be inherent in its very constitution, the Pestalozzi Institute achieved great fame all over Europe. Whether at Burgdorf, Münchenbuchsee or Yverdun, it remained, for quarter of a century, a place of pilgrimage for all those who were interested in questions of education. Many of the visitors came from Germany where *How Gertrude Teaches Her Children* received a great deal of publicity. On their return they wrote accounts of what they had seen, but it mattered little whether they approved or disapproved of the new theories. Pestalozzi's methods had become a matter of general interest and his Institute the cynosure of every teacher's eye.

Herbart stayed for some weeks at Burgdorf in 1801 and afterwards acknowledged his debt to the great Swiss reformer in his *Pestalozzi's Idea of an ABC of Anschauung*,[18] which appeared the following year. Froebel visited Pestalozzi on two occasions, once in 1805 and again in 1808 when he stayed for two years with three of his pupils. Talleyrand, Wilhelm von Humboldt, Madame de Staël and Catherine the Great likewise came to see the renowned Institute.

More important than such visits, however, was the interest which individual countries began to take in Pestalozzi's work. Fichte, in his celebrated *Addresses to the German Nation*,[19] declared wholeheartedly that the Prussian reform of education should begin with a consideration of the new methods of instruction. The Prussian Government, in reply to Fichte's eloquent appeals and inspired by the wise counsel of Nicolovius, decided to send young men to learn what they could of the new methods. Other parts of Germany followed Prussia's example and Holland, too, despatched a number of young masters to Pestalozzi.

From such information we can readily appreciate how great a subject of interest the Swiss reformer became during the first half of the nineteenth century. Yet how much of his theory was genuinely understood is difficult to say. One may surmise that such explanations of it as were given in *Report of the Method* and *How Gertrude Teaches Her Children* were usually taken to indicate that teaching should fulfil the following tasks: develop man as a whole, guide and stimulate self-activity, foster the growth of knowledge through the training of the senses, and observe a right gradation and progression in development. But that was by no means all that Pestalozzi said and ignored one of his basic contentions—that all instruction should be based on 'Anschauung'. Such a highly abstruse consideration, however, signified little to the average teacher, who was quite content to leave its interpretation to other educational philosophers such as Herbart and Froebel.

It would seem, indeed, that the more recondite educational truths, such as that of 'Anschauung', which Pestalozzi sought to

---

[18] *Pestalozzis Idee eines ABC der Anschauung*
[19] *Reden an die deutsche Nation*

perpetuate, were revealed to him in moments of illumination when he achieved complete union with a child's mind and saw, clearly and unmistakably, all the difficulties in a particular problem. He held his views precisely because of that faculty of vision. That was his distinguishing mark. That was what differentiated him from the logician or philosopher, for he based his belief not on demonstrated facts but on an intuitive inner knowledge. The doctrines which he tried to propound were new and difficult. Systematic psychology had barely begun and Pestalozzi moved into a new world of thought and practice as a pioneer, being beset with all a pioneer's difficulties and discouragements. It was an impossible undertaking at that time of day to base a system of education on an adequate psychological foundation, because psychological analysis was in its infancy. Pestalozzi had a twofold task: whereas his main aim was to establish education on the basis of the laws of mental operation, it was no less important to explain what the laws of mental operation were. Complete success could not be his, not because the man was too small, but because the task was too great.

It would be unfair, however, because of a limitation which was not of his making, in any way to minimize the tremendous results of Pestalozzi's work. By a series of careful experiments, he elaborated and formulated the new theory of education started by Rousseau, which sought its inspiration in the influence of Nature. By a completely fresh approach to the whole problem of the child's acquisition of knowledge, he prompted further investigations by such eminent thinkers as Herbart and Froebel. By improved methods of individual approach to the pupil's needs, he produced a new creative impulse in education. By demonstrating that teaching could be a kind and considerate form of guidance instead of a cruel and repressive means of discipline, he forced the whole scholastic world to revise its ideas not only on formal training but on the nature and destiny of man himself. And finally, by means of all these achievements, he aroused and inspired his contemporaries to such tremendous efforts that countless thousands of children, who might otherwise have been forced to forgo the advantages of a formal education, were enabled to enter into a richer and fuller life.

4

THE NATURE SCHOOL IN SWITZERLAND—DE FELLENBERG

'And he gave me it for his opinion that whoever could make two ears of corn, or two blades of grass, to grow upon a spot of ground where only one grew before, would deserve better of mankind and do more essential service to his country, than the whole race of politicians put together.'

JONATHAN SWIFT—*Gulliver's Travels*

AMONG the contemporaries and fellow countrymen of Pestalozzi who occupied their lives interpreting the message that Nature held for education, none was more important than Philippe Emanuel de Fellenberg (1771–1844). He was an agriculturist of distinction, who possessed a more intimate knowledge of the natural world than almost anyone of his time, and a man of culture, who founded one of the most interesting educational estates that Europe has ever known. Yet his own generation was in many ways loth to acknowledge his greatness and history has tended to ignore his achievements.

This was principally owing to the fact that de Fellenberg's enemies early dubbed him a thinker of little consequence, who was content merely to copy Rousseau and Pestalozzi, and thus attached a stigma to his name which was difficult to erase. By so doing, however, they rendered him an injustice and misinterpreted his attitude towards his two compatriots. He was not, as were they, primarily concerned with formulating a theory of education. Rather was he a man of practical skill who, once that theory had satisfactorily been enunciated, was prepared to devote his energy and money to seeing that it was interpreted in the best possible manner. To consider him as a plagiarist, therefore, is false. The debt he owed to Rousseau and Pestalozzi was enormous, but he was at all times prepared to acknowledge it.[1]

---

[1] See *The Education of the Peasantry in England; what it is and what it ought to be* by B. F. Duppa (pp. 24–28)

It would be strange if that had not been the case, for de Fellenberg, alone among the Nature School of teachers, was given an education which resembled that of Emile. He was, for instance, entrusted to the care of a private tutor from his earliest years and allowed to spend his time roaming the countryside near his father's castle at Wildenstein on the bank of the river Aar. The tutor, who was given sole charge of the boy's training, was Albert Rengger, the friend of Pestalozzi who later became Minister of the Interior to the Swiss Republic. As might be expected, therefore, de Fellenberg was early introduced to the educational ideas of his great contemporary. Indeed, before he was fifteen, he was not only familiar with *Leonard and Gertrude* but had found therein the inspiration which was to shape his life's work. As he himself said: 'The book made a deep impression upon me. Every time I read it, I was more and more convinced of its truth, and it was in an excess of deep feeling after studying its message that I vowed to my mother that I would dedicate my life to poor forsaken children.' [2]

It is important to remember these words in any estimate of de Fellenberg's character for his sense of mission was always intense. He had no taste for purely frivolous pursuits, such as his position and wealth would have made possible. He was merely anxious to do some useful work in the world. Accordingly, at the age of sixteen, in order to prepare himself for the cause to which he was committed, he left the family home and, for the next ten years, did little save investigate the cultivation of land and the living conditions of rural populations. On foot and with his knapsack slung across his shoulder, he visited the most remote regions of Germany, the Tyrol, Hungary and Switzerland, offering his services as a voluntary workman and willingly enduring many privations in order to harden his mind and body for the testing time which, he felt, awaited him.

This period of preparation was of great importance to de Fellenberg for it was then that he conceived the idea that, by means of a system of education based on agriculture, he could solve many of the social problems which confronted his compatriots. Accordingly, in 1796, with that thought in mind, he returned to Berne. He soon found, however, that the times were unpropitious for any far-reaching plans of social amelioration. His family was dispirited, an atmosphere of impending evil overhung his native land and members of

[2] *Monumenta Germaniae Paedagogica*, Vol. 25, 58

the aristocracy went about in fear of their lives because of the dangers that threatened from the neighbouring French Republic. Such a mood of gloom boded ill for his long-cherished schemes and so he temporarily laid them aside. It was well that he did so, moreover, for, in 1798, the French armies invaded Switzerland and he was forced to seek refuge in Würtemberg.

Throughout these months of waiting he would appear to have suffered great mental agony and to have lost all faith in humanity and in his capacity to help it. Once he returned to Switzerland, however, he became so forcibly impressed by the depths of misery into which thousands of families had sunk that an urge to alleviate their misery soon reasserted itself. It seemed to him that the misery which his fellow citizens had endured as a result of the war had served only to increase their viciousness. Many had abandoned their offspring and taken to a life of vagabondage. Large gangs of undisciplined children wandered the roads in search of food. Poverty and disease confronted him on every hand and, amidst it all, drunkenness and immorality flourished. The spectacle was one upon which de Fellenberg could only look with horror and, in a spirit of bold resolve, he determined to do everything in his power to banish it. In an act of self-dedication, written in 1799, he stated in simple terms the task he set himself to perform:

'Born as I am one of the aristocracy of Switzerland, let me show myself worthy of pre-eminence by deserving it. I will place every distinction of rank, which is inconsistent with the welfare of my fellow creatures, upon the altar of my country, and embrace a profession "despised and neglected of men". . . . All that I wish is "peace on earth and goodwill towards men". *I will turn schoolmaster*—a somewhat bold resolve, when one considers the general contempt in which that important office is held.' [3]

In order to realize his ambition de Fellenberg purchased the estate of Hofwyl on the outskirts of Berne and moved there towards the end of 1799. His father's death shortly afterwards put him in possession of a considerable fortune, so he was able to embark on his life's work without any financial qualms in a way that Pestalozzi at Neuhof had never been able to do. He pursued it conscientiously for the next forty years and, during that time, succeeded in making Hofwyl

[3] Quoted by B. F. Duppa in a footnote to Appendix I of *The Education of the Peasantry in England; what it is and what it ought to be* (1834)

famous throughout Europe. Yet, before discussing how he accomplished so remarkable a feat, it is perhaps wise, in view of the fact that his theories underwent no radical change from 1799 onwards, first to examine what rôle he expected education to play.

As he contemplated the world at large de Fellenberg was disgusted by the way in which society consistently refused to accept responsibility for the enlightenment of its members. Man, he said, had two sides to his nature—the temporal and the spiritual—but society refused to recognize so obvious a fact. It continued to pay lip service to such qualities as humility and mercy whilst inwardly extolling pride and profit. The result was that nation despised nation, every man hated his neighbour and virtue fought a losing battle with vice. But so distressing a state of affairs was by no means necessary. Enormous changes in the well-being of individuals and peoples could be effected if only men would submit to the discipline of hard work and endeavour to improve themselves. That was why education alone could provide an escape from the impasse in which the world found itself.[4]

With that thought in mind de Fellenberg determined to bring about a reformation of the appalling conditions which threatened the very foundation of the Swiss constitution. But such a task was by no means easy for, as a result of the revolution, all community of spirit had been destroyed. Members of the aristocracy, bourgeoisie and peasantry had forgotten their mutual responsibilities and were bitterly hostile one to another. What was needed, it seemed to him, was some force that would bind them together and make them conscious of their interdependence. After some deliberation, therefore, he decided that the most efficacious way of achieving his objective was to provide a wholly distinct education for all three sections of the community.

Thus he embarked on his life's work and made agriculture the basis of his plan because in it he saw a source of development for nations which so far had received but scant consideration. The nurture of the soil held many advantages. If pursued with skill it was favourable both to physical health and intellectual growth;

---

[4] See p. 273 of *Publications of the Central Society of Education* (second volume), 1838. Letter from de Fellenberg entitled 'Mes observations sur les rapports qui existent entre l'éducation et la politique'

if allied to science, it gave promise of being a source of economic wealth which would bring untold benefits to the labouring classes.

De Fellenberg began, therefore, by giving consideration to the needs of the servant men whom he employed on his estate. 'The peasant who follows the plough,' he stated, 'like the ox which goes before it, sinks from day to day deeper into a state of hopeless inanity and insensibility.' [5]

After experimenting for some years he founded, in 1804, his ' Practical School for Agriculture and Manual Work', which was designed to show the peasants how to set about their work and how to make use of recent agronomical improvements. To help them he constructed a forge and mechanics' workshop where revolutionary implements for land cultivation were made. They included an 'exterminator' for destroying weeds, a 'scarificator' for paring soil, a new type of plough copied from a model imported from England and a drill, designed by de Fellenberg himself, for sowing seeds. A portion of the estate was given up to an experimental farm where elementary tests with regard to crop production, tillage and fertilization were tried and noted.

The work could not proceed rapidly because de Fellenberg had first to win the confidence of those whom he sought to help. This was by no means easy and, during the initial stages, he frequently encountered fierce opposition. Once he was able to show his employees the results of his experiments, however, their attitude changed and large numbers of young labourers came to him begging to be allowed the advantage of his special tuition. Within five years, therefore, de Fellenberg was in a position to demonstrate two facts of importance: first that, as a result of scientific labour, the land of the estate had increased to five times its former worth; and secondly that, by reason of his training, humble country folk had been turned into efficient farmers. Attracted by so bold a claim visitors began to arrive at Hofwyl to see exactly what had been achieved, to whom de Fellenberg rarely missed an opportunity of pointing out the peculiar advantages to be gained from a life closely connected with the soil. Above all he stressed the fact that such work demanded great powers of concentration and was beneficial both to the bodily strength and moral worth of the peasants. In addition it was capable of improving

[5] *Report of M. le Comte de Capo d'Istria*, p. 38

their standard of living and so could provide a solid basis for the social structure of the country. Such an improvement was obviously necessary and to the advantage of everyone. If it were brought about, it would be achieved by the efforts of the lowest classes. A healthy labouring population, he maintained, would act as a moral lever to the rest of the community and thus, in time, effect a regeneration of society from the bottom upwards.

Having first considered the labourers, de Fellenberg next turned to those who supervised them. In 1807 he created his 'Advanced Institute of Agronomy' to provide a scientific training for young men who, one day, would be bailiffs or direct the development of rural areas. The education he offered them endeavoured to keep them abreast of the latest developments in agricultural research. He expounded, for instance, the new principles of crop production and soil management which Dr. Albert Thaër had been advocating in Hanover since 1794 and enlarged on the successes and failures of Tschiffeli, who had introduced the growing of madder into Switzerland. Theory, however, was by no means all that de Fellenberg insisted upon. In addition each student was made to take charge of a group of peasants, to supervise their labours, to see that their machines were kept in constant repair and to be answerable for the general welfare of their lives. The course, therefore, held many advantages. It kept the students occupied from morning until evening, provided an excellent training in responsibility and linked the destinies of the bailiff and peasant in a way that many previously would have deemed impossible.

As early as 1804 de Fellenberg considered the idea of inaugurating summer courses for the elementary schoolmasters of Berne. The project was shelved at the time, however, because of the arrival of Pestalozzi in the neighbourhood. The renowned teacher had recently been expelled from Burgdorf, and the authorities of Berne had given him the monastery of Münchenbuchsee in order to carry on his educational experiments. Hofwyl lay close by and there seemed little point in de Fellenberg's opening a rival institution especially as a plan was soon under consideration to associate them in a joint enterprise. De Fellenberg with his remarkable powers of organization was to make himself responsible for the administration of a Normal School for the training of teachers, whilst Pestalozzi undertook the actual instruction. But the results were unhappy and

Pestalozzi soon showed that he would brook no kind of interference with his plans.[6]

This contact with Pestalozzi, however, was not without influence upon de Fellenberg. Indeed, as a result of it, he came to realize that, if Hofwyl were truly to fulfil its destiny, it would have perforce to cater for the needs of children as well as adults. From 1805 onwards, therefore, he gave a great deal of thought to the manner in which youth should be trained.

As far as educational theory was concerned he declared boldly that he was a disciple of Pestalozzi.[7] No one, he stated, who had studied *Leonard and Gertrude* and *How Gertrude Teaches Her Children* could fail to realize the importance of their discoveries. They showed unmistakably that, if a teacher would but follow certain rules, he could 'light up a torch in the mind of every pupil'—a torch which would enable that pupil to see the natural world not merely as a storehouse of information but also as a wellspring of the formative influences which shaped his character. Thus the greatest contribution which Pestalozzi had given to contemporary thought was undoubtedly his proof that all true education rested on 'Nature, the great book of God'.[8]

If once that fundamental truth were understood, argued de Fellenberg, then society, which in the past had been so blind to the needs of individuals, would quickly realize what the early disciples of Pestalozzi had set out to accomplish. 'They commenced their task', said he, 'with the conviction that the destination of every child was indicated by Divine Providence in the natural turn of his mind, and that no educator should allow himself to misapprehend or pervert, according to his contracted ideas, that which the Creator had ordered in infinite wisdom.'[9] In consequence their first consideration was to preserve as far as possible 'the child-like innocence of youth' and 'that cheerfulness which was its inseparable companion'. In order to do so they endeavoured to turn themselves into the

[6] Despite the fact that de Fellenberg was prepared at all times to acknowledge the genius of Pestalozzi, he had no liking for him as a man. Indeed their relationship from 1804 onwards was steadily to worsen and to drag on in a series of unhappy quarrels until Pestalozzi's death in 1827

[7] See p. 280 of *Publications of the Central Society of Education* (second volume), 1838. Letter from de Fellenberg entitled 'Mes observations, etc.'

[8] See *The Education of the Peasantry in England; what it is and what it ought to be* by B. F. Duppa, 1834, Appendix II

[9] *Ibid.* Appendix II

friends and not the tyrants of their pupils. They strove hard to 'occupy every moment of a boy's life in well-directed and useful activity so that nothing evil should find room to develop itself', and kept 'sound religious principles continually in view in every branch of study'. Only by so doing could they promote a feeling of communal responsibility among their charges and teach them 'to comprehend Christianity thoroughly and to embrace it cordially'.

With these thoughts in mind, therefore, de Fellenberg returned to his idea of forming a summer school for elementary teachers. The project was finally carried out in 1808 and the course, which consisted of a detailed exposition of the theories enunciated in *How Gertrude Teaches Her Children*, lasted six weeks. At its close, however, the education authorities of Berne decided that in future no teacher under their jurisdiction should be allowed to attend. Their decision was prompted by a quarrel with de Fellenberg, who insisted on his right to run the course in the way he considered best.

Undeterred by the edict of the Berne authorities, he immediately issued invitations to other cantons to send their teachers during successive summers, and it was thus that he made the acquaintance of Wehrli, who, in 1810, began a 'School for the Poor' which is discussed in the next chapter.

Thus far in his educational schemes de Fellenberg had catered for the needs of farm labourers, bailiffs, elementary school-teachers and peasant children. His own sons, meanwhile, had reached an age when he desired them to have a classical education, and so, in 1811, he decided to found a boarding school for the sons of gentlemen. Within the space of a few years it became the most fashionable academy of its kind in Europe and attracted pupils from countries as far distant as Russia, Scotland and America. By means of it de Fellenberg hoped to train those who, sometime in the future, would have direct responsibility for their country's welfare or assist in Councils of State. As might be expected, therefore, it was both exclusive and expensive. The number of pupils, for instance, was limited to a hundred, each of whom paid approximately £300 per annum for board and tuition. This large fee was rendered necessary because de Fellenberg insisted that, from a boy's entry into the school at the age of eight, until he left when he was eighteen, he should receive the maximum amount of care and attention. For that reason no fewer than thirty-five masters were in constant attendance, each of whom was an expert in the particular subject he taught. Thus no pains were spared to make these young aristocrats proficient in all the accomplishments which befitted their station in life.

De Fellenberg's principal aim was to allow his pupils to reach maturity by a cautious and well-directed teaching, and never under any circumstances to force them. The masters used the Pestalozzian method of instruction, and were careful always to appeal to the reasonable part of their pupils' characters. Rewards, honours and divisions of a class into first, second or third places, formed no part of the educational system, and punishments were exceedingly rare. The internal management of the school was administered to a large extent by the pupils themselves, who appointed their own officials for posts of responsibility, under the supervision of the principal. All the teaching was conducted in French or German.

De Fellenberg was a great believer in the benefits to be obtained from a life in the open air. Besides the numerous games the boys played, therefore, they were made to spend some of their time cultivating the land. Each pupil had a small garden, which he was required to till with care, whilst the entire school was made jointly responsible for a patch of ground that provided the school vegetables. In the winter months, when the weather became so severe as to preclude all outdoor activity, de Fellenberg insisted that his pupils drive forth in an enormous sleigh, specially designed by him to accommodate about eighty people and drawn by fourteen horses.

Contrary to what one might expect, however, the boys were never pampered. They rose at 6.0 a.m. in winter and 5.0 in summer. They had breakfast at 7.0, dinner at noon, light refreshment at 5.0 and supper at 8.0. Eating at other times was strictly forbidden. Five hours in the morning and four in the afternoon were given to study, whilst the rest of the day was devoted to the pursuit of individual interests such as riding, swimming, dancing, practising musical instruments and performing gymnastic exercises. Special buildings were provided in various parts of the estate for these various activities.

The curriculum embraced the following subjects: Greek, Latin, German, French, History, Geography, Mathematics (Pure and Applied), Natural and Mental Philosophy, Chemistry, Music, Drawing, Gymnastics and Divinity. Great attention was paid to the first and last of these subjects.

The language and literature of the Greeks were emphasized 'because of the very polished civilization of that people'. When once the Grammar had been mastered, the pupils were introduced to Homer, Herodotus, Thucydides, Xenophon and finally to Plato. It was not uncommon, we learn, for the children of twelve to recite the hymns of *The Odyssey* as they went to their sports, and some became so enthusiastic in their studies that they had to be checked. Count Capo d'Istria, writing to the Emperor Alexander of Austria in 1814, stated: 'A short time ago, the young Baron de Bissing and the youngest of the three Princes de Wrede rose at one o'clock in the morning, to return to their Homer, and it was necessary to send them again to their beds.' [10]

A knowledge of Greek was also of considerable use in the study of the New Testament, to which particular care was devoted. Pupils of the Catholic Church were taught by a priest, those of the Protestant Church by a pastor, and those of the Greek Orthodox Church by a special tutor who came from Russia. Thus due respect was paid to every religious persuasion but, in order that those points of doctrine should be emphasized on which Christians everywhere agreed, all boys were likewise expected to attend communal prayers both night and morning. De Fellenberg was anxious that everything possible should be done to stress the harmony rather than the discord of Christendom for he regarded religious principles as the basis of all that was excellent in man. His boys were encouraged, therefore, constantly to watch for opportunities of doing good to others. On summer evenings they often walked to the neighbouring villages to discover the needs of the poor families. In winter, when the roads were so thick with snow that it was impossible to proceed on foot, they would go in sleighs to distant hamlets ready to give what help they could to the unfortunate peasants. In that way the privileged young gentlemen were taught that the best way to serve God was first to do one's duty towards one's neighbour.

From 1827 onwards de Fellenberg gained great satisfaction from the knowledge that his experiments at Hofwyl prompted others to follow his example. In 1827 an agricultural school was founded at Kathrinelyst, near Sorø in Denmark, which proved so successful that others were opened within a few years at Boggildgaard, Holsteinsminde and Flakkebjerg—all of them modelled closely on

[10] See Count Capo d'Istria's report to the Emperor Alexander, p. 18

Hofwyl.[11] In 1834 an extensive educational establishment was started by the Prince de Chimay in his park at Menars, near Blois.[12] Such projects were watched with interest by the ageing de Fellenberg, who began to cherish the hope that his life's work would survive him in its entirety and thus prove a source of inspiration to those who were striving to perpetuate his ideals. With that thought in mind, from 1839 until the time of his death, he made repeated requests to the authorities of the Swiss Government that his estate should be taken over as a National Institute. They felt compelled to refuse his offer, however, since the whole of the undertaking seemed to them too much bound up with the ideals of a single individual to be perpetuated by a public body. In consequence Hofwyl came to an end when its creator died on 21st November, 1844.

To appraise de Fellenberg's achievements is no easy task. Certainly as a social benefactor and reformer of agricultural methods he was pre-eminent. Hofwyl had originally numbered 220 acres. At his death it comprised 650. Around the ancient castle, which, in 1799, had been the only habitable place, there arose over the years more than twenty buildings housing a population of between three and four hundred people from every section of society. All those individuals were engaged peaceably in pursuing the multifarious activities that de Fellenberg planned to satisfy the divers needs of their lives, and his object in bringing them together, not under one roof but in one colony, was to provide a model for the Governments of Europe. He wished to illustrate how society could effectively be organized on an agricultural basis by the provision of schools that offered to each class the culture appropriate to its position. It may well be that his rigid social distinctions limited the appeal of his work to future generations, but that he gave a highly individual contribution to educational and sociological practice cannot be questioned. In fact he succeeded, far better than he himself would allow, in attaining the objective which he placed before himself as early as 1799: 'to demonstrate by means of an extensive series of experiments what education ought to accomplish for the human race'.[13]

[11] See *Vor Skole* (*Our School*) by Hans Kyrre, p. 116
[12] See article on the institution of the Prince de Chimay in the first book of the *Publications of the Central Society of Education*, p. 380
[13] See *The Education of the Peasantry in England; what it is and what it ought to be* by B. F. Duppa, Appendix II

5

THE NATURE SCHOOL IN
SWITZERLAND—WEHRLI

'Aimer les hommes est la première condition pour les former dans
l'enfance et dans la jeunesse, pour les conduire et les gouverner dans
l'âge mûr.'

JULLIEN DE PARIS—*Essai général d'éducation
physique, morale et intellectuelle.* 1808

HOFWYL will always be associated in the annals of educational
history with two remarkably contrasted characters—Philippe
Emanuel de Fellenberg, the aristocrat who founded it, and Johann
Jakob Wehrli, the peasant who directed its school for orphans.
So different, indeed, were these two men both in temperament
and social position that, at first sight, one cannot easily reconcile
their alliance. The more one studies their lives, however, the clearer
it becomes not only that they strove ardently to perpetuate the
same ideals but also that they enjoyed a warm and lasting friendship.

To understand the Poor School at Hofwyl, therefore, it is necessary to stress the harmony that existed between these two men—a
harmony which is inexplicable save in the light of their love of
Nature. That was the force which bound them together, the foundation of their friendship and the inspiration which shaped their
destinies. Without it there would have been no identity of purpose
and no common educational creed.

We do well, therefore, before investigating Wehrli's contribution
to educational practice, to remind ourselves of the degree to which
Nature influenced his tender years for, just as de Fellenberg's upbringing was remarkably similar to that of Emile, his conformed
with almost equal exactness to that advocated by Pestalozzi in his
first novel. Indeed, but for the fact that his father was a schoolmaster, the circumstances of Wehrli's life were precisely those of one

of Leonard and Gertrude's children. He was born to poverty and early made aware of the fact that, had his mother not supplemented the family income by means of a loom, he would frequently have gone hungry. He was trained by her not only to work in the house and on the land but also to worship regularly and to give whatever help he could to neighbouring families. He owed her a great debt of gratitude, therefore, and later expressed thanks to her early training, for it gave him, he asserted, bodily strength, supple limbs, a quick eye and a steady hand.

When the time came for him to choose a career Wehrli decided, as his father had done before him, to become a teacher. Accordingly, in 1804, when he was fourteen years of age, he was sent to the municipal public day school at Frauenfeld. He stayed there almost three years, but the headmaster was such a tyrant that he drove all thoughts of teaching from his pupil's mind. Nor did any interest revive until Wehrli attended a series of lectures, given in Frauenfeld during January and February 1807, when the principles of Pestalozzi were expounded in detail. At the end of the course he returned to Eschikofen full of enthusiasm for the new learning and was soon given an opportunity of translating it into practice as headmaster of a small school in Leutenegg—a period of his life which he later described as 'the first of four steps in my pedagogical career'.

In 1809 the Thurgau Government decided to send one of their teachers to a Summer School lasting six weeks at de Fellenberg's institute at Hofwyl, and Wehrli's father, Thomas, was chosen to attend. The course interested him greatly but, on its completion, he felt himself too old to undertake the reforms it suggested. The thought came to him, however, that perhaps another might prove more suitable, and so the old man begged de Fellenberg's permission to send his son in his place the following year. Thus, in the summer of 1810, when he was nineteen years of age, young Wehrli came to Hofwyl, which was to be the chief scene of his life's work.

His first intention was to stay only as long as the course lasted, but de Fellenberg perceived in him an unusually gifted teacher who would be able to carry out a plan of reform that he had long contemplated. This was a school for vagrant children which de Fellenberg was anxious to inaugurate in order to complete his provision of educational facilities for every walk of life. Accordingly he offered the post of director to Wehrli who decided to accept it.

It was a hard life that he led, particularly at the beginning, for not only had he to learn to understand the far-seeing de Fellenberg, who invariably carried a number of grandiose schemes in his head, but also to stand up for his own point of view. Indeed, on more than one occasion, he was tempted, certainly in the initial stages, to return home, but de Fellenberg, through kindness, always succeeded in defeating such plans.

As a beginning Wehrli was allowed to experiment with twenty-five boys whose parents were employed on the estate, and so admirably did he succeed that de Fellenberg soon asked him to embark on the more ambitious project of rescuing abandoned children. The first pupil arrived in June 1810 and was handed over to Wehrli's exclusive care. By December there were seven boys from six cantons. They all arrived in a pitiable condition, having existed for months without proper food, clothes and shelter. De Fellenberg described them later as 'Beggars, afflicted with scrofula and itch, who had been snatched from the hands of the police; filthy street urchins, covered in lice; starving subhumans, who bore in their faces the symptoms of consumption.' [1] To such outcasts Wehril gave himself wholly with the same spirit of self-sacrifice that Pestalozzi had shown at Stanz. 'I was their father,' he wrote. 'I was with them the whole day long without interruption, and if I sometimes went to bed later than they, I never slept longer, but rose with them.' [2]

In August the number of pupils grew to thirteen and towards the end of December, a fourteenth was added. Wehrli was wise to insist on rescuing them one by one. A sudden influx would have ruined everything. The boys were so different in age and so disparate in character that they had to be handled separately. There was one, for instance, almost six years old, who had never known his parents and was physically so backward that Wehrli had literally to act as his nurse. Another, fourteen years of age, was a hardened liar, who spent much of his time feigning sickness. When the other children went into the fields to work he would stay indoors and steal whatever he could lay his hands on. Gradually, however, his viciousness was curbed by kindness and affection. In such a manner, slowly and painfully, a moral code was built up amongst the young vagabonds,

---

[1] See p. 2990 of *Dictionnaire de Pédagogie et d'Instruction Primaire*. Article on Wehrli. Vol. II, Part 1

[2] See *Wehrlis Lebensgang und Pädagogische Bedeutung* by Philipp Hartleb. *Encyklopädisches Handbuch*, Vol. X, p. 129

and they learnt to treat one another as if they really had passed their lives together and were brothers. Thus, although hard work was his constant lot, Wehrli found his labours rewarding.

In the autumn of 1812 de Fellenberg asked that the 'Poor School' be reported on publicly by the Swiss Government, and four commissioners, headed by the former Minister of the Interior, Albert Rengger,[3] duly arrived at Hofwyl in February 1813. The results of their enquiry, published in September of that year, gave a detailed account of the workings of the institution.[4]

The examiners reported that the living accommodation was adequate. The twenty-six pupils, including Wehrli, occupied two large rooms, one of which was used for sleeping, and the other for work. They used an outer building for meals and, when the weather permitted, took lessons in an open shed in a neighbouring wood. The dormitory had no artificial heat and was furnished with camp beds, palliasses, straw bolsters, sheets and thick quilts. The boys' clothing was made of coarse cotton for summer wear and of wool for winter. They invariably went bareheaded and, in warm weather, barefooted. They rose at 5.0 a.m. in summer and 6.0 in winter. The first task of the day was to make the beds and air the dormitory, after which, in strict order, they washed, said morning prayers, received instruction for thirty minutes, breakfasted and did manual work until 11.30. Dinner was served at noon when Wehrli sat at the head of the table and divided out the portions of food. After the meal the boys had a lesson lasting one hour and then went to work on the land until 6.0 p.m. Supper came shortly afterwards, followed by recreation and half-an-hour's instruction, after which everybody joined in prayer and retired to bed between 8.0 and 9.0. The commissioners noted that Wehrli himself had no privileges which he did not share with his pupils, and that his food and clothing were similar in all respects to theirs.

The report gave a full account of the work that was undertaken by the boys. As long as the weather was fine, they were employed in the fields on such tasks as hoeing, weeding, gleaning and picking beans, peas and potatoes. The young ones, who were mostly employed on gathering vegetables, had a small cart drawn by a donkey

[3] The same Albert Rengger who had been de Fellenberg's tutor at Wildenstein

[4] See *Translation of the Reports of M. le Comte de Capo d'Istria and M. Rengger, upon the principles and progress of the Establishment of M. de Fellenberg at Hofwyl, Switzerland,* by *John Attersoll, Esqre.* London, 1820

which was their special responsibility. The older boys, on the other hand, spent much of their time ploughing with horses and oxen.

When the season did not allow them to labour in the fields they made baskets, plaited straw for chairs, cut up roots for the cattle, sawed wood and knitted stockings. Some of the senior boys were allowed to learn the trade of wheelwright and to assist in making farm implements at the mechanics' workshop. Thus the pupils were kept fully occupied from morning until night.

The commission found the performance highly satisfactory and laid stress on the fact that the 'Poor School' was not primarily one of instruction but of work. It added that education, far from limiting itself to the classroom, lasted the entire day. As a result many subjects such as Speech Training, Singing and Nature Study were taught indirectly, in the manner advocated by Rousseau in *Emile*. Whenever the boys were out of doors they talked in high German instead of in dialect. While toiling in the fields or returning home after the day's labours, they practised the songs they had learnt in the classroom. And, as they followed the plough, they were reminded by Wehrli of the incomparable beauty of the Swiss countryside that stretched before them as far as the eastern Alps.

In all his teaching, we learn, Wehrli followed the Pestalozzian method. It was, for instance, only after considerable practice in writing upon slates that the boys were allowed to proceed to a study first of Drawing and later of other subjects. 'Drawing may be considered as a supplement to the art of writing,' Wehrli asserted, 'and affords great assistance in the explanation of those objects of sense which we can but imperfectly describe.' [5] The theory was precisely that outlined in *How Gertrude Teaches Her Children*. Once the pupil had 'acquired the properties of the compass in his eye' and could recognize right angles, circles, cubes, etc., he was ready to start measuring them. 'The purpose of Geometry is to be able to measure objects accurately.' [6]

The subjects selected for the boys' study included Reading, Writing, Arithmetic, the elements of Geometry, Speech Training, Nature Study, Geography, the history of the Fatherland and Singing. It would seem, at first sight, that the curriculum was meagre compared with that of the boarding school for young gentlemen,

[5] Rengger Report, p. 5 [6] *Ibid.* p. 11

but it has to be remembered that only two hours a day were spent
in the classroom, and that the last thing at which the school aimed
was any kind of academic distinction.

If one subject were stressed more strongly than the rest, it was
religious instruction. Every morning and evening the pupils fore-
gathered for prayer, and part of Sunday was always devoted to
reading passages from the Old and New Testaments. On that day,
also, the boys of the 'Poor School' joined with those of the boarding
school for a religious service in de Fellenberg's parlour. It was their
one time of meeting in the week, and the reunion was said to be 'a
most solemn act of devotion'. More important still, however, were
Wehrli's constant reminders of the presence of God when he was out
of doors with his pupils. 'One lovely evening I walked out with my
children,' he wrote in his Journal. 'The sky was serene, a faint
twilight was still visible in the west, while, on the opposite side, the
moon rose majestically above the mountains; she was at the full,
shining beautifully, and very finely reflected on the sheet of water
which lay in front of us. My children gazed delighted on the firma-
ment. The moon in particular attracted their attention. Two of
them began singing the hymn, of which the first words are "The
planet of the night which rises in silence", in which we all joined.
I seized the opportunity of reminding them that the Almighty had
created all the magnificent objects which they beheld and, when
we returned home, I read over with them the hymn, "There is a
God by whom we are watched, by whom we are beloved." This had
more effect upon their youthful hearts than if I had read the Bible
or any book of devotion to them. They were talking to each other
of this beautiful evening, till the instant they fell asleep.' [7] One sees,
in such a passage, how closely the spirit of Christianity and that of
Emile approximated in Wehrli's mind.

The high quality of the moral and religious instruction received
special praise from the Rengger commission, which concluded its
report by commending the unsparing devotion of Wehrli, without
whom the 'Poor School' could never have achieved such remarkable
results.

As the years passed more and more destitute children arrived at
Hofwyl. From fourteen in 1811, twenty-six in 1813 and forty in
1820, the total must have approached the hundred mark about

[7] Rengger Report, p. 30

1830. Gradually, therefore, Wehrli's work came to be revered throughout Switzerland and, as a tribute to his name, de Fellenberg decreed, in 1813, that the institution should thenceforth be called the 'Wehrli School' and its pupils the 'Wehrli Boys'.[8] Many visitors were attracted to Hofwyl by what they had heard of the regeneration of social outcasts, and were frequently so impressed by the boys' good manners and excellent behaviour that they begged de Fellenberg to supply them with masters qualified to conduct schools for the poor.

It was for this reason that de Fellenberg decided, as early as 1813, to bring young teachers to his estate and allow Wehrli to train them. From that date, therefore, the institution became not only a school for poor boys but also a small training department for future teachers. As the number of children increased it proved helpful to have a few assistant masters and Wehrli devised a simple method of training them which ensured that the running of his school was in no way neglected. Systematic instruction he cut out completely and, as a substitute, encouraged the young men to join in the life of the school whether in the fields, the gardens or the house. When the day's work was done and the boys were asleep, Wehrli would gather his colleagues around him and examine their opinions and judgments. Sometimes he discussed the teachings of Pestalozzi, offering advice on problems that were presented to him; sometimes he counselled the young teachers to imitate his own methods in so far as their individuality would allow them; but, most frequently, he spent the time encouraging them by pointing out noteworthy tasks which he had seen them performing for his boys. Thus the same spirit of mutual regard and love grew up in the training centre as reigned in the school.

In January 1826 de Fellenberg inaugurated plans for an establishment where the sons of the middle classes could be educated. Wehrli was asked to direct it and, after some hesitation, promised to do so, meanwhile relinquishing charge of his own institution. The 'Middle School' was not a success, however, and was soon supplanted by a seminary at Münchenbuchsee, as mentioned in the preceding chapter. Yet the confidence Wehrli gained from his new experience stood him in good stead. Indeed, as a result of it, he was prepared to widen his sphere of activity and, in 1830, to undertake

[8] The actual names were 'Wehrlischule' and 'Wehrliknaben'

the direction of the Summer School, which had been in existence at Hofwyl since 1808.

The Summer School usually attracted between thirty and forty teachers annually, but so speedily did its reputation grow between 1830 and 1833 that an increased number of applicants sought admission from almost every canton. The majority of them came from remote districts, and Wehrli, remembering the advantages that both he and his father had gained from the Hofwyl courses, strove hard to impress upon the village schoolmasters the benefits that resulted from an education closely connected with cultivating the soil. What he could never have anticipated was that his success with them would result in his having to leave Hofwyl.

It so happened that a number of teachers who attended the Summer Schools had been sent to Hofwyl by the education authorities of Thurgau. On their return they spoke in glowing terms of their experiences and, in particular, of Wehrli. The result was that his native canton decided to confer upon him a signal honour. A new Training College, specially designed for Thurgau teachers, was constructed at Kreuzlingen on the shores of Lake Constance and Wehrli invited to direct it. The request put him in an embarrassing position for the last thing he desired was to part company with de Fellenberg. And, though the latter was full of understanding, it was only after much deliberation that Wehrli brought himself to accept the offer and, in September 1833, to bid farewell to Hofwyl where he had worked for twenty-three years.

At the age of forty-three, however, Wehrli was still sufficiently vigorous to embark on his new career with enthusiasm. Accordingly he set to work to build up an establishment which would perpetuate the same ideals that de Fellenberg had striven to foster at Hofwyl. He stressed to his students the importance of agricultural work and gave many examples of the peculiar advantages to be gained from it. He showed how it developed intellectual and bodily strength; how it accustomed both infants and adults to orderliness, vigilance and cleanliness; and how it lifted the human mind towards God and thus became a most effective means of fostering true piety. He emphasized in his teaching that children should be made self-reliant and that they should be shown how to handle such implements as the axe, saw, plane and drill in order to perform any number of tasks by themselves. He made a special point, too, of drawing his students' attention to the sacredness of their self-chosen work. The primary duty of a teacher, Wehrli said, was not to impart knowledge but to guide and help those who had been entrusted to his care. With that thought in mind the teacher would soon come to realize that one duty was more important than all others with regard to training children. It was to see that the vocational impulse was quickened and developed aright. If it seemed not to be present then the master could blame one of two things—either his teaching or the fact that his pupil was ill. Both these difficulties were surmountable, however, and, once they had successfully been combated, the vocational impulse would soon manifest itself. Then, by means of careful handling, infinite patience and emphasis on the fact that every deed without an end in view was nothing worth, the pupil, no matter what his difficulties, could be set on the right path and encouraged to greater efforts. Constant attention to such details, Wehrli assured his students, would ultimately be rewarded with success.[9]

The course of instruction he devised for them to follow included the following subjects: Grammar, Writing, Arithmetic, Geometry, Biblical History, Drawing, Geography, History, Gymnastic Exercises and the Art of Teaching. Special consideration, too, was given to Outdoor Labour, Gardening and Music—a fact that is readily discernible from the time-table overleaf which was in use during the summer of 1839.

Wehrli remained as director of the Kreuzlingen College for twenty years. During that time he worked untiringly to make his students conscious of the fact that a teaching career was not merely a means of earning a livelihood, but an apostleship which demanded a great spirit of self-abnegation. Perhaps he asked too much of them. Certainly, after a time, a spirit began to show itself that was alien to Wehrli's way of thinking. The students were not happy to accept so humble an idea of their future station in life. They accused him of being old-fashioned and made light of his motto, 'Work and Pray'. In 1852 a political change brought new men to power and Dr. Scherr, the idol of those who demanded reform, was elected to the educational council of Thurgau. A reorganization of the Kreuzlingen College was decided upon and a new time-table forced upon

[9] See Hartleb, *Wehrlis Lebensgang und Pädagogische Bedeutung*, pp. 134 and 135

its director. Wehrli felt himself unable to share any part of it and retired from his work in the spring of 1853. At a later date he

COURSE OF INSTRUCTION PURSUED AT THE NORMAL SEMINARY IN THE CANTON OF THURGOVIA, SWITZERLAND, UNDER THE SUPERINTENDENCE OF M. WEHRLI, IN THE SUMMER HALF-YEAR OF 1839

Hours	Class	Monday	Tuesday	Wednesday	Thursday	Friday	Saturday	Sunday
5 to 7	First	Outdoor Labour	Outdoor Labour	Art of Teaching	Outdoor Labour	Outdoor Labour	Art of Teaching	Attending Divine Service, Sacred Music, Teaching in Sunday School
	Second	Outdoor Labour	Outdoor Labour	Outdoor Labour	Art of Teaching	Outdoor Labour	Outdoor Labour	
7 to 8		Breakfast	Breakfast	Breakfast	Breakfast	Breakfast	Breakfast	
8 to 9	First	Natural History	Biblical History	Profane History	Natural History	Biblical History	Profane History	
	Second	Profane History	Biblical History	Management of Land	Profane History	Biblical History	Management of Land	
9 to 10	First	Grammar	Grammar	Natural History	Grammar	Grammar	Natural History	
	Second	Geometry	Arithmetic	Grammar	Geometry	Arithmetic	Grammar	
10 to 11	First	Singing	Singing	Singing	Singing	Singing	Grammar	
	Second	Grammar	Grammar	Grammar	Grammar	Grammar	Geometry	
11 to 12	First	Arithmetic	Geometry	Geometry	Arithmetic	Geometry	Arithmetic	
	Second	Natural History	Natural History	Art of Teaching	Natural History	Natural History	Art of Teaching	
12 to 1½		Dinner and Gymnastic Exercises	Dinner and Gymnastic Exercises	Dinner and Gymnastic Exercises	Dinner and Gymnastic Exercises	Dinner and Gymnastic Exercises	Dinner and Gymnastic Exercises	
1½ to 3	First	Singing	Writing	Drawing	Singing	Writing	Drawing	
	Second	Writing	Drawing	Violin	Drawing	Singing		
3 to 4	First	Geography	Arithmetic	Arithmetic	Geography	Arithmetic	Writing	
	Second	Arithmetic	Geography	Natural History	Arithmetic	Geography		
4 to 5	First	Geometry	Reading	Repetitions	Geometry	Reading		
	Second	Reading	Geometry	Arithmetic	Reading	Geometry		
5 to 6		Supper	Supper	Supper	Supper	Supper	Supper	
6 to 9		Garden-work House-work Conversation	Garden-work House-work Conversation	Garden-work House-work Conversation	Garden-work House-work Conversation	Garden-work House-work Conversation	Garden-work House-work Conversation	

Included in Four Periods of Public Education by Sir James P. Kay-Shuttleworth (1862)

founded an agricultural college at Guggenbühl but unfortunately was prevented from seeing it prosper. He died, quite suddenly, on 15th March, 1855.

Two phases of Wehrli's life must be differentiated if any idea is to be formed of his educational significance—the one as director of students, the other as a teacher. His work at Kreuzlingen was not particularly successful for, possibly as a result of de Fellenberg's training, he had little time for such questions as an improved social status for teachers. Enduring on the other hand was his work among indigent children. Wehrli will always be remembered as the kindliest, gentlest and most lovable of masters—a master whose belief in his mission and fervent devotion to duty made him serve to the limits of self-sacrifice. He will also be remembered, and this is perhaps even more important, as a shining example to his contemporaries of what a humble teacher, versed in the theory of Pestalozzi and obedient to the voice of Nature, could accomplish for those rejected of men.

6

THE EMERGENCE OF THE IDEA OF
A STATE SYSTEM OF EDUCATION

'Nous touchons à l'époque désirée qui va mettre fin aux abus de
l'éducation, pour en produire une nouvelle qui fera honneur à notre
siècle.'

From a speech by the Procureur de Tours, 12th August, 1763

AFTER examining the educational work of de Fellenberg and Wehrli
we are able to appreciate not only the tremendous extent to which
Pestalozzi influenced his contemporaries, but also the way in which
the Nature School developed during the first half of the nineteenth
century—a development which Rousseau could never have anticipated. For *Emile* may well have been designed by its author to
enlighten the select few, but it was certainly not intended to disclose
a secret by which the masses could be educated.

By 1801, however, when *How Gertrude Teaches Her Children* was
published, the Nature School had developed into something very
different from its essentially aristocratic beginning. It had broadened and deepened with the passing of the years and had finally
produced a most effective means of teaching large numbers of
children to read, add and write. The importance of this revelation
was even greater than would otherwise have been the case because
it was given to the world at a peculiarly opportune moment when
such countries as Switzerland, Prussia and Holland were not only
giving serious consideration to improved methods of teaching, but
were likewise actively engaged in laying the foundations of state
systems of education.

Before examining the way in which the doctrines of the Nature
School and the demand for popular instruction eventually coalesced
in the countries concerned, however, it is necessary, as nearly as one
can, to trace the gradual development of the idea of a state system

of education. So bold and interesting a conception, which eventually envisaged nothing less than instruction for all children regardless of wealth or position, was not a new scheme that suddenly sprang to life at the beginning of the nineteenth century. It was rather a product of the same forces that shaped both the French Revolution and the Nature School of educators, and its origin lay concealed, as did theirs, in that peculiarly fertile period of French history when so many of the influences that have fashioned modern democratic Europe first became evident.

About half-way through the eighteenth century there was an outpouring of ideas in France that was to have far-reaching effects. Politicians were beginning to realize the importance of greater freedom, scientists were busily engaged on detailed research, and philosophers were everywhere occupied with new and interesting speculations. Never subsequently has the French nation had so many eminent men who, at one time, were all engrossed with bold discoveries. A spirit of enquiry was abroad which was without parallel since the time of the Renaissance and which showed itself nowhere more clearly than in the flood of instructional works that flowed from the press.

A cursory glance at some of the major publications of the period gives some indication of the consuming interest in knowledge that was everywhere manifest. In 1743 Montesquieu published *The Spirit of the Laws*—the product of twenty years' intensive study which was destined to awaken a desire for freedom and a hope of political progress that materially changed the thought of France. At the same time Buffon was engaged on his *Natural History*, published in forty-four volumes between 1749 and 1804, which inspired all classes with an interest in its subject that was quite without precedent in French history. In 1759 Voltaire published his satirical novel *Candide*, which ridiculed the facile optimism current at the time, and, in 1760, established himself at Ferney to start a vigorous campaign against the flagrant injustices of the Ancien Régime. In 1761 and 1762 Rousseau published *The New Heloise*, *The Social Contract* and *Emile*, whose important consequences have already been noted.

The individual efforts of these men were to some extent united by means of the famous French Encyclopaedia or Dictionary of Arts and Sciences. This colossal enterprise, started in 1751 under the joint editorship of Diderot and d'Alembert, set out to embody the whole sum of human learning then existing. In its character, significance and results it became the most striking production of its day, and no summary of knowledge ever assembled achieved the dominating position which this work held in the civil and literary history of France during the second half of the eighteenth century. At its outset the Dictionary of Arts and Sciences attempted to be a non-contentious work, modelled on Ephraim Chambers' *Cyclopaedia* of 1728, but within five years it had changed into a vehicle for vaunting the power of human reason, attacking the beliefs of the past and disseminating anti-religious propaganda. For that reason the first two volumes were condemned by the Paris Parlement in 1757 —a step which resulted in the suspension of its publication and d'Alembert's resignation as co-editor. In 1765, however, the authorities withdrew their embargo, and from then until 1772, when the last of its thirty-five volumes was published, the French Encyclopaedia became an effective means of drawing together a group of intellectuals who were antagonistic towards the old order of things. They were invited by Diderot to contribute articles which would arouse public opinion to the cruelty and constant miscarriage of justice that were everywhere apparent in monarchical France, and amongst those who responded to the appeal, with varying shades of political enthusiasm, were Montesquieu, Buffon, Voltaire and Rousseau.

Not all the contributors were of one mind politically nor would they have agreed among themselves on an unwavering policy, but the cumulative effect of their writings was such as to make readers conscious of a new force in their midst. Every indication was given that a body of thinkers had emerged who visualized nothing less than a complete reorganization of the existing means of government. Some of them, moreover, seemed anxious to demonstrate that their objective could never be achieved so long as clerical influence remained all-powerful in education, and a few even went so far as to give premonitory hints of a widespread system of secular instruction. Conspicuous among the latter were such men as Turgot, Condillac, Helvétius and, more especially, d'Alembert, Faiguet and Diderot. In 1753 d'Alembert wrote a bitter criticism of current educational theory and practice which demanded that 'the yoke of prejudice be lifted from the necks of young people'. Three years later Faiguet reaffirmed the same argument whilst reminding the French Academies that their prime duty was to extend and reform the existing means of instruction. And in 1775 Diderot drew up his *Plan of a Russian University* at the request of the Empress Catherine II which adumbrated a scheme whereby all children could be educated and supplied with school meals from funds provided by the state.[1]

These contributors to the French Encyclopaedia were not the only people who gave earnest consideration to the necessity of providing systematic instruction for the people. Indeed many intelligent men throughout the country had for some time been pondering the same question. There were, for instance, Guyton de Morveau in Dijon, La Chalotais in Rennes, Montclar and Saissin in Grenoble, and Lavardy and Rolland d'Erceville in Paris—all of whom were anxious to secure a more effective means of education.

Of the vast number of reports that flowed from their pens perhaps two may be selected as of more than passing interest: La Chalotais' *Essay on National Education or plan of studies for young people* (1763) and President Rollin's *Compte-rendu* (1768).

In his work La Chalotais stated categorically that the current methods of instruction were wrong since they were obviously designed to produce good clerics rather than responsible citizens. Such a policy was bound to have disastrous results for it was based on a false pedagogical ideal. The most important person to be considered in any system of training was not the master but the pupil. La Chalotais saw no virtue in a young boy being surrounded by celibates, often himself to become a celibate. The teaching orders of the Catholic Church apparently subscribed to the theory that, because a man had no children of his own, he was thereby rendered the more capable of teaching the sons of others. Yet their viewpoint was surely mistaken. What was needed was the immediate introduction into schools of lay teachers and, in particular, of married men. They would, of necessity, provide a type of training different from that which the Church supplied, and that was precisely what was needed. The children of the state should be instructed by members of the state as was the case in ancient Greece.

President Rollin's report reaffirmed many of the same arguments. Much of it was a detailed consideration of the teaching of Latin, and Rollin gave it as his considered opinion that too great

---

[1] 'Depuis le premier ministre jusqu'au dernier paysan, il est bon que chacun sache lire, écrire et compter' (Diderot, *Plan d'une Université russe*, 1775)

an emphasis on that particular language was at the root of many of the nation's educational difficulties. He did not wish to see it banished, but he thought that at least equal consideration should be given to French.[2] In addition he pleaded eloquently for the widening of University curricula. He would have less emphasis on theology and philosophy and more on science and natural history. He demanded the introduction of new professors to teach mathematics and physics, and suggested the creation of Normal Schools to train lay teachers. These institutions, he affirmed, should be maintained at the expense of the state and should ensure that all new methods of teaching were given careful consideration, that new text books in French were supplied in considerable numbers, and that a body of 'Visitors' or inspectors was formed to offer advice. Rollin wished finally that a central office be constituted to make certain that an official educational policy was pursued throughout France, and expressed the belief that this newly created organ would become the most effective means yet devised of securing a sound national unity.

From 1763 onwards, then, there were several thinkers in France who were actively considering an extension of educational facilities throughout the kingdom. Undoubtedly they were the bolder spirits of the time, but even among less ardent members of the population there was a readiness to accept a change in the general direction of their lives towards greater freedom. A new feeling had arisen that was to become nation wide and eventually to merge with the very ideals that inspired the Revolution. Indeed it is no exaggeration to say that it was those same ideals, embodied in the reports of such men as Mirabeau, Talleyrand and Condorcet, that first gave expression to a new conception of education as a 'right' of every citizen and as a responsibility of the state.

Mirabeau wrote four reports of which the most important was *Concerning public instruction or the organization of a teaching body* (1790).[3] It began by emphasizing the need of all men to acquire worthy moral habits. Morality, education and the customs of the people were more closely linked than many suspected. Since customs varied so considerably in different countries, however, it was obviously not possible to define the essentials of educational truth in a form equally

---

[2] 'Je veux que dans l'enseignement la langue française marche d'un pied égal avec la latine.' *Compte-rendu* by Rollin, 1768
[3] *De l'instruction publique ou de l'organisation du corps enseignant*

acceptable to thinkers of different nationalities. The purposes of education differed too greatly for that and had always done so down the ages according to the nature of the society which, at a given period, was attempting to mould its citizens. Legislators in former days had used public instruction as the most convenient method of maintaining their institutions and propagating their beliefs. Youth was regarded as the preserve of the Fatherland, and parents were merely given the satisfaction of knowing that their sons would be trained in the duties demanded by their native country. The state had thus on many occasions brought about a complete change in the nature of its young people. But that was not the aim of enlightened thinkers in France whose only object was to render men more capable of using their faculties and enjoying their rights. It was, therefore, the duty of French legislators and distinguished citizens to busy themselves with the question of popular instruction in order thereby to free the people from ignorance and ensure a lasting progress.

The *Report on Public Instruction*,[4] written by Talleyrand, was read to the Constituent Assembly in September 1791. It was full of the new revolutionary enthusiasm and proclaimed in the strongest terms a belief in reason, progress, liberty and the rights of man. Since public instruction belonged to the people its purpose was to perfect them either collectively as a nation or singly as individuals. In its efforts to improve them as a nation it should attempt ceaselessly to enhance the good qualities of the constitution by infusing into it a sense of morality. In its attempts to help them as individuals it should strive to render their lives better, happier and more useful, and to fortify their physical, intellectual and moral faculties. Only thus could it possess a soul. The whole structure of public instruction, Talleyrand maintained, should be based on the sound principle of liberty, otherwise it would be impossible to encourage local differences in the interest of the common good.

Condorcet presented his report to the Legislative Assembly on the 20th and 21st April, 1792. It was perhaps the most significant account of all for it was written by a man who thoroughly understood the advantages of education and by a scholar who was a former pupil of Turgot and the last important survivor of the Encyclopaedists. He demonstrated how necessary it was for an

---

[4] *Mémoire sur l'instruction et sur l'éducation nationale*

organized system of instruction to achieve the two basic ideals which the Revolution proclaimed—liberty and equality. He argued that, without the diffusion of education, liberty could not endure. Anarchy or despotism would inevitably be the lot of a people that had become free before becoming enlightened. Instruction as an instrument of liberty and equality was the true source not only of public morality but also of progress. All the vices of humanity sprang from intellectual impotence. They came either from a desire to escape boredom or a reliance on sensation rather than on thought. To encourage men to pass from the life of the senses to the life of the intellect, to render study agreeable so that more elevated pleasures might replace the appetite for enjoyment of material things, to substitute the book for the bottle of wine, the library for the tavern—such were the basic problems which confronted education.

Condorcet maintained faith in the progressive development of mankind and in instruction as the best means of hastening it. Education, he asserted, was able to put a light at everyone's door by whose radiance hidden talent had a chance of being discovered. The oftener ability and skill were thus revealed, the clearer was the way left open to a limitless progress. He would have the light of education shine impartially on boys and girls, on young and old.

The permanent value of the work done by Mirabeau, Talleyrand, Condorcet and others for education has perhaps not been sufficiently stressed. In the view of these idealists there was no duty more compelling or more sacred for the state than to ensure that all its citizens, whether rich or poor—especially the poor—had regular instruction. Furthermore their reports demonstrated how far the interest in popular instruction had developed since the middle of the century. Indeed they showed more clearly than any other means yet devised how a state system of education could benefit the children of all ranks and classes. But unfortunately France had neither the funds nor the power to realize so ambitious a project at that time, and Condorcet's prophecy that despotism would be the lot of a nation which became free before becoming enlightened was amply fulfilled. Ironically enough, then, it was not France that first benefited by the educational reports of Mirabeau, Talleyrand and Condorcet, but three of her neighbours—Switzerland, Holland and Prussia.

Previous to 1798 the state authorities in Switzerland had left all matters concerning education in the hands of the Church, whether Catholic or Protestant. In that year, however, when the Swiss Directory was established under French tutelage among the loose confederation of forty-five states, the new Government appointed Albrecht Stapfer, Professor of Theology at Berne, to be its Minister of Arts and Sciences, entrusting all matters concerning education to his department.[5]

One of the main clauses of the new Constitution declared that education was the chief foundation of public welfare, and accordingly Stapfer set to work to devise a scheme whereby the existing means of instruction could be improved. In particular he directed his attention to the primary schools and drew up a bill of reform which he presented to the Legislative Council on 18th November, 1798. Unfortunately national events precluded its consideration at the time, but, undeterred, the Minister forthwith submitted a detailed questionnaire to all elementary teachers asking for information about their schools. The results of this enquiry were most revealing for they showed that many of the country districts were suffering shameful neglect. It was obvious, therefore, that no reforms would be of the slightest use unless they could simultaneously be introduced throughout the country and, as Stapfer had no clear notion as to how this might be achieved, he made a request to his more enlightened compatriots that they should give their opinions on a national system of education. Many hundreds responded to his appeal and, after studying their suggestions, he drew up his plan for a general reorganization. In each canton a Council of Education was formed consisting of eight members—five citizens, two teachers and a minister of religion. This council, in turn, appointed an inspector of schools for every district within the canton. Both the councils and inspectors were made answerable to the Minister, who was enjoined to maintain the closest contact with them either personally or through correspondence. The plan as originally conceived was exceedingly simple, but it possessed one inestimable merit. It kept the Minister constantly abreast of educational developments everywhere in the country.

We may judge of this particular quality if we consider some of the instructions which Stapfer addressed to his inspectors. He encouraged

---

[5] This Government lasted only from May 1798 to March 1803 and Stapfer himself was Minister for but two and a half years

them to pay great attention to the planning of school buildings, the cleanliness of the teachers' homes and the ventilation of class-rooms. The pupils' desks, he informed them, should be neither too high nor too low and should always be so arranged as to receive the maximum amount of light. A recreation ground, partly covered, should be provided adjoining the school premises. An atmosphere of gaiety and cheerfulness should be encouraged whenever possible, for it was of prime importance in fostering confidence and good will amongst the young. These and other instructions clearly showed that no matter, however seemingly trivial, escaped the Minister's notice.

To Stapfer, then, subsequent generations of legislators and teachers owed a special debt of gratitude for, though his reforms unfortunately were neglected when he quitted office, he was the first responsible Minister of State in any country to give practical appli-cation to the ideals which emerged from Revolutionary France. Thanks to his efforts Switzerland, if only for a short period, became the first nation in Europe to adopt a state system of education as we now understand the meaning of those words.

It was not long, however, before two other countries were likewise seeking a drastic reorganization of their schools. In Holland there had been a growing interest in the subject ever since La Chalotais' *Essay on National Education* had been translated into Dutch in 1767, and in Prussia several enlightened men had applauded the efforts of the French legislators, among whom was von Rochow, who personally undertook a translation of Mirabeau's reports.

What could never have been foretold was that both these countries would fall under the conqueror's yoke or that this fact, in itself, would prove responsible for an early maturing of their educational schemes. As each country was overrun, Napoleon stripped it of all power—of laws, revenue, excise, foreign relations and commerce. One thing, however, he left untouched, and neither country was long in seizing the loophole left open to it. The solitary exception was education.

At the beginning of the nineteenth century, therefore, when both Holland and Prussia began seriously to consider laying the founda-tions of a state system of education, it was to Switzerland, the pioneer in this field, that they turned for an example. In particular they became interested in the work of Pestalozzi whose method depended for its success on a regular supply of trained teachers. One of the first tasks which they undertook, in consequence, was the creation of Normal Schools or Training Colleges and, though the initial cost of their schemes was great, they each contrived to lay sound foundations to their educational edifices on which they could continue to build. Thus, when a large part of Europe fell under the monitorial spell after 1814, Prussia and Holland resolutely refused to be beguiled. In the former country the mutual method of instruction had no influence whatsoever, and in the latter it was tried only to be abandoned. This gave them a great start in the educational field, for when other nations decided to abandon the Bell-Lancaster system, they had either to compromise by turning the monitor into a pupil teacher or virtually to start afresh. In the 1830's, therefore, when several European countries including France and England were giving serious thought to the shaping of their individual educational destinies, it was to Prussia and Holland that they looked for guidance.

7

THE ADOPTION OF A STATE SYSTEM
OF EDUCATION BY THE NETHERLANDS

'It is with a certain pride that we say: study the history of the schools
of the Netherlands; study the history of its education laws; study the
liberty of education which it practises.'
F. J. TH. RUTTEN, Dutch Minister of Education, in the preface
to P. J. IDENBURG's *Education in The Netherlands*. 1951

IF we examine the state of education in Holland prior to 1784
we find that it was in the same deplorable condition as elsewhere
in Europe. There was no general law to regulate either primary
or secondary instruction, the superintendence of schools was non-
existent, masters were mostly ignorant, teaching was calculated
more to stifle than to stimulate the minds of pupils and the interest
taken by parents was negligible.

The first improvements that took place came from a charitable
organization called 'The Society for the Public Good',[1] founded in
1784 by Jon Nieuwenhuysen, a Mennonite Minister of Monniken-
dam in North Holland. It accepted as its mission the improvement
of existing educational facilities, the spread of useful knowledge and
the moral relief of the masses. So successful was it that within one
year it had spread throughout the country. The central administration of the Society remained in the hands of a committee of
twelve, all resident in Amsterdam, but local needs were met by
means of several departments, created in various parts of the country. By 1809 the organization contained more than 7,000 members,
and its numerous branches extended as far as the Cape of Good
Hope.

'The Society for the Public Good' spent a great deal of its time

[1] 'De Maatschappij tot Nut van 't Algemeen'

74

and money publishing small, cheap and easily comprehensible books on such subjects as morals, domestic economy and mechanical science. It also supplied information gratuitously on a variety of other matters, some of them as widely separated as agriculture, vaccination and the training of midwives. Its principal object, however, was education. Accordingly it issued text books for the benefit of teachers, encouraged research into the physical well-being of children, and created a number of model schools. The majority of these were designed for boys and girls whose parents could afford to pay for their children's education, but a few were established expressly to provide free training for the neglected offspring of the peasants—a bold and interesting development which was not without its effect on subsequent legislation.

In 1795, when the French Army entered Amsterdam and the Batavian Republic was proclaimed, there were some doubts as to whether the Society would be allowed to continue its work. The turn of events, however, soon showed otherwise. In the spring of 1796 the National Assembly decided to hold an enquiry into the existing means of instruction and, with that purpose in mind, formed a special commission which was instructed to draw up a questionnaire on education and submit it to 'The Society for the Public Good'. The existence of Nieuwenhuysen's charitable organization was thereby officially recognized and, with a feeling of relief, its committee members set about collecting the detailed information that the Government required. Their reply was sent at the end of 1796 and subsequently published under the title of *General Ideas on National Education*.[2] So excellent was it in every way and so penetrating in its analysis of the nation's educational wants that the Government decided not only to accept the whole of its recommendations but likewise to grant them official sanction.

The first law to attempt a realization of the Society's recommendations was passed on 15th June, 1801. It was drawn up by van der Palm, the celebrated oriental scholar, who had been appointed Commissioner of Public Instruction for the Batavian Republic, and it formed the basis of all enactments subsequently adopted. Certain minor difficulties presented themselves once it was put into operation, however, and accordingly it had to be revised, first in 1803 and again in 1806, but after the necessary adjustments had been made

[2] *Algemeene Denkbeelden over het Nationaal Onderwijs*

and the law of 1806 finally promulgated, all parties were agreed that an outstanding example of educational legislation had resulted.[3]

By the law of 1806 all schools then in existence in Holland were recognized, but all became immediately subject to one regular and uniform system of superintendence. A Secretary of State for the Home Department was appointed to take charge of official matters concerning education, and a Chief Commissioner or Inspector General for Primary Schools was attached to his office. The latter had as one of his duties that of choosing men of sound learning and probity to serve as district inspectors.

In addition the law enacted that no primary school should be established without the authorization of the Secretary of State for the Home Department, and that no one should be allowed to teach / unless he could produce both a 'certificate of competency'[4] and a 'licence for a special place'.[5] Both these qualifications were obtained by virtue of a written examination, set and marked by the district inspectors, the results of which were made known through a list of successes issued by the Inspector General.[6]

A further clause of the bill decreed that one supervisor should be appointed for every province in the country, and that he should be held responsible for all educational activities in the different districts under his control. He was also given the task of ensuring that the Government's policy was at all times carried out. He did so by acting as chairman of the united body of district inspectors, which formed the 'Provincial Board of Public Instruction'. Once a year the supervisor went to The Hague with his corresponding members from the other provinces to sit on a general committee presided over by the Secretary of State for the Home Department. The Inspector General for Primary Schools acted as secretary for this meeting and drew up the minutes. It was his duty afterwards to summarize what had been discussed and to supply the provincial boards with a copy of his memorandum.

With regard to the educational policy formulated by the Govern-

---

[3] In 1836 Cousin described the Dutch law of 1806 and the Prussian law of 1819 as 'the two greatest monuments to the cause of popular education yet existing in the world'

[4] 'Algemeene toelating tot het geven van onderwijs'

[5] 'Speciale beroeping, aanstelling of admissie'

[6] See pp. 22–24 of *Publicatie van Hun Hoogmogende vertegenwoordigende het Bataafsche gemeenebest, aangaande het Lager Schoolwezen en Onderwijs in de Bataafsche Republiek* 1806

ment, it is interesting to note that, from 1808 onwards, more and more emphasis was placed on the advantages that would be gained if teachers were to follow the Pestalozzian method of instruction. This was owing primarily to the influence of W. van Wapperen of Haarlem and H. Scholten of Rotterdam who, after studying for three years at the Yverdun Institute, returned to Holland full of enthusiasm for what they had learnt.[7] There were, however, other contributory causes such as the interest created by a Dutch translation of *How Gertrude Teaches Her Children* in 1806, and the appointment of van den Ende as Inspector General for Primary Schools in 1808. The latter, who was a great admirer of the eminent Swiss reformer, remained in office from 1808 to 1833 and, during that period, did more than any of his contemporaries to fashion the outlines of official educational policy. One result of this was the creation in 1816 of two Normal Schools, the first at Haarlem and the second at Lierre, whose purpose was to train elementary schoolmasters to apply the principles of instruction outlined in *How Gertrude Teaches Her Children*. For a variety of reasons, therefore, the gradual development of the Dutch state system became identified, as far as teaching was concerned, with an interpretation of Pestalozzi's views.

Fortunately we are able to appraise the success both of this procedure and of many other developments connected with the 1806 law if we examine two official documents drawn up by distinguished Frenchmen, who personally investigated education in the Netherlands during the first half of the nineteenth century.

The first was by Georges Cuvier and Jean-François Noël,[8] two professors from the University of Paris, who undertook a journey to Holland in 1811, at the express command of Napoleon, in order to devise a method by which the Dutch and French universities could become affiliated. Though Institutes of Higher Learning were their prime concern, the French visitors also availed themselves of the opportunity to inspect several Dutch primary schools, and it is from their observations on the latter that we are able to form some idea of the progress that had been made by 1811.

In their report Cuvier and Noël commended the excellence of 'The Society for the Public Good' and the 1806 Act, both of which

---

[7] See *Paedagogische Studien, 27e jaargang, afl. 4*, pp. 117–123. April 1950

[8] The report was published in Paris in 1811 under the title *Rapport sur les établissements d'instruction primaire en Hollande*

had given a tremendous impetus to popular instruction. In fact
Holland, at that time, was able to boast no less than 4,451 primary
schools housing 190,000 pupils. These institutions, moreover, contrary to expectation, were clean, efficient and well organized. They
had been designed in the first place to supply instruction free of
charge in Reading, Writing, Arithmetic, Spelling, Drawing, Geography and Music to poor children who would otherwise have remained deprived of a formal education. So admirably had they succeeded, however, that within five years they had been asked to accept
many boys and girls who had previously been educated privately,
and the result was that they were full to capacity. This the professors could well understand, and attributed it in large measure to
the high quality of the Dutch primary teachers.

In Amsterdam the two professors visited a number of institutions
designed especially for vagrant children and were sensibly affected
by the extraordinary care with which these social outcasts were
trained to become useful members of society. In one such establishment they saw the senior girls practising Sewing and Dressmaking,
whilst the older boys did Cobbling and Carpentry. Such a well-
devised means of social regeneration struck them as particularly
noteworthy, and they commented on the extent to which Holland
applied it. In Amsterdam alone there were eleven institutions for
indigent children.

Finally, in their general summary of what they had seen, the
Frenchmen noted three characteristics of Dutch primary schools
which seemed to them unique—namely, that they were remarkably
orderly, despite the fact that corporal punishment had been abol-
ished; were co-educational and were non-denominational. The last
feature did not mean, however, that they ignored religious instruction altogether. It simply indicated that the particular tenets of
sectarianism were not allowed to be mentioned during Scripture
lessons. Yet both Cuvier and Noël were amazed to discover that all
children of the Christian faith, no matter what their religious persuasions, were expected to attend school on Saturday mornings in
order to learn the history of the New Testament. When questioned
about the wisdom of such a procedure the Dutch authorities pointed
out that Sundays were left free for denominational teaching, and
that the religious instruction given in schools was merely intended to
emphasize those points of doctrine on which all Christians funda-

mentally agreed. They commented further that no attempts at proselytism were permitted and that religious instruction took place on Saturday mornings for the sole purpose of allowing Jewish children during that interval to attend the synagogue. Thus a wide degree of toleration was manifest throughout the whole of their scheme.

A second report on the educational system of the Netherlands was written by Victor Cousin, the distinguished philosopher and member of the French Academy, who spent six weeks in Holland in 1836.[9] At the time of his visit the 1806 law was still in force and had been modified but little since the time when it was reviewed by Cuvier and Noël. The only difference that Cousin could detect was that meanwhile the entire state system had gained greater solidarity and firmness of structure. This he attributed to the excellent work of the district inspectors—the very corner stone on which the Dutch educational edifice rested.

On his arrival Cousin asked particularly to be shown the Dutch primary schools, and was informed that there were three kinds in existence: the Poor,[10] the Intermediate,[11] and the French.[12] Accordingly he began his tour of inspection by visiting a Poor School in The Hague where a large number of indigent children were being educated free of charge. All that was required of these pupils was that they should come to school as well washed, well combed and well clad as their poverty allowed. In charge of them were eleven male members of staff and a number of 'apprentice-assistants'. The latter ranged in age from fourteen to eighteen and were mostly former pupils of the school who were being trained as teachers. They spent a period of four years in the primary schools where, in addition to their work with children, they were expected to study for the qualifying examination set by the district inspectors. During this period of preparation they remained under the close supervision of the director of the school where they were employed and, in the evenings, attended classes on teaching-method and the principles of education. Though Cousin did not comment on this unique method

[9] Cousin's report *De l'instruction publique en Hollande* was published in Paris in 1837. One year later it was translated into English by Leonard Horner and published under the title of *On the State of Education in Holland as regards Schools for the working classes and for the poor*. London, 1838

[10] 'Armen-School'

[11] 'Tusschen-School'   [12] 'Franse School'

of training teachers, he was, in fact, witnessing an early manifest-ation of the 'Pupil Teacher' system—a system which was later to spread to Great Britain and to enjoy considerable success there until well into the twentieth century.

What Cousin did comment on, however, were the same three features that Cuvier and Noël had instanced some twenty-five years previously: first, that all the masters used the Pestalozzian method of instruction; secondly, that boys and girls were permitted to sit side by side; and thirdly, that the pupils belonged to a variety of religions. In one class he found Catholics, Calvinists, Lutherans, Remonstrants, Anabaptists and Jews mingled indiscriminately to-gether. 'I had', he remarked, 'an anticipation of what I should find throughout Holland—that entire toleration which pervades it in every part.' [13]

Cousin afterwards paid a rapid visit to the other primary insti-tutions in The Hague and, once again, was impressed by their broad religious attitude. The Intermediate School he found in many respects similar to the Poor School save that it was smaller and non-coeducational. The French School, however, immediately impressed him as unusual. It was a select and fairly expensive establishment, designed expressly for boys and girls of better class families who pur-posed eventually to enter a 'Gymnasium'. In consequence it main-tained a high standard of work and placed particular emphasis on the teaching of languages. Cousin commented favourably on the amount of individual work which the pupils undertook and, with obvious delight, laid aside the services of his interpreter to converse with them in French.

After inspecting the three types of primary school Cousin ex-pressed a desire to see any other educational establishments that Holland had devised in order to implement her 1806 Code. Accord-ingly he was taken first to a village school on the outskirts of Haar-lem, and afterwards to a nursery school in Rotterdam.

The former was situated in what appeared to be a private house 'of perfect Dutch neatness'. On one side was a large classroom cap-able of holding all the village children of school age; on the other the living accommodation of the schoolmaster and his family. The classroom was light, pleasant and scrupulously clean. It was kept constantly aired by means of several large ventilators and furnished

[13] Cousin Report (Horner Translation), p. 18

with small wooden tables that were so placed as to receive the maximum amount of light and to allow of easy passage to the teacher's blackboard. Cousin delighted in the atmosphere of freshness that surrounded him and was happy to find, yet again, that the village schoolmaster and his assistant were able to speak French.

The same impression of order and cleanliness was conveyed by the Nursery School in Rotterdam. As he entered the building Cousin found, on the left, a place where the pupils washed and, on the right, a large well-ventilated classroom. The school housed about a hundred infants who were divided into three classes. In the first were those of two years of age; in the second those from three to four, and in the third those from four to five. Each class was under the care of an assistant mistress, whilst the entire school was managed by a headmistress or directress. The children were taught elementary reading, writing and arithmetic. They did their work on slates, in the approved Pestalozzian manner, and spent much of their time playing games. For that purpose a large recreation room had been constructed at one end of the building, which was in constant use during the winter months or whenever the weather was inclement. In summer, Cousin learnt with satisfaction, the entire school worked and played out of doors.[14]

There can be no doubt whatsoever that Cousin's appreciation of the Dutch state system grew steadily keener the further he journeyed, for he spoke with increasing enthusiasm not only of the individual institutions that he encountered but also of the teachers who staffed them. The latter, by their industry, efficiency and never-failing courtesy, seemed to him to personify the very ideals which had inspired the 1806 Code. Undoubtedly, therefore, the highlight of the tour, as far as he was concerned, was the visit he paid to 'The Royal Seminary for the Training of Schoolmasters'[15] in Haarlem, whither he was conducted by its director, Prinsen. Cousin discovered that it

[14] There would seem to be little doubt, if one studies his comments on them, that Cousin regarded the Dutch nursery schools as a complete innovation. Yet how he was able to do so is hard to imagine for, as early as 1769, Oberlin, in the Ban-de-la-Roche, had conceived the idea of collecting the young children of his parishioners and entrusting them to the care of 'conductrices de la tendre jeunesse'. In 1829, moreover, Frédéric Cuvier had awarded 'le grand prix de vertu de la fondation Monthyon' to Louise Scheppler, Oberlin's chief assistant, precisely because of her work in nursery schools. Why Cousin made no mention of this is difficult to understand

[15] 'Rijks Kweekschool voor Schoolonderwijzers'

was a day school and that almost every student there was in receipt
of a Government grant. No one could be admitted under the age of
fourteen and no one accepted without first having served a pro-
bationary period of training lasting three months. During that interval Prinsen made it his duty to get to know each of the new
candidates personally and to sort out those who were obviously
unsuited for teaching. At the time of Cousin's visit there were forty
students in regular attendance, together with a number of older
teachers who had returned for supplementary training. They did
their work in the college but lived in lodgings in Haarlem. Their
studies usually kept them occupied from eight to ten hours daily
and, during the rest of the time, they were free to amuse themselves
as they wished, save that they were strictly enjoined not to enter
public houses or places of entertainment—offences that necessitated
instant dismissal. Few of them, however, were guilty of such irregular
conduct, first because they came to Haarlem voluntarily, and
secondly because they deemed it a great honour to have been
accepted at the 'Royal Seminary'.

The course of study which they followed lasted four years and
comprised the following subjects: History, Geography, Mathematics, Natural Science, Singing, Drawing, Penmanship, Philosophy, Pedagogics and Religion. Cousin remarked on the fact that all
students attended lectures on the Old Testament, but that Jews
were exempted from those on the New Testament and the life of
Christ. He also noted that Prinsen personally directed the courses on
Pedagogics. These consisted of three series of lectures on Pestalozzi's
educational principles which were delivered in the evenings during
the period when the students were engaged as under-masters or
assistants in the Haarlem primary schools. Thus, Prinsen asserted,
theory and practice went hand in hand.

Whilst in Haarlem, Cousin likewise took the opportunity of paying his respects to van den Ende, who had been responsible for starting the 'Royal Seminary' in 1816, and who, though old and infirm,
still maintained an active interest in its welfare. Cousin regarded him
as the foremost promoter of popular instruction then alive in Europe
and was anxious to seek his advice on three subjects of general
importance with regard to primary education. The first, as might be
expected, concerned the way in which religious instruction should be
given in schools, and van den Ende was emphatic that the method

then in existence in Holland was the right one. 'The primary schools must be Christian,' he asserted, 'but neither Catholic nor Protestant. They ought not to belong to any particular church, nor ought they to teach any separate creed: nothing ought to be admitted which tends to produce a division of the schools; a school for the people ought to be for the whole of the people.' [16] Cousin's rather laconic comment was: 'You are in Holland, where a Christian spirit is widely disseminated, but where, at the same time, a great degree of toleration has existed for centuries amongst the members of different communion.' [17]

The second question concerned the way in which inspectors should be chosen—a subject on which van den Ende could not be drawn but which solicited from him the following pregnant observation: 'Take care whom you choose as inspectors; they are a class of men who ought to be searched for with a lantern in one's hand.' [18]

And the third question concerned the merits or demerits of the system of mutual instruction which, Cousin pointed out, enjoyed considerable popularity in several European countries, but was nowhere to be found in Holland. 'This by no means arises from our not being sufficiently acquainted with the system,' replied van den Ende. 'We have studied it well, and it is because we have studied it that we have laid it aside. . . . Do you expect that, by such a mode of tuition, the instruction given in the primary schools will ever form men? For that, in truth, is the real purpose. The different things taught in school are but means, and their whole value depends upon the degree of relation they bear to that object. It never will be attained unless the system of mutual instruction be given up; it does well for the purpose of conveying a certain amount of information, but will never *educate* the pupil; and, I repeat it, education is the object of all instruction.' [19] With this expression of opinion Cousin readily agreed, and added: 'Both as a philosopher and moralist I maintain that simultaneous teaching (individual tuition being unobtainable) is the only method that is suitable for the education of the moral being.'

There is no doubt that this conversation was emphasized by Cousin because it seemed to him not merely to give a reasoned commentary on educational problems that were very real to many thinking

[16] Cousin Report (Horner Translation), p. 29

[18] *Ibid.* p. 31

[17] *Ibid.* p. 30

[19] *Ibid.* p. 33

people at the time, but also to afford an insight into the mind of the man who, as Inspector General for Primary Schools from 1808 to 1833, helped to fashion and fortify the Netherlands' state system of education. Throughout his tour Cousin was repeatedly made aware of the religious toleration, the wise system of inspection and the enlightened methods of teaching which van den Ende advocated. Yet he could not bring himself to accept these three guiding principles as equal either in value or importance. As far as inspection and methods of teaching were concerned, he was wholeheartedly in support of the Dutch policy. On the subject of religious teaching, however, he remained doubtful. 'I confess', he said, 'that the absolute separation of the school and the church is, to my mind, in no degree better than the undue interference of the one with the other. There is a happy medium in the matter, which Holland is far from being in any disposition to adopt.' [20]

It was precisely because he included criticism as well as praise in his account that Cousin gave so valuable a commentary on what he saw in Holland in 1836. Never for one moment did he allow his enthusiasm for what he admired to run away with him or to prevent his censuring what he felt to be unsatisfactory. His balanced judgment kept a correct perspective throughout. Yet the final impression that his report conveyed was one of sweetness and light. Cousin showed the tremendous strides that Holland had made since the foundation of 'The Society for the Public Good' in 1784. He commended the wisdom and effectiveness of her 1806 Code. He demonstrated the way in which she had carefully built up her educational establishments and promoted the Pestalozzian principles of instruction. He pointed out the high standard of work maintained by her teachers and inspectors, and he praised the toleration and breadth of vision which infused the whole of her state system of education. With the possible exception of Prussia, he said, no country in Europe had done more to promote the happiness and well-being of her people, and it would be both salutary and inspiring if other nations were to follow her example.

[20] Cousin Report (Horner Translation), p. 42

8

THE ADOPTION OF A STATE SYSTEM OF EDUCATION BY PRUSSIA

'From foreign sources Germany has been infected with self-seeking. She must be built up on a loftier moral plane, for which we require a new system of education. . . . The new education must completely destroy freedom of will. The pupil must not even hear that our impulses and actions may be directed towards our own interests. . . . The foreign genius is like a bee; the German spirit is like an eagle; to have character and to be a German undoubtedly mean the same.'

J. G. FICHTE—*Reden an die deutsche Nation.* 1808

In the early years of the nineteenth century, when Holland was striving to promote the welfare of her people by means of systematic instruction, another of Napoleon's victims was giving careful consideration to the same subject. This was Prussia, a young and vigorous nation, whose desire for enlightenment was immense, but whose ideas and ideals, apart from a common interest in Pestalozzi, were strangely at variance with those of Holland. The result was that she created a state system of schools which, though remarkably efficient, was as different from that of her neighbour as was well-nigh conceivable. In order to appreciate this contrast, however, and to understand how it arose, it is necessary briefly to examine the state of primary instruction in Prussia during the latter half of the eighteenth century.

The sordidness, poverty, squalor and neglect which characterized primary schools in France, Switzerland and Holland prior to the Revolution were likewise to be found in Prussia. Indeed, if we study social history during the reign of Frederick William II, it is clear he believed that no advantage could possibly accrue from an educated proletariat and that the instruction of poor children could happily be left to such unenlightened preceptors as old soldiers, night watchmen and shepherds. The background to the history of educational

85

reform in Prussia, therefore, differs not one whit from that of other European countries.

Such a gloomy state of affairs, however, was happily not allowed to continue by Frederick William III, who early evinced a desire to promote the prosperity of his people. It was, indeed, largely because of his interest that a complete transformation eventually took place in the state of popular instruction. He began his reign, for example, by appointing as Minister of Education, von Massow, a man of considerable administrative ability who had already held a number of influential posts. On 3rd July, 1798, moreover, in order that the new Minister be conversant with what he required, Frederick William addressed a directive to him in which he summarized under three headings his views on the education of the people. First, he stated that it was solely by means of instruction that the poor child was rescued from a life of vagabondage and moulded into a good citizen; secondly, that this had never been accomplished in the past because large sections of the peasantry had remained deprived of the advantages of a formal education; and thirdly, that it was clearly the first duty of the new Minister to inaugurate a state system of schools.[1]

In his reply von Massow adumbrated a plan whereby primary institutions should be created throughout the realm. When he submitted it for the king's approval, however, he took care to point out that it was bound to prove ineffective unless the Government backed it financially—words of counsel that did not go unheeded. So anxious was Frederick William that the scheme be implemented that he decided to give an annual grant of 6,000 thalers from his own purse for the construction and maintenance of educational establishments in the March of Brandenburg. Of this sum 1,000 thalers were to be spent on building industrial schools for the peasantry, 500 on schools for girls and the remaining 4,500 on any other educational improvements that the Minister deemed necessary. Previous to that date the instruction of girls had been sadly neglected, and no institutions existed for their benefit save a few exclusive academies for the daughters of the nobility. There was, in consequence, some difficulty in finding a person suitable to take charge of the venture when, quite unexpectedly, Ernestine von Krosigk, a woman of letters, declared her willingness to do so. In 1797 she started a number of

[1] See p. 253 of Vol. 5 of *Geschichte der Erziehung* by Dr. K. A. Schmid

private schools in Berlin for the daughters of the soldiers and, three years later, helped to train school-mistresses by personally directing the first Normal School for women. Meanwhile von Massow made headway with the provision of primary schools and Frederick William himself, anxious to achieve a unity of outlook amongst his people, ordered the most competent men in the realm to prepare a book of readings, songs and prayers which would prove suitable to all denominations. Over and above all this, considerable interest was created in new methods of teaching by the publication of Pestalozzi's *How Gertrude Teaches Her Children* in 1801 and of Herbart's *Pestalozzi's Idea of an ABC of Anschauung* in 1802. Every indication, therefore, was given that the nation was preparing seriously to tackle the problems of ignorance and illiteracy when suddenly the turn of national events put an end to these beginnings.

The early years of the nineteenth century were fraught with anxiety for Prussia. From the time of his accession in 1797 Frederick William III studiously avoided any clash between the Prussian and French forces, but from 1803 onwards it became obvious to him that the latter's numerous incursions into Germany would some day have to be challenged. The situation was further aggravated when, on the way to Austerlitz, Napoleon seized a number of states which looked to Prussia for protection. Accordingly, in 1806, Frederick William promptly ordered Napoleon to retire behind the Rhine—an unwise injunction which achieved naught for his country save a conqueror's yoke and her own dismemberment. Prussia was reduced by half after the battles of Jena and Auerstadt (1806) and again after the treaty of Tilsit (1807). Her losses were huge, her armies were scattered and disaster faced her on every hand. At such a time, it might be imagined, Prussia would have little desire for educational reform. Oddly enough, however, even during those days of defeat and despair, she turned to popular enlightenment as the one means left open to her to regain her glory. Frederick William and Queen Louise breathed patriotism into the souls of their subjects. Members of the nobility emulated their efforts. Fichte gave his inspiring *Addresses to the German Nation* and, as if by magic, public instruction began not only to grow but to flourish.

'We have sacrificed a great deal in the length of our lands,' said Frederick William. 'Our state has lost much in external power and splendour, but that is all the more reason why we should direct our attention towards winning for it an internal power and splendour. It is my formal desire that the most minute attention be given to popular instruction.'

His Minister, Baron von Stein, replied: 'In order to transform the people, to inspire them with confidence and to make them ready to endure any sacrifice for independence and national honour, we must educate the youth of the country. All the forces of the spirit must be developed and no ability on which the dignity of man rests must be neglected. We shall thus see a generation growing up which is physically and morally of such vigour that a better future will open before us.' [2]

Perhaps the most significant factor of the urge for enlightenment that swept through Prussia from 1806 onwards was the interest which her philosophers and politicians took in the teachings of Pestalozzi. This was primarily because of Fichte who, in the ninth of the fourteen addresses that he delivered in Berlin during the winter of 1807–8, placed the eminent Swiss teacher along with Luther as a national saviour. 'In spite of obstacles of every kind,' he declared, 'Pestalozzi, inspired by the mighty and invincible sentiment of love of the poor and the outcast, has succeeded in making an intellectual discovery that is destined to revolutionize the world. He has sought an education for the common people and, by the force of his genius and his love, he has created a true national education that is capable of rescuing the nations and humanity as a whole from the deplorable situation into which they have now fallen.' [3] Such was Fichte's tribute in a dark hour of Prussia's history. He was, however, by no means the only person who, at that time, was looking to Switzerland for inspiration. Others, such as von Stein and Wilhelm von Humboldt, their subordinates Nicolovius and Süvern, and the directors of Normal Schools, Harnisch and Diesterweg, also had their eyes fixed on the Yverdun Institute.[4] Of this number two at least could claim the distinction of being friends of Pestalozzi—Fichte and Nicolovius. Both had stayed with him in Switzerland and both had maintained

[2] See *Dictionnaire de Pédagogie et d'Instruction Primaire*. Article on Prussia on p. 2472 of Vol. II

[3] See Ninth Address of Fichte's *Addresses to the German Nation*, translated by R. F. Jones and G. H. Turnbull, 1922

[4] For a detailed consideration of the extent to which Fichte influenced his more prominent contemporaries in their admiration of Pestalozzi, see *The Educational Theory of J. G. Fichte* (pp. 85–89) by G. H. Turnbull, 1926

an active correspondence with him over the years. There were, therefore, several influential men in Prussia who, in the period of national reconstruction following Jena, were anxious that the teaching principles enunciated in *How Gertrude Teaches Her Children* receive careful consideration.

An interest in Pestalozzi was further stimulated when, at the beginning of 1809, Wilhelm von Humboldt was appointed Director of Ecclesiastical Affairs and Public Instruction. A man of learning and high ideals himself, he readily seized the opportunity afforded him by his new position to spread the gospel of enlightenment to others, and the result was that, though he remained in office only until 23rd June, 1810, he left an indelible imprint on Prussian education. His three greatest undertakings were the creation of the University of Berlin (1810), the reorganization of the system of admission to universities and the introduction of a qualifying examination for secondary schoolmasters. It would be unfair, however, because of the magnitude of these achievements, to ignore two rather special contributions which he also gave to primary education. In 1809 at his insistence, Zeller opened a Normal School in Königsberg, which was devoted entirely to furthering Pestalozzi's principles, and Preuss, Kaweran and Henning, three student teachers, were despatched to Yverdun to study the new educational gospel at its source. They were joined soon afterwards by fifteen others and, from that date onwards, there began a steady pilgrimage between Prussia and Yverdun which was to continue as long as the famous Institute remained in existence.[5]

When these students returned to their native land they were anxious not only to demonstrate what they had learnt, but also to impress on their fellow countrymen two fundamental truths with regard to the future development of primary instruction: that the first condition of having good schools was to have good schoolmasters, and that to have good schoolmasters it was necessary to train them. The years succeeding 1810, in consequence, saw the creation of several Normal Schools in Prussia and the gradual penetration into her primary institutions of a number of capable teachers all of whom were conversant with Pestalozzi's methods. Third-rate tailors and disabled soldiers were supplanted by young men who held a firm conviction that no duty was more sacred than that of

[5] See p. 241 of Friedrich Paulsen's *German Education Past and Present*, p. 908

providing a proper training for the youth of the country, many new districts were provided with schools and serious consideration was given by the Government to the best means of ensuring a uniform educational policy.

During this period of steady growth Public Instruction remained a branch of the Ministry of the Interior. Gradually, however, the conviction grew in Frederick William's mind that more authority would be given to education if a severance were to be effected, and so, on 3rd November, 1817, he created an independent Ministry of Public Instruction and Ecclesiastical Affairs,[6] which he entrusted to Baron von Altenstein. The latter nominated as his assistants Süvern and Nicolovius, and the three of them set to work to revise Prussia's educational enactments. The task was by no means easy as a mass of statutes confronted them, some of which were obsolete and others in need of considerable modification. In 1819, however, after months of toil, they completed their work and the famous Prussian law of Public Instruction was promulgated which remained in force, more or less undisturbed, until von Raumer became Minister of Education in 1850.

Fortunately we are able to form some idea of the intricate workings of this enactment by virtue of an official account written by Victor Cousin whose comments on Holland have already been noted. He spent three weeks in Prussia in June 1831 and, on his return to Paris, published his *Rapport sur l'état de l'instruction publique en Prusse*,[7] which gave a detailed description of all he had seen.

In 1819, Cousin affirmed, Prussia devised two authorities for the internal management of the state. The first was the Ministry of the Interior, which controlled all institutions relating to commerce, public works and factories, and the second was the Ministry of Public Instruction, of Ecclesiastical and Medical Affairs. The latter, in view of its tripartite constitution, was housed in three separate offices in charge of each of which was a director whose responsibilities were clearly defined. The first took charge of Public Instruction, the second of Church Affairs and the third of Medicine. To

[6] Ministerium des öffentlichen Unterrichts, der geistlichen-und-medicinal-Angelegenheiten

[7] Cousin's report was translated into English by Sarah Austin and published under the title *Report on the State of Public Instruction in Prussia* in 1834

assist each director was a body of twelve councillors who met twice a week to discuss developments in various parts of the realm.

Prussia, at that time, was divided into ten provinces, each of which possessed a separate council [8] under the charge of an official known as the 'over-president'.[9] These provinces were themselves divided into departments,[10] which likewise had separate councils controlled by a 'president'.[11] Continuing further down the scale, each department was once more divided into circles [12] and finally all circles were subdivided into parishes.[13] Thus, by means of his director, councillors, over-president, president and various other officials, the Minister in Berlin was kept constantly abreast of educational developments even in the remotest parts of the kingdom.

An interesting feature of this carefully graded series of steps was the way in which the various levels made themselves answerable for different kinds of public instruction. Thus, whilst the universities became the responsibility of the state, Normal Schools and Gymnasia were controlled by the departments, and primary schools either by the circles or parishes.

Every parish, by reason of the 1819 law, had to possess a school which was inspected by the local pastor or priest. Associated with this member of the clergy was a committee of superintendence,[14] which was composed of the most distinguished persons in the parish. In urban districts, however, where there were frequently several schools in a parish, it was necessary to have a higher education committee. This was known as the 'school commission'.[15]

In addition to the local inspectors there was, in the chief town of the circle, another inspector [16] whose authority extended over all the schools within the circle and whose duty it was to maintain close contact with his subordinates. He was almost always a clergyman. As may be seen, then, the first degrees of authority in primary instruction were in the hands of the Church, but there the ecclesiastical influence ceased.

At the next stage, the civil power began to exercise its authority. The president of the council had several advisers under his control, one of whom was specially charged with the task of supervising primary schools. He was known as the 'Schulrat' and was a man of

---

[8] 'Regierung' [9] 'Oberpräsident' [10] 'Regierungsbezirke'
[11] 'Präsident' [12] 'Kreise' [13] 'Gemeinde'
[14] 'Schulvorstand' [15] 'Schuldeputation' [16] 'Kreisschulinspektor'

considerable importance because he acted as a link between public instruction and the civil administration of the province. He had, in fact, a dual rôle. He was nominated by the Minister of Public Instruction but, on his nomination, became one of the president's advisers and thus responsible to the Minister of the Interior. The 'Schulrat' made reports to the council which then decided by a majority vote what action to take. He inspected schools and kept close contact with committees and teachers. Reports from inspectors were addressed to him and he conducted all correspondence relative to schools in the name of the department. The 'Schulrat' was thus the true director of primary instruction in each department.

As a brief summary one might say that all primary instruction in Prussia was parochial and departmental. At the same time it was subject to the Minister of Public Instruction and thus had a double character. The double character was represented by the 'Schulrat', who had a seat on the council of the department and was responsible both to the Minister of the Interior and to the Minister of Public Instruction.[17]

Such was the intricate legislation which Prussia introduced in 1819 to promote the enlightenment of her people—a code of law as different from the Dutch enactment of 1806 as was imaginable. In order to realize the implications of what von Altenstein, Nicolovius and Süvern had done, however, it is profitable, along with the Cousin report, to study two papers on Prussian education written in 1837 and 1838 by W. Wittich, a native of Tilsit, who taught German in University College, London. The first he named 'On the Former and Present Conditions of Elementary Schools in Prussia',[18] and the second 'On the Seminaries for Schoolmasters in Prussia'[19]—two highly detailed accounts that serve not only to show the Prussian law translated into practice but also to amplify the observations of the French philosopher.

From both Cousin and Wittich, then, we learn that, as a result of the 1819 statute, three kinds of primary institution were recognized by Prussia. The first was the free 'Poor School'[20] for indigent children, which was situated in the cities and large towns; the second was the fee-paying 'Elementary School'[21] for poor and working-

[17] See Cousin Report (Austin Translation), pp. 13–19
[18] See *The Publications of the Central Society of Education*, Vol. I
[19] *Ibid.* Vol. II   [20] 'Armenschule'   [21] 'Elementarschule'

class boys and girls, which was to be found in both urban and country districts, and the third was the more expensive 'Burgher School' [22] for better-class children, which existed only in towns. Few differences were perceptible between them save that the last gave considerable attention to the teaching of Latin because many of its pupils purposed to enter a 'Gymnasium'. In other respects, however, the three types of primary institution were remarkably similar. All catered for children between the ages of seven and fourteen; all used the Pestalozzian method of instruction; and all, with the solitary exception already noted, taught the same subjects. Furthermore the lines of demarcation between them were not so strongly drawn as might be imagined. Thus, if an indigent child lived in a district where no poor school existed, he was admitted free of charge to the nearest elementary school.

The course of instruction in the primary schools was divided into four periods each of two years. In the first of these, from the entrance of the child into school until the completion of his eighth year, his senses were exercised for three hours daily in the approved Pestalozzian manner. He was introduced, for example, to a great number of objects of different shapes and sizes and asked to take note of any special qualities they possessed. This served as a preparation for 'Weltkunde' or 'knowledge of the external world'—a subject which included the first elements of Geography, History, and Nature Study, and trained the pupil to estimate distances, examine the growth of trees and plants, and recognize different sounds and scents, etc. Not until his five senses had thus been stimulated could he proceed to more advanced study. Indeed, during this initial period of sense-training, all attempts at forcing him to learn were strictly forbidden. He was simply expected to absorb impressions and gradually to unfold in the manner of a flower. After some weeks, however, when a well-marked desire to learn facts asserted itself, he was introduced to Reading, Writing and Arithmetic. These subjects, in addition to 'Weltkunde', then occupied the whole of his time and so, at the completion of his eighth year, he generally knew how to read, write, add, subtract, multiply and divide, and could name the properties of those objects of the external world which confronted him in his immediate environment.

In the second period, when the children varied in age between

<hr>

[22] 'Bürgerschule' or 'Stadtschule'

eight and ten, instruction usually lasted four hours a day. At the completion of this course they were expected to be able to narrate in their own words the Bible stories they had studied; do arithmetical problems; write legibly, speak correctly and read accurately; sing from music; name the most important plants and animals; repeat historical events and express their ideas with exactness.

In the third period, from ten to twelve, the pupils were in school four and a half hours each day. During this time they committed to memory a large number of Biblical passages and religious songs; worked advanced problems in Arithmetic; began Algebra and Geometry; studied German Grammar; practised part-singing and learnt to read with accuracy and expression.

Finally, in the fourth period, from twelve to fourteen, the children were instructed five hours a day. By the end of this course they were supposed to have acquired a clear conception of the dogmas of their respective churches; a knowledge of accounts and algebraic equations; a familiarity with reference books; a sound training in penmanship; an intimacy with the geography of Europe; a mastery of their native tongue, and the power to express their thoughts with lucidity and precision.[23]

Wittich admitted that such a course was not universally applied in Prussian primary schools, but that it had been tried with good results in many country districts and was strongly insisted on in towns. He acknowledged, too, the necessity of small classes if the plan were wholly to succeed. In 1837 many schools were still overcrowded, particularly in Silesia where as many as a hundred children were to be found in one class. Legislation, therefore, was needed to determine how many pupils a teacher should have under his control. The town of Bremen had led the way in this respect by enacting that the number of boys or girls in any class should never exceed twenty-five.[24]

The mere fact that such matters were under discussion clearly demonstrated the amazing transformation that had been effected in primary education since the disasters of Jena and Auerstadt—a transformation which was obviously attributable in no small measure to the high quality of the Prussian Normal Schools. In 1837 there

[23] Wittich—*On the Former and Present Condition of the Elementary Schools in Prussia*, pp. 166–169
[24] *Ibid.* p. 171

were no less than fifty such establishments—all of them busily engaged interpreting the Pestalozzian principles of instruction. Of this number about ten were known as 'large' and the remainder as 'small' seminaries. The former, of which the most famous was Dr. Diesterweg's Academy in Berlin, were usually situated in cities. They catered for better-class students, who purposed eventually to teach in the burgher schools, and therefore included Latin in their curricula. The latter, however, which were mostly to be found in towns of moderate size, were the true nurseries of the teachers of the poor.

At first sight, as with the burgher and elementary schools, one might imagine that the large and small seminaries were totally dissimilar. The truth of the matter was, however, that they both strove ardently to promote the teaching principles outlined in *How Gertrude Teaches Her Children* and, in consequence, provided a training that was in many respects identical.

A student usually entered a Normal School at the age of sixteen and remained there until he was nineteen.[25] During the first year, in view of the fact that his studies had usually been neglected since he left the primary school, he spent a great deal of time revising German Grammar and Literature, Mathematics, History, Geography, Biology, Natural Science, Drawing and Singing. In addition he learnt to play the organ because many education authorities insisted that teachers should also act as choirmasters. The subject to which he gave the greatest attention, however, was Religion—a fact that may readily be discerned from the time-table overleaf which was in use at the Normal Seminary in Eisleben during the summer of 1838. All students were compelled to attend lectures on ecclesiastical history, the Old and New Testaments and the tenets of the particular church to which they belonged. They were likewise directed to present themselves daily for morning and evening prayers in the college chapel, to attend a place of worship at least twice every Sunday, and to write out summaries of all the sermons they heard.

During the second year, in addition to the subjects already mentioned, the students were introduced, by means of three courses, to the principles of teaching. These included 'Pädagogik' or the science of training, 'Didaktik' or the art of instruction and 'Methodik' or

[25] Cousin Report (Austin Translation), p. 169

COURSE OF INSTRUCTION PURSUED IN THE TWO CLASSES OF THE NORMAL SEMINARY IN EISLEBEN, PRUSSIA, IN THE SUMMER HALF-YEAR OF 1838

Hours	Classes	Monday	Tuesday	Wednesday	Thursday	Friday	Saturday
7 to 8	First	Religious Instruction	Religious Instruction	Art of Teaching	Religious Instruction	Religious Instruction	Religious Instruction
	Second	Religious Instruction	Profane History	Logic	Religious Instruction	Profane History	Logic or Sacred History
8 to 9	First	Profane History	Logic	Geography	Profane History	Logic or Prussian History	Geography
	Second	Arithmetic	Thorough Bass and Organ	Geometry	Grammar	Arithmetic	Geometry
9 to 10	First	Reading	Organ	Thorough Bass	Art of Teaching	Reading	Arithmetic
	Second	Thorough Bass and Organ	Religious Instruction	Drawing	Writing	Religious Instruction	Thorough Bass and Organ
10 to 11	First	Arithmetic	Grammar	Violin	Arithmetic	Grammar	Organ
	Second	Grammar	Singing	Drawing	Thorough Bass and Organ	Singing	Writing
1 to 2	First	Art of Teaching	Natural Philosophy		Examination	Natural History	
	Second	Natural Philosophy	Reading		Natural Philosophy	Reading	
2 to 3	First	Geometry	Drawing		Geometry	Writing	
	Second	Composition	Geography		Composition	Geography	
3 to 4	First	Thorough Bass	Drawing		Violin	Writing	
	Second		Violin			Violin	
4 to 5	First	Organ			Organ		
Note:							

Note: Three hours of singing, and one hour of instruction in the Art of Teaching are also given weekly at indeterminate times

Included in *Four Periods of Public Education* by Sir James P. Kay-Shuttleworth (1862)

the theory of method.[26] As might be expected, the greater number of these lectures were detailed expositions of the fundamental educational truths advanced by Pestalozzi. A few, however, dealt with topics of more general interest such as the maintenance of discipline, the responsibilities of the teacher with regard to the community and the attitude which the schoolmaster should adopt towards the various educational officials with whom he came in contact.

At the beginning of the third year, by which time the students had attained a reasonable standard of learning together with some knowledge of teaching method, they were allowed to act as assistant masters in the primary schools attached to their seminaries. In order that they should receive the maximum amount of experience, moreover, they were divided into small groups, each member of which taught two subjects for eight weeks. At the end of this period he changed to two other subjects and so, in the course of the year, gradually worked his way through the entire curriculum. Teaching practice, however, rarely occupied more than twelve hours weekly and so, in order that no time be wasted, further educational courses and conferences took place in the college. The latter were frequently conducted by the director himself, who discussed with the students the difficulties they encountered in their work and impressed upon them the importance of their self-chosen profession. Much, therefore, depended on the quality of this man. If he were able, he could quickly turn the poorest seminary into something of account; if, however, he were incapable, the results of his weakness would be quickly manifest in all branches of the establishment. Fortunately, Cousin asserted, the Prussians attached great importance to the maxim 'As is the master, so is the school' and, in consequence, exercised extreme vigilance in the choice of directors for their Normal Schools.[27]

Such were the estimable features of the state system of education that Prussia devised in 1819—features which prompted an American visitor named Calvin E. Stowe to exclaim: 'I think the system in its general outline as nearly complete as human ingenuity and skill can conceive.'[28]

It remains to be noted, however, that though the 'general outline'

---

[26] See Cousin Report (Austin Translation), p. 200
[27] *Ibid.* p. 149
[28] See p. 307 of *Reports on European Education* edited by Edgar W. Knight, 1930

of the scheme was admirable, certain minor details were distinctly arbitrary. Under the 1819 law it was the duty of all parents to send their children to school from the age of seven to fourteen. As Cousin so sapiently remarked: 'This obligation is so national, so rooted in all the legal and moral habits of the country, that it is expressed by a single word "Schulpflichtigkeit".[29] It corresponds to another word similarly formed and similarly sanctioned by public opinion "Dienstpflichtigkeit".[30] These two words are completely characteristic of Prussia; they contain the secret of its originality as a nation, of its power as a state, and the germ of its future civilization.' [31] The fact that school attendance became compulsory at so early a date in the nineteenth century was, of course, highly commendable. The means adopted to ensure it, however, were unfortunately less so. One is amazed on studying the 1819 Code to-day to discover the extra-ordinary powers which the state assumed to coerce unwilling or negligent parents to have their children educated. Such authoritarianism reveals only too clearly what Cousin described as 'the germ of Prussia's future civilization'.

The following is a typical example. Every year, after Easter or Michaelmas, the committees and municipal authorities made enquiries concerning all families under their jurisdiction which had not provided private tuition for their sons and daughters in lieu of public instruction. For this purpose a census of all children of school age was made. Baptismal registers and the records of the civil authorities were laid open for inspection and the police were asked to give every assistance. The significant fact was that, when this information had been obtained, it was used not merely to coerce unwilling parents to send their offspring to school, but also to ensure that the children arrived at school punctually. Thus the state increased its power over the very lives of the people. 'If parents and masters neglect sending their children punctually to school . . . coercive measures are then to be resorted to against the parents, guardians or masters. The children are to be taken to school by an officer of police, or the parents are to be sentenced to graduated punishments or fines; and in case they are unable to pay, to imprisonment or labour, for the benefit of the parish.' [32]

Again, one is astonished to discover how the Jews were singled out

---

[29] 'School-duty or school-obligation' [30] 'Military service'
[31] Cousin Report (Austin Translation), p. 24 [32] Ibid. p. 28

for special treatment by the 1819 Act. They were forbidden to take part in the management of any state institutions, strictly enjoined not to admit the children of Gentiles into their schools and deprived of their civil rights if they refused to have their children educated. In the year 1817 Prussia numbered among its inhabitants some 7,000,000 Protestants, 4,200,000 Catholics and 170,000 members of other religious denominations including Jews.[33] Such a minority could hardly have been dangerous it would seem. The fact remains, nevertheless, that a strong antipathy towards Jewry was shown by those who framed the 1819 Code—an antipathy that stands in remarkable contrast to the toleration and breadth of vision which inspired the Dutch enactment of 1806.

Cousin was undoubtedly conscious of these limitations when, on presenting his report to the Minister of Public Instruction in Paris, he stressed the fact that certain modifications of the 1819 law would have to be made if it were to suit the French character. On such imperfections, however, he did not dwell. He merely contented himself with fostering much that was of value in what he had observed —the efficiency of Prussia's administration, the excellence of her primary and Normal schools, the faith of her teachers in Pestalozzi and, above all, the zeal of her people for enlightenment. If such advantages accrued from a state system of education, then it would be well if France and other European countries were to look to Prussia for guidance. 'The true greatness of a people', he said, 'does not consist in borrowing nothing from others, but in borrowing from all whatever is good, and in perfecting whatever it appropriates.' [34]

[33] Cousin Report, Introduction by Mrs. Austin, p. xxxvi
[34] Cousin Report (Austin Translation), p. 292

9

THE ORIGIN OF THE MONITORIAL SCHOOL AND ITS INFLUENCE ON EUROPE

'On accuse cette méthode (d'enseignement mutuel) d'être d'origine anglaise et, le croirait-on! on lui en fait un tort, un tort impardonable pour certains esprits. Je pourrais, comme plusiers de mes com-patriotes, revendiquer cette invention pour ma patrie, et ce ne serait pas sans fondement. Mais qu'importe cette puérile querelle? Personne, je crois, ne contestera à la France l'esprit d'invention. Elle en a un supérieur encore, celui de croire qu'elle s'honore elle-même, en mettant à profit toutes les découvertes, toutes les inventions de quelque lieu qu'elles viennent, si elles sont utiles au bonheur des hommes.'

LA ROCHEFOUCAULD, President of the Society for Elementary
Instruction in France, 1818–19 and 1821–22

IT will be noted that Cousin concluded his reports both on Holland and Prussia by suggesting that France and other countries should pay the strictest attention to what he had described if they were to achieve any kind of scholastic distinction—a suggestion that is useful not merely in establishing the educational pre-eminence of the two countries concerned, but also in tracing the pattern of primary in-struction in Europe during the first half of the nineteenth century. For, if the Dutch and Prussians looked to Switzerland for guidance in their tentative gropings after a satisfactory educational creed, there is no doubt that the majority of nations chose quite a different course. Indeed one may ponder long on the reason why, for instance, Denmark, Spain and France manifested scarcely any enthusiasm for Pestalozzi's revelation when such pains were taken to make them aware of its advantages. In 1803, the Danish Government sent two teachers, Strøm and Torlitz, to Burgdorf where they stayed for six months in order to familiarize themselves with the renowned teacher's educative principles. On their return they established a model school in Copenhagen and worked hard to interest their fellow-countrymen in what they had learnt, but their efforts were largely ineffectual and, by 1808, their school had ceased to exist.[1] In 1805 Voitel de Soleure inaugurated a campaign to familiarize the Spaniards with the Pestalozzian doctrines and, on 5th April, 1806, started a day training college for teachers in Madrid with a subsidiary branch in Santander. He hoped later to establish Normal Schools in other important cultural centres, but the scheme never matured. A complete apathy on the part of the public killed it.[2] In 1808 Alexander Boniface, for a time teacher of French at Yverdun, established a Pestalozzian school in Paris, and, in 1812, Jullien de Paris published his *Esprit de la méthode de Pestalozzi*—but neither won any acclaim.[3] The more one studies the growth of primary education in Europe, the clearer it becomes that the majority of nations either could not afford or were not prepared to inaugurate the reforms which Pestalozzi advocated. Odd as it may seem, therefore, in their search for an alternative means of instruction, they looked towards England—a country by no means distinguished for educational reform. Nevertheless, in England as elsewhere, there was a growing demand for education—a demand which was temporarily satisfied, as far as primary instruction was concerned, by the efforts of Andrew Bell and Joseph Lancaster. Each of these individuals made the establishment and maintenance of schools possible by falling back on the age-old expedient of setting children to teach one another, and each contrived to turn his particular brand of mutual instruction into a recognizable system.

The history of the monitorial movement in Great Britain is, of course, too well known to need further elaboration here. It is perhaps relevant to remark, however, that its progress, certainly in this country, was so closely bound up with the bitter quarrels that arose between Bell and Lancaster as to which of the two first decided to employ monitors, that it is almost impossible to obtain a dispassionate view of the system. Indeed the heat generated by their disputes was sufficient to ensure not only that the two teachers despised one another thoroughly, but also that their disciples

[1] See p. 247 of *Vor Skole* (*Our School*) by Hans Kyrre
[2] See p. 312 of *Pestalozzi* by H. Holman
[3] See p. 1442 of Vol. II of *Dictionnaire de Pédagogie et d'Instruction Primaire*. Article on Jullien de Paris

banded themselves into unbelievably hostile camps. This cleavage was further accentuated by the formation of two societies. In 1811 the 'National Society for the Education of the Poor in the Principles of the Established Church' allied itself with the monitorial system as laid down by Bell, and, in 1814, the 'Royal Lancasterian Association' renamed itself 'The British and Foreign School Society'. Thus two rival groups came into being whose points of divergence, more religious than educational, appeared irreconcilable. Furthermore, when the monitorial system spread to the Continent, the contentions still continued and French educationists, with a Gallic love of fine distinctions, chose to style themselves as either 'Belliste' or 'Lancastrien'.

The differences between the competing schools were, however, fewer than such disputes indicated. Bell held that a class should contain between twenty-four and thirty pupils or, in large schools, forty; Lancaster considered ten the ideal number and consequently required more monitors.[4] Bell expected his masters to take an active interest in the teaching: Lancaster looked to his merely to supervise and watch the almost automatic working of the system. In the teaching of reading Bell made use of books, whilst Lancaster resorted to sheets of printed paper pinned on the walls. Bell's rewards and punishments were few; Lancaster's were many. None the less, though their systems were not identical, these bitter antagonists had more in common than they suspected, and subsequent generations of Englishmen, exercising a native love of compromise, reconciled all points of divergence by hyphenating their names and referring to their respective establishments as the Bell-Lancaster schools.

It was about 1814 that the work of Bell and Lancaster began to attract the attention of foreign thinkers and, in particular, of Frenchmen. The reason for this is hard to discover, especially if we recall that at the beginning of the nineteenth century we were dubbed 'the worst educated nation in Europe', but possibly foreigners tended to be enamoured of most things British because of the turn of international events. For some twenty years England had been the heart of the coalition which had struggled to over-

---

[4] This does not mean that the classes were held in separate rooms. Indeed the reverse was the case. In the schools of both Bell and Lancaster all children were taught in an enormous hall so as to be continuously under the Headmaster's supervision

throw the revolutionary dictatorship of Europe and, though Waterloo had not yet taken place, Napoleon seemed powerless enough on Elba.

Whatever the cause of this interest, the achievements of the monitorial system began to receive considerable publicity on the Continent. One of its most enthusiastic promoters was La Rochefoucauld, an influential member of the nobility, who was well acquainted with this country. He had been given asylum in England at the time of the French Revolution, when he stayed for some months with Arthur Young at Bury St. Edmunds, and had never subsequently forgotten this kindness. In 1815 he translated and published certain extracts from Lancaster's writings under the title *Système anglais d'instruction ou Recueil complet des améliorations et inventions mises en pratique aux écoles royales en Angleterre.*[5]

In 1814 two other distinguished Frenchmen, Jomard and the Abbé Gaultier, also visited this country expressly to study the methods of mutual instruction, and, in 1815, they were followed by de Laborde, who was so impressed by the spectacle of several hundred children under the charge of monitors that he wrote a pamphlet on the subject entitled *Plan d'éducation pour les énfants pauvres, d'après les deux méthodes combinées du docteur Bell et de M. Lancaster,* which was published in London in 1815 and reprinted in Paris in 1815 and 1816.[6]

A further analysis of the mutual system came in 1815 from de Lasteyrie, which ran into three editions and bore the name *Nouveau système d'éducation et d'enseignement pour les écoles primaires, adopté dans les quatre parties du monde; exposé de ce système, histoire des méthodes sur lesquelles il est basé, de ses avantages et de l'importance de l'établir en France.*[7]

The result of this interest was that on 17th June, 1815, the eve of the Battle of Waterloo, an association was formed in Paris whose purpose was to spread amongst the lower classes the kind of intellectual and moral training most appropriate to their needs. It called itself the Society for Elementary Instruction and announced that it was by means of the mutual method that it hoped to achieve its object.[8] Such quick success attended its endeavours, moreover, that

[5] See p. 1510 of Vol. II of *Dictionnaire de Pédagogie et d'Instruction Primaire.* Article on La Rochefoucauld-Liancourt

[6] *Ibid.* Vol. II, p. 1460. Article on Laborde

[7] *Ibid.* Vol. II, p. 1524. Article on Lasteyrie

[8] The 'Société pour l'instruction publique' had, among its founder members,

within a year 1,500 monitorial schools were created. This number was greatly increased in 1816 when the sum of 50,000 francs was voted by the Government for the erection of further primary institutions and again in 1817 when a substantial grant for the same purpose was received from the Royal Purse. From then onwards, therefore, the monitorial schools were securely established in France —a fact that we may appreciate the more readily if we recall that in 1818 they were chosen as the subject of the prize poem of the year by the French Academy. Indeed during the next two decades they were to achieve such popularity that eventually they became the chief means by which French youth was educated and thus incurred the bitter opposition and rivalry of the Brothers of the Christian Doctrine whose authoritative sway over primary instruction had hitherto been unchallenged.

An interesting feature of this new movement was the influence it exerted on Guillaume Wilhem (1781–1842), who was Professor of Music at the Napoleon Lycée (Collège Henri IV) at the time when the Society for Elementary Instruction was formed. In 1815 he was present at the opening of the primary school of Saint-Jean-de-Beauvais where he saw some three hundred children being instructed by monitors without the active participation of a master. So greatly did this spectacle impress him, moreover, that he determined forthwith to study the mutual method in the most minute detail. In so doing he discovered that it was necessary not only to isolate difficulties before presenting new subject matter to the child, but also to divide and subdivide the classes so as to have, in a given group, a collection of pupils of roughly the same standard of attainment. If this were done he saw no reason why vocal music should not take its place in the school curriculum along with other subjects. All that was necessary was to devise a simple method of sight-reading which could effectively be taught to the monitors so that they, in their turn, could pass on their knowledge to the other pupils. Accordingly, with that thought in mind, he began two preparatory classes at his own expense—one at his home, No. 374 rue Saint-Denis, and another in a room hired for the purpose in the rue Saint-Louis-au-Marais.

On 23rd June, 1819, moreover, M. de Gérando, having recently

de Laborde, Jomard, the Abbé Gaultier and de Lasteyrie, whilst de Gérando and the Duc de La Rochefoucauld-Liancourt became successive presidents

observed the success with which choral music had been introduced into German schools, submitted a request to the Society for Elementary Instruction that singing be included among the subjects taught by monitors. The poet Béranger [9] suggested Wilhelm as the only man to whom such an experiment could safely be entrusted and, in August, 1819, the first trial was made. It took place in the primary school in the rue Saint-Jean-de-Beauvais where Wilhelm had first seen the mutual method in operation.

This experiment had not long been under way, however, when grave difficulties began to present themselves, for many people saw in the growth of singing a direct threat to their preconceived ideas on education. They felt it to be too radical a step which inevitably would turn the school into a preparatory department of the theatre. But Wilhelm was determined that such fears should be allayed and, with tremendous zeal, set himself to discover the simple method of teaching singing which he knew to exist but which as yet he had been unable to perfect. Accordingly he prepared further elaborate charts for his monitors and choristers, experimented with a new 'harmonic hand' and vocal scales, wrestled with such problems as how best to interpret the duration of notes, understand clefs, determine keys, transpose, etc., and finally, after months of research,

[9] This famous couple were the greatest of friends. Indeed few tributes are more moving than the letter that Béranger wrote in 1841, after the final concert of the 'Orphéon'.

> 'Mon vieil ami, ta gloire est grande:
> Grâce à tes merveilleux efforts,
> Des travailleurs la voix s'amende
> Et se plie aux savants accords.
> D'une fée as-tu la baguette
> Pour rendre ainsi l'art familier?
> Il purifiera la guinguette
> Il sanctifiera l'atelier . . .
> La musique, source féconde,
> Épandant ses flots jusqu'en bas,
> Nous verrons ivres de son onde
> Artisans, laboureurs, soldats,
> Ce concert, puisses-tu l'étendre
> A tout un monde divisé!
> Les cœurs sont bien près de s'entendre
> Quand les voix ont fraternisé.
>
> .   .   .   .
>
> Sur ta tombe, tu peux m'en croire,
> Ceux dont tu charmes les douleurs
> Offriront un jour à ta gloire
> Des chants, des larmes et des fleurs'

evolved a method of teaching singing which became known to subsequent generations as the 'fixed doh' system.[10]

This discovery completely altered the French attitude towards music in schools. As a result of it there grew up a real enthusiasm for singing, and those who had formerly derided Wilhelm's efforts became his most ardent admirers. From that time forward, therefore, his reputation grew apace. In 1820 he was awarded a silver medallion by the Society for Elementary Instruction. In 1826 he was granted their highest distinction—a gold medallion—and, on 6th March, 1835, he was appointed Inspector General of Singing for the primary schools of Paris. Undoubtedly the greatest of his honours, however, came in 1836 when he founded the 'Orphéon'—a society which provided evening classes in part-singing for workpeople. This venture, in its initial stages, was a modest attempt to teach the bare rudiments of music to labourers and apprentices in the neighbourhood of the rue Saint-Denis. So rapidly did it capture the imagination of Paris, however, that after a few months Wilhelm

[10] The following extract on the 'fixed doh' system is taken from John Curwen's *How to read music and understand it*, pp. 16 and 17.

'*THE KEY OF C*. To call a certain key the "natural key" is a licence. But it is highly convenient to have some generally understood standard of pitch, so that we may know exactly at what part of the voice we are to begin every tune. The key which has been fixed upon is that which is sounded on the white digitals of the pianoforte and organ. The 'Doh' of this key is called C, and the other notes follow each other, descending in the way indicated in the margin. The sounds of these letters are the same as those of the scale already learnt, thus:—

```
 C'
 B
 A
 G
 F
 E
 D
 C
```

```
d'  :—  t  :l  s  :f  m  :r  d  :—  ||
C'       B  A   G    F   E    D   C
```

and a convenient way of remembering the descending order is to note that after C come the words "bag" and "fed". These notes C, B, A, etc., unlike the Sol-fa syllables, are absolutely fixed. C, for example, may be "Doh", "Ray", "Te", according to the key we are in; and conversely, "Doh", may be C, F, D, etc. But C, theoretically at least, is always one sound, though "Doh" may be a hundred different sounds. The modern Continental practice is to call C always "Doh", whatever the key. This plan is called the "fixed doh", to distinguish it from the "movable doh", a system which has prevailed in England for two or three hundred years and is founded on the scientific basis of key-relationship'

and his assistant, Huber, were called upon to inaugurate choral groups in the Halle aux draps, rue de Fleurus, rue d'Argenteuil and other centres. Hundreds of sopranos, altos, tenors and basses began to assemble each week who previously had manifested no interest in singing. Under Wilhem's baton they came together from all social groups—children from monitorial schools and private academies, workmen and their employers, peasants and their masters. They were trained to read music at sight, to pronounce their words distinctly, to sing with expression and finally, after considerable practice, to give recitals of well-known masterpieces. Around 1840, therefore, it was commonplace for Parisians to hear more than a thousand voices participating in various festivals.[11]

Thus a great revival of choral music arose from a method of teaching singing that was first invented for use by monitors—a revival which had further success when, in 1841, the 'fixed doh' system, under Wilhem's personal direction, was introduced into the schools of the Brothers of the Christian Doctrine. This was an unhoped-for triumph for an innovation derived from the mutual method and a 'rapprochement' of some educational significance since, for the first time, these bitter rivals, if only in the realms of music, were prepared to sink their differences.

It would be unfair, however, in treating of the important rôle which the monitorial method played in the diffusion of learning merely to confine our attention to England and France. Indeed some brief indication must be given of its rapid transition through Spain, Greece, Italy, Denmark, Sweden and Norway if the pattern of primary instruction in Europe is successfully to be traced during the first half of the nineteenth century.

The mutual method was introduced into Spain in 1817 by an Englishman, Thomas Kearney, who quickly interested King Ferdinand in its possibilities for rendering instruction available to the children of the poor. Soon afterwards the Government afforded

[11] The history of this movement in France provides a fascinating story. After Wilhem's death in 1842, his assistant, Huber, assumed direction of the 'Orphéon' and he, in turn, was succeeded by no less an illustrious figure than Gounod. A group of 'Orphéonistes' crossed over to London in 1851 to render choruses at the Great Exhibition. In the second half of the nineteenth century these musical societies achieved so great a reputation that composers of the calibre of Delibes, Massenet and Saint-Saëns deemed it an honour to write compositions for their performance

protection for his scheme, funds were advanced for the dissemination of Bell's and Lancaster's ideas and, by a royal decree of 10th March, 1819, a Normal School for the training of monitors was established in Madrid.

A further extension of the principle was effected in 1818 when George Cleoboulos of Philippoli, who had studied in Paris, decided to promote mutual instruction amongst the Greeks. He composed reading tables, had them printed in Paris, and returned to his native land with all the visionary enthusiasm of a missionary. In Athens he succeeded in interesting a number of prominent people in his plans and together they formed the Society of the Philomuses. As a result of their activities two monitorial schools were started in 1818, one for girls and one for boys. Later similar institutions were founded in Delos, Patmos, Syros, Tripolitza and Nauplia, and, in 1819, the mutual method was introduced into the schools of the outermost Ionian Isles under the inspectorship of Athanese Politis, as well as into the Greek colonies in Bucharest and Odessa.[12]

A similar movement to that which had produced the Society for Elementary Instruction in Paris took place in Italy in 1822. Conscious of the benefits that France had already received from the introduction of monitors into her day schools, a group of liberal thinkers decided that Tuscany, too, might gain something of value if she were to adopt the same expedient. Such men as Lambruschini, Enrico Meyer, Thouai, Tommaseo and Francheschi were amongst their number. They extolled the system of mutual teaching, reorganized the existing Infant Schools and started a newspaper called the *Guida dell' educatore* as the official organ through which to propagate their views. From Tuscany the monitorial system spread rapidly to Lombardy and Piedmont and was flourishing there as late as 1844 when its merits were praised at some considerable length by Vitale Rosi.[13]

Another country which derived great benefit from this singularly inexpensive means of instruction was Denmark. King Frederick VI first learnt of its success in 1816 from reports that were sent to him from the French Embassy in Copenhagen. In 1818, however, his

[12] See article 'Grèce Moderne', p. 1204, of *Dictionnaire de Pédagogie et d'Instruction Primaire*, Vol. I
[13] *Ibid.* Vol. II, p. 1391. Article 'Italie'

interest was further stimulated when Captain Josef Nicolai Abrahamson was appointed a member of his personal staff. The latter had recently returned from Northern France where he had served with distinction in the Danish forces of occupation. There he had been introduced to the system of mutual instruction and there he had conceived the idea that, by means of it, he could confer a signal benefit on the poor children of his native land. Towards the end of 1819, in consequence, with the king's approval, he started a model school in Copenhagen and soon afterwards inaugurated a movement which sought nothing less than the diffusion of the monitorial system throughout the primary schools of the kingdom. So ardent a propagandist was he, moreover, and so ruthlessly did he counter opposition that he earned for himself the title of 'the red bishop'. Indeed it was largely owing to his personal zeal that the monitorial system remained in force in Denmark until 1837.[14]

Sweden, unlike her neighbour, adopted the system direct from England. Count Jacob de la Garde, who had studied the monitorial schools during a period of residence in London, published a full account of all he had seen in 1821. This attracted the interest of King Gustavus IV who immediately sent one of his secretaries, J. A. Gerelius, and a Government official, H. Svensson, to make further enquiries in London. On their return they became, with de la Garde, the leading spirits of a society which was established in 1822 to promote the construction of monitorial schools throughout Sweden. From then onwards, therefore, the Bell-Lancaster system was generally accepted and, as late as 1841, five hundred schools were still being conducted according to its principles.[15]

And the mutual method also enjoyed considerable prestige in Norway. In 1814 a teacher named Sölling, after studying in England, opened a monitorial school at Larvik. Then, in 1818, William Allen visited Norway, lecturing on Lancaster's methods and arousing much interest in his subject. The following year Bishop Christian Sörenssen undertook a journey to London expressly to visit the Borough Road School and later published an account of what he saw in a highly successful work entitled *The Lancasterian Education*

---

[14] See *Den Danske Landsbyskoles Historie til 1848* by L. Koch. Abrahamson published three reports on the mutual system in collaboration with a clergyman named Mønster under the title *Den Indbyrdes Undervisning*

[15] See article on Sweden in *A Cyclopaedia of Education* by P. Munroe

System and its importance with regard to the Norwegian common schools.[16]
And finally, C. F. G. Bohr, a disciple of Abrahamson, started mutual
schools in various parts of Norway and invited specialists from Denmark and Sweden to lecture on the monitorial system in Oslo.
Indeed there can be little doubt that in Norway, as elsewhere
in Western Europe, the mutual method was soon recognized as a
singularly inexpensive means of instructing the offspring of the
poor.[17]

The dissemination of the Bell-Lancaster system through England,
France, Spain, Greece, Italy, Denmark, Sweden and Norway con-
stitutes one of the most amazing educational movements of all time.
True one may say that its success was due to its comparative
effectiveness at a time when cheapness was the prime consideration,
and that it weakened in its influence in proportion as nations were
prepared to spend more money on education, but the fact remains
that it was by far the most widely spread method of instruction
used on the Continent in the twenty years succeeding Waterloo.
Furthermore its speedy transition across Europe may be taken as
nothing more than an illustration of the debt which many countries
owed to British enterprise and initiative, were it not for the important fact that the mutual method was used by two prominent individuals abroad whose work was not without influence upon this
country. The first was Guillaume Wilhem who, as has already been
noted, brought about a powerful revival of choral music as a direct
result of his contact with the mutual schools in Paris. And the second
was Father Girard, a Franciscan monk from Fribourg in Switzerland, who, whilst relying on the services of monitors, likewise strove
ardently to perpetuate the educational ideas of Pestalozzi. To him,
therefore, special consideration must be given, for not only did he
bring the mutual method to a high level of efficiency, but also
devised an educational compromise which was quite without parallel
in Europe.

[16] *Det Lancasterske Underviisnings-System med Henayn til dets Andendelighed i Norges
Almueskoler* (1821)

[17] For this information I am personally indebted to Mr. Oddvar Vormeland
whose thesis, *Vekselundervisningen og dens andendelse som pedagogick metode i vare skoler—
The monitorial system and its use as an educational method in this country*, was approved by
the University of Oslo in 1950

10

FATHER GIRARD'S COMPROMISE—
THE UNION OF THE MONITORIAL AND
NATURE SCHOOLS IN SWITZERLAND

'Now compromise may be of two kinds, and of these two kinds one
is legitimate and the other is not. It may stand for two distinct attitudes of mind, one of them obstructive and the other not. It may
mean the deliberate suppression or mutilation of an idea, in order to
make it congruous with the traditional idea or the current prejudice
on the given subject, whatever that may be. Or else it may mean a
rational acquiescence in the fact that the bulk of your contemporaries
are not yet prepared either to embrace the new idea, or to change
their ways of living in conformity to it. In the one case, the com-
promiser rejects the highest truth, or dissembles his own acceptance
of it. In the other, he holds it courageously for his ensign and device,
but neither forces nor expects the world straightway to follow.'

LORD MORLEY—*On Compromise*

IN treating of the many well-known men who, during the period
under review, saw in the diffusion of learning an effective means of
helping poor children, it is impossible to avoid the conclusion that
such progress as they achieved was frequently marred by fierce contentions. In this respect mention need only be made of Pestalozzi's
differences with de Fellenberg, of the opposition of the Brothers of
the Christian Doctrine to the founders of the Society for Elementary
Instruction and of Bell's hostility towards Lancaster. In some in-
stances these disputes arose between members of opposed schools of
thought; in others, between advocates of the same system. It would
seem, indeed, that partisanship on far too many occasions acted as a
motivating force in the lives of those who strove to help the poor
and that, in consequence, their common mission was obscured by
discord.

Much of this bitterness disappears, however, if consideration be given to Jean-Baptiste Girard of Fribourg (1765–1850).[1] He was an advocate of the monitorial method and perhaps the most distinguished teacher who ever used it, yet he was also a cleric of wide sympathies, born and bred in Switzerland, who fully appreciated the significant contribution to educational thought and practice, which some of his compatriots, inspired by Rousseau, were giving. In him, then, we find a rare individual—a member of the Order of St. Francis, a scholar of some stature and an able teacher who, apparently with little difficulty, succeeded in reconciling many outstanding differences between the Nature and monitorial schools.

Perhaps we understand this unusual gift for compromise the better if we examine the circumstances of his upbringing and note that, quite early in life, he manifested two interesting characteristics —both of which, we are told, he inherited from his mother. The first was a wise and boundless toleration, and the second an avid taste for learning. Indeed the acquisition of knowledge and the desire to impart it went hand in hand from infancy and, before he was twelve, he evolved a system of mutual instruction for his younger brothers and sisters which not only proved singularly successful but also laid the foundation of his own pedagogical career.

From such information we are able to gain some small insight into Father Girard's mentality, for his love of toleration and scholarship in no way diminished with age. Indeed the memory of his home was not merely a source of constant inspiration to him, but likewise an important factor in determining his educational philosophy. On the one hand it led him to adopt the mutual system which was irrevocably associated with his early childhood and, on the other hand, predisposed him to accept with readiness many of the educational doctrines which were enunciated, for example, in *How Gertrude Teaches Her Children*. To consider Father Girard and Pestalozzi as rivals, then, would be false, for they shared too much in common for such a suggestion to have any credence. Both placed particular emphasis on the importance of a mother's love, both conceived of the art of education as the re-creation in the school of the atmosphere of mutual trust enjoyed in the home, and both maintained that the family unit was an institution more powerful than

---

[1] He took the Christian name of 'Grégoire' on becoming a member of the Order of St. Francis in 1781

any other in developing the intellectual, moral and religious faculties of mankind. It was merely in their teaching methods that they differed.

The beginning of Father Girard's educational career, like that of de Fellenberg, was intimately bound up with the Swiss Revolution. It will be recalled that, when Albert Stapfer assumed control of the Ministry of Arts and Sciences, he promptly issued an appeal to his more enlightened compatriots to give their views on the organization of national education.[2] Father Girard, then an obscure priest in a Franciscan house in Fribourg, was one of many who responded to this request. In 1798 he wrote and in 1799 despatched to Stapfer his *Plan of Education for the whole of Switzerland*.[3] This document, which unfortunately no longer exists among the Girard manuscripts, was said to have been a defence of Christian principles and to have stated categorically that no system of national instruction would be of any avail which did not first consider the spiritual welfare of the people. Such a theory seems plausible, for Stapfer was so impressed by the clarity of its suggestions that he promptly invited the unknown Franciscan to come to Berne.

On his arrival Father Girard was nominated chaplain to the new Government—a difficult position for him to fill since it was the first time since the Reformation that a Catholic priest had received an official appointment in this stronghold of Protestantism. So marked was his self-restraint, however, that, within a year, he had won the respect of all men. He shared a place of worship with a pastor of the Reformed Church, established friendly relations with members of all religious denominations and started a number of charitable organizations for the victims of the revolution who poured into Berne from the outlying districts. It was, in fact, largely because of the latter that he first considered becoming a teacher. Distressed by the sight of the vagrant children whom he encountered in search of shelter he conceived the idea of building a new primary school. Accordingly, with that thought in mind, he went to Burgdorf to consult Pestalozzi, who begged him earnestly to proceed with the undertaking. Stapfer also encouraged him by insisting that what Pestalozzi had done in Stanz he, too, could do in Berne and so, towards the end of 1803 when sufficient funds had been collected, a start was made. Scarcely had the foundation stone been laid, however,

[2] See chapter 6 of present work   [3] *Plan pour l'éducation de la Suisse entière*

when Father Girard received word from his Order to return to his native town. It appeared that in Fribourg, [too, a scheme was afoot to erect a new primary school and that the municipal council was anxious for the Franciscans to direct it. They, in their turn, declared their willingness to do so provided they could count on the services of Father Girard. So it was that in 1804, to the sorrow of all sections of the community, he left Berne.

For several months after this, however, Father Girard rarely emerged from his cell. His sole desire was to implement the instructions which Stapfer had addressed to the district inspectors and to produce a model educational establishment that would do credit to Fribourg. Accordingly, with that purpose in view, he worked most conscientiously, eventually producing the plan of a spacious school, complete with large classrooms and a recreation ground, which proved satisfactory alike to the municipal authorities and to the Franciscans. Building, therefore, began almost immediately and, towards the end of 1804, sufficient progress had been made for the first pupils to be admitted.

Even at this stage of the undertaking, however, Father Girard did not emerge as the leader of a bold, new enterprise. He effaced his efforts behind those of the other Brothers and chose the youngest class of pupils as his particular preserve. The trouble was that doubts began to assail him as to what method of teaching he should adopt and what steps he should take in order to create within the school the feelings of inter-dependence that existed in a large family. For several years, therefore, he did little save experiment. In the initial stages he was assisted by his colleagues from the cloister, but soon realized that that was not what he wanted. Next he tried lay teachers, but that again did not satisfy him. And finally he came to use by turn the direct spoken word of a master supplemented by the services of monitors. Thus, by a process of trial and error, he devised his ideal method of teaching—a method that enabled him not merely to transmit his personal influence to all his pupils but also to build up an atmosphere of cheerfulness and brotherly love such as he had known in his own home.

In treating of Father Girard's teaching methods, however, it is obviously important to note that his successful use of the mutual method was directly consequent upon the moral and intellectual improvement of his school. In other words, had he introduced it at the start, it would have proved fatal, for his first pupils were forty vagrant boys, who had somehow managed by dint of stealing to survive the rigours of post-revolutionary Switzerland. From such material he could hardly have made monitors and that is why, in the early stages, he concentrated almost exclusively on his youngest pupils. He had faith that, if only their allegiance could be won, many of his difficulties would disappear. In this view he was fully justified, moreover, for when, in 1807, the senior class was composed entirely of boys who had passed through his hands he was able satisfactorily to call upon their services. Nor was the secret of the metamorphosis difficult to discover : Father Girard had finally succeeded in creating the family atmosphere which he prized so dearly.

The school had, none the less, its detractors—people who were opposed to the cause of popular instruction and complained that if all the 'chimney sweeps and mole catchers' were given some sort of tuition there was no knowing where the process might end. By 1809, moreover, these accusations would have degenerated into open persecution had it not been for several enlightened members of the Government, headed by Count Louis d'Affry,[4] who readily came to Father Girard's aid and stated publicly that his educational work had their sanction.

It was possibly because so many people were anxious to denigrate his efforts that, as early as 1807, Father Girard decided to extend his sphere of influence. In that year he became Commissioner of French Schools in Fribourg—a position which he held until 1823. This did not mean, however, that he had to abandon his own school. It simply called upon him to act in an advisory capacity to other educational establishments. From 1807 onwards, in consequence, he spent much of his time counselling teachers and addressing public meetings. The task he set himself was to make the principle of compulsory education understood by all. Once that was done he felt there was a chance of its being adopted, but he fought against great odds. A written statement, published in 1816, gave his considered opinion of the matter: 'The common folk have little sympathy with the idea of compulsory education. If they feel about it at all, their feelings are soon swept aside by other considerations. For the ordinary man, who is much the same everywhere, instruction is a

---

[4] Count Louis d'Affry was on two occasions 'Landamman' of Switzerland

great blessing, but it requires a bit of violence to make him think so!' [5]

To his work as commissioner Father Girard gave the same unremitting attention that he afforded his duties as headmaster; but it was in many ways unrewarding. Frequently, for instance, he was asked to submit reports on educational establishments where his friends were employed and to comment on their activities. With such problems, troublesome though they were, he was usually able to cope. But in November 1809 he was given a peculiarly distasteful assignment which caused him untold worry. Along with Frederick Trechsel and Abel Merian he was called upon by the Swiss Diet to pay a three-day visit to the celebrated Yverdun Institute.

At that time, it must be realized, Pestalozzi was almost sixty-five years of age and had to a large extent lost control over the college. Indeed, as the three commissioners discovered, the Institute was virtually run by Niederer who seemed anxious not only to claim credit for everything that happened there but also to prevent, whenever possible, direct contact with Pestalozzi. Throughout the first two days, for example, he did little save discuss metaphysics with his visitors and succeeded in irritating Father Girard to such an extent that he dubbed him a fraud who spent his time 'saying what everybody knew in language nobody could understand'. [6]

As might be expected, therefore, the commissioners were of one mind that the Yverdun Institute had lost much of its former glory —thanks to Niederer. Father Girard, moreover, had the painful task of explaining this unfavourable judgment in his report, though he sought to mollify any criticism of Pestalozzi himself by referring to the latter's noble work at Stanz and his amazing contributions to educational theory. Had it not been for such works as *Leonard and Gertrude* and *How Gertrude Teaches Her Children*, he asserted, the theory of education by Nature would have advanced but little since 1762 when it was first outlined by Rousseau in *Emile*. The world as a result owed a special debt of gratitude to 'this modest and self-sacrificing man who passed his days in the midst of children and

[5] See *Rapports sur l'organisation morale d'une maison de Travail—sur l'immoralité de la ronde des pauvres—sur les soins à donner aux familles pauvres—sur l'assistance due aux pauvres isolés; inserés dans les Mémoires de la Société économique de Fribourg, 1813–1816*

[6] See *Pestalozzi Blätter*, 1828, p. 193

d evoted his time, his fortune and his heart to their betterment'.[7]

Thus a thoroughly unpleasant task was completed, but no sooner
was the report in the hands of the Swiss Diet than its author fell ill.
He had been working without respite for many years, and the strain
eventually had proved too great. But it was the visit to Yverdun
which, more than anything else, precipitated the breakdown. He
became perturbed that his criticism of Niederer might do harm to
Pestalozzi and the thought of it preyed on his mind. To make
matters worse, as he lay feverish in his cell, news was brought him
of the death of Count Louis d'Affry, his supporter in many times
of trouble. Life, as a result, seemed black indeed and for some time
he contemplated renouncing all connection with education. But the
local magistrates and his fellow Franciscans refused to countenance
so drastic a decision. It was well that they did, moreover, for, after
several months' complete rest, he began to regain his health and
with it his old enthusiasm. Towards the end of 1810, therefore, in a
spirit of thankfulness for having been spared to carry on his work,
he solemnly pledged himself to perform two important tasks—first
to bring his school to a higher level of efficiency, and secondly to
devote the remainder of his days to helping the poor youth of
Fribourg.

As may be seen, then, the inspection of the Yverdun Institute was
an important step in Father Girard's career for, despite the fact that
it caused him much despondency, it spurred him on to greater
efforts. Up to the time of his illness he had formulated no definite
rules for the guidance either of his masters or of himself. In the years
succeeding his recovery, however, he made a determined effort not
merely to improve his school but also to sort out his pedagogical
theories. Thus, by 1815, he was in a position to state categorically
that all teaching should be based on three principles: 'interrogation', 'invention' and the 'integration of graduated courses'.[8]

Of these, he asserted, the first was by far the most important. In
consequence, during the initial stages of training, a teacher should
do little save ask and answer questions, for it was principally by that
means that a child acquired information. Yet, even in dealing with

---

[7] See *Rapport sur l'Institut de Monsieur Pestalozzi à Yverdun présenté à la Diète
helvétique*
[8] See *Notice Biographique sur le Père Girard de Fribourg* by Ernest Naville, pp. 24–30

so tender an age, there were definite pitfalls to be avoided. It was, for example, by no means sufficient for a boy to repeat parrot-fashion what he had been told. To exercise his ingenuity he should be called upon to reproduce any statement in words different from those previously used by the instructor. By so doing his powers of observation, concentration and judgment were strengthened. That was why, in the early stages of school life, questioning was so vitally important. A child was naturally inquisitive and, unless his curiosity were fostered, he would never develop that urge constantly to add to his knowledge which eventually made learning a joy instead of a drudgery.

Once he manifested a predisposition to obtain information by personal enquiry, however, a pupil was ready to pass to the next stage of his training, which was that of invention. There the study of Language became all important to him. By means of it he was enabled both to develop his personality and to enrich his conceptions. Indeed, from personal experience Father Girard was able to attest that, if only a child could be persuaded constantly to increase his vocabulary, eventually he would take increasing delight in using words appositely. The study of Language was thus a real factor in his development, for the less ambiguous his statements grew the more his powers of invention increased.

After interrogation and invention came the integration of gradu-ated courses. This educative principle—in essence an attempt to wrest from Nature the secret of her influence upon mankind—was obviously based to a large extent on the researches of Rousseau and Pestalozzi. In fact, to expound it, Father Girard relied on the same two theories with regard to the acquisition of knowledge which were contained in *How Gertrude Teaches Her Children*: first that man, if placed in an alien environment, would strive with every fibre of his being to orientate himself; and secondly that, by so doing, he was merely reverting to childhood and discovering anew the means by which he initially acquired information. The Franciscan, however, differed from Rousseau and Pestalozzi in describing the source whence this knowledge came. Significantly enough, it was no longer 'Nature' but 'God working through Nature'. The Almighty, in His wisdom, did not take the young child and show him the marvels of creation singly. Rather did He set them out in all their variety and allow the infant to choose such as interested him most. Thus, every day, the child's familiarity with certain objects grew until the time arrived when he was not only thoroughly familiar with them but could name and describe their separate properties whenever and wherever they manifested themselves.

The graduated courses attempted to follow this manner of natural selection. In the teaching of Geography, for example, Father Girard encouraged his pupils, during their first year, to bring to school any scraps of information about Fribourg which particularly interested them. These he collected and added to as he deemed necessary until eventually he built up an accurate picture of the town. During the second year he did much the same thing save that he took into consideration the surrounding countryside also. In the third year, still beginning with Fribourg, he extended his field of enquiry to the canton; in the fourth to Switzerland; in the fifth to Europe. All investigation, he maintained, should begin with a consideration of the most familiar objects—a statement which proves conclusively that Father Girard did not remain oblivious to the truths enunciated in *How Gertrude Teaches Her Children*.

Interrogation, invention and the integration of graduated courses were then the means used in the Fribourg School to develop the pupils according to a wise and carefully conceived plan. But all development, the Franciscan pointed out, was a gradual advancement towards a definite objective—an objective which, to all who professed and called themselves Christians, was clear and unmistakable. 'We have no ambition', he said, 'other than that of guiding to their Saviour the children who have been entrusted to us.' [9]

With such a goal before him Father Girard naturally placed great importance on the teaching of Religion, for only by so doing was he able to turn his poor youngsters into morally responsible human beings. In consequence, from their entry into the school at the age of six, he took pains to impress upon them the importance of the Christian message. He soon found, however, that they attached little meaning to such words as 'body' and 'soul' unless he exercised his ingenuity. In order to help them to more precise notions, therefore, he enlivened his religious talks with simple illustrations. On one occasion he might bring dolls and leaden soldiers to the classroom so as to demonstrate the uselessness of a body without any animating force. On another occasion he might take his boys to some

[9] *Discours pour la distribution des prix de 1821*

neighbouring workshop and introduce them to a stone-mason or cabinet-maker. There he would show them first the rough material with which the craftsmen worked and afterwards the finished product. Obviously without stone and wood nothing beautiful could have been fashioned, yet stone and wood in themselves were not beautiful. It was the labour and skill of the workmen which transformed these rough materials into objects of worth. So it was with our lives, whose effectiveness likewise depended on great care. Such illustrations abounded in Father Girard's teaching. He felt that children could become interested in almost any subject if only the teacher would start from their point of view.

This idea of striving constantly to ennoble his pupils' lives had a particular appeal for the Franciscan. In fact so convinced was he of its necessity that he insisted on every subject in the curriculum being treated as a means of leading children to nobler conceptions of life. Thus Natural Science was taught to demonstrate the wonders of God's handiwork; Geography was used to awaken the pupils' commiseration for peoples plunged in ignorance; Arithmetic furnished lessons in economy, and Language was shown to be the great universal expression of the thoughts of mankind and the chief instrument for spreading the gospel to distant lands. The strong moral bias was deliberate. The Franciscan wanted Christianity to permeate everything without itself being obvious. As a visiting Brother from the poor schools in Genoa remarked to him: 'I observe that you moralize the whole time but "quasi aliud faciendo".' [10]

From such information we are able to appreciate not only the care with which Father Girard thought out his educational theories but also the earnestness with which he applied them. Indeed so strenuously did he work during the years immediately following his illness that, by 1815, he had succeeded in bringing his school to the forefront in the battle against ignorance. That in itself was a remarkable achievement, but what was even more remarkable was the fact that he did so whilst relying on the services of monitors. Perhaps, therefore, in endeavouring to analyse the secret of his success, we do well to bear in mind the following considerations: first that he himself was an unusually gifted teacher who, by the force of his personality, was able to inspire a zest for learning in others; secondly that his monitors were older and better trained than was usually the case

[10] See p. 30 of *Notice Biographique sur le Père Girard de Fribourg* by Ernest Naville

in mutual schools; and thirdly that, in addition to his young assistants, he invariably had a small nucleus of efficient lay teachers who saw to it that his policy was at all times carried out. In 1815, for example, there were six masters and twenty-seven monitors for four hundred pupils. Thus, when the simultaneous method of instruction was used, the pupils were divided into six sections and the masters were thereby spared the difficulty of presenting their lessons to widely disparate groups of age and attainment. When, on the other hand, more detailed work was required and the mutual method was in force, the school was divided into about thirty sections each containing from twelve to fifteen pupils.

The remarkable thing about all this was that Father Girard thought it out and started to practise it long before the work of Bell or Lancaster attracted attention on the Continent. It was, in fact, not until 1815 that he learnt of the success of the British reformers through the reports of Count de Lasteyrie and Count de Laborde. As soon as he studied their accounts, however, he determined to ally himself with the new movement. But the trouble was that his theories did not conform with complete exactness to those of either Bell or Lancaster. He was quite unable, for instance, to cut rewards to a minimum in accordance with the former's advice, or to leave the whole of the instruction to monitors as recommended by the latter. After much deliberation, therefore, he decided that, since the use of teachers was really the vital issue, he was 'plus Belliste que Lancastrien'—a decision expressly recognized in his souvenirs written towards the end of 1815.[11]

Doubtless Father Girard was rather puzzled by this wholly illogical contention for, having decided that he was a disciple of Bell, he gave no indication that he was prepared in any way to abandon his belief in the efficacy of rewards and punishments. Indeed, during the years 1816 and 1817, he added considerably to his list of prizes and began to award them not only for progress and achievement but also for cleanliness, orderliness, punctuality and public spiritedness. Thus, by 1818, he was in a position to state openly that almost every boy in the school was in receipt of some token of commendation. Yet such a pronouncement was perhaps not wise. It afforded an excellent opportunity for his enemies openly

---

[11] This decision is also mentioned by John Griscom in *A Year in Europe* published in 1823. See p. 36 of *Reports on European Education*

to criticize both his school and his educational policy. And, as might be expected, several people soon voiced their opinion that the Franciscan's rather expensive system of remuneration was wholly out of keeping with a school for indigent boys. But such charges were soon rebutted by the Franciscan. He condemned those who uttered them as slanderers who had no thought for anyone save themselves. His whole system of teaching, he said, was founded on a true conception of morality and, if people sought to oppose Good with Evil, he would fight that Evil, be it in the inclinations of human nature or in the defects of a country's constitution.

It is perhaps important to note, however, that such criticisms as Father Girard incurred had little effect either upon him or his reputation. Indeed, between 1816 and 1818, his school won such great renown that it attracted visitors from all parts of the world—Englishmen, Frenchmen, Italians, Russians and Americans. In December 1816, for example, the ex-queen of Sweden visited the school and took particular delight in talking to the youngest class. 'Pourquoi viens-tu ici, mon enfant?' she demanded of one pupil. 'Pour m'amuser' was the answer. 'Comment? est-ce que l'école t'amuse?' she demanded further. 'Oui, Madame,' said he, 'nous nous amusons ici toujours.' [12] In October 1818, John Griscom, Professor of Chemistry and Natural Philosophy in the New York Institution, also came to Fribourg expressly to see Father Girard and commented as follows: 'The principle which he relies most upon, as an excitement to the energies of the boys, is emulation. This principle, properly directed, he is confident does not produce envy or any other injurious feeling. So anxious are the boys in his school to improve that they are known often to rise in the night to study; and so lively and interesting to them has he rendered the exercises of the school that very young children are fond of attending.' [13] Girard's methods were likewise studied with great care by his fellow-countrymen and in Berne, Lausanne, Geneva, Neuchâtel and Zurich schools called 'les Girardines' sprang up, all of them modelled on the Fribourg institution. So popular were they that, during the summer of 1817, Pestalozzi himself decided to visit the parent foundation. He deplored the use of monitors but was greatly impressed by the Franciscan's educational zeal. 'Girard performs

[12] See *Reports on European Education by John Griscom, Victor Cousin and Calvin E. Stowe.* Edited by Edgar W. Knight, p. 38   [13] *Ibid.* p. 38

miracles,' he said to Archdeacon Fontaine, who accompanied him round the premises, 'he makes gold out of mud.' [14]

With such commendations it is perhaps wise to conclude an account of the Fribourg School for, within a year of Pestalozzi's visit, it fell on evil days. The trouble was that Father Girard's success inspired great jealousy in Mgr. Jenny, Bishop of Fribourg, who decided to recall the Jesuits as an effective means of counteracting the Franciscan's influence. The Society of Jesus, be it known, had long been forbidden in Fribourg and was exceedingly unpopular. As a result angry quarrels swept through the canton and caused a deep split in the heart of the Government. It was, in fact, only after many heated debates that Mgr. Jenny succeeded in getting his policy adopted. But when, on 15th September, 1818, his wish became law, the Fribourg School was doomed. As an American visitor to Switzerland remarked: 'The Jesuits were not able, at one stroke, to put Father Girard's school out of action, but from the moment they were reinstated, they strove persistently for its destruction.' [15]

During the next five years Father Girard struggled against ever increasing difficulties, hoping against hope that his life's work would somehow be spared. On 21st June, however, unable any longer to resist the combined onslaught of the Jesuits and Bishop Jenny, he decided to quit his work and retire to Lucerne.[16] 'Frightful means have been used to snatch me away from my large family,' he wrote to a friend on the eve of his departure. 'I regret it, but am resigned to it and feel calm as usual. . . . The children assembled in the Church to hear Mass for the last time here, and I said it. On coming out of the vestry I saw a catafalque before my eyes. It represented to me the death and burial of my school. But when I came to the

---

[14] See p. 1180 of *Dictionnaire de Pédagogie et d'Instruction Primaire*, Vol. I. Article on 'Le Père Girard'

[15] See *Reports on European Education*, p. 37

[16] Though Father Girard's retirement virtually ended his work with indigent children, it did not put paid to his career. At Lucerne he was persuaded to occupy a seat on the Council of Education and to act as an adviser on schools. Thus, in 1823, he gave a paper on the mutual system of instruction to the Swiss Society of Public Utility. In 1827 he published an account of his old school, which he called *Explication du plan de Fribourg en Suisse*. In 1844 came the introductory book to his treatise on language, *De l'enseignement régulier de la langue maternelle*, which was awarded the Monthyon prize by the French Academy, and in 1847, the publication in six volumes of *Cours éducatif de la langue maternelle à l'usage des écoles et des familles*

altar I saw that the sacerdotal vestments were green and Hope immediately filled my mind. I cannot tell you what passed within me during those few minutes. . . . The school leaves a happy memory behind it—a memory which, sooner or later, will grow as a seed grows under the kindly influences from above.' [17]

So it was that one of the most interesting experiments of its day ceased to exist—a school that was not perhaps great in the way of Yverdun or Hofwyl, but one which deserves special mention if only for its brave attempt to reconcile the ideas of Pestalozzi and Bell. During the first half of the nineteenth century, when Europe was greatly divided on the question of simultaneous and mutual instruction, Father Girard quietly demonstrated, to his own and other people's satisfaction, that the services of trained teachers and monitors could be co-ordinated. That was why his work was so important. It clearly showed that compromise, too often a refuge for indecision, could be both a solution of difficult issues and a presage of new understanding.

[17] See letter of 21st June, 1823, to F. M. L. Naville quote on p. 42 of Ernest Naville's *Notice Biographique sur le Père Girard*

11

A SUMMARY OF THE MAIN EDUCA-TIONAL FORCES AT WORK IN EUROPE DURING THE LATE EIGHTEENTH AND EARLY NINETEENTH CENTURIES

> 'It is the most serious difficulty of the history of civilization that a great intellectual process must be broken up into single, and often into what seem arbitrary categories, in order to be in any way intelligible.'
>
> JACOB BURCKHARDT—*The Civilization of the Renaissance in Italy*

AFTER treating of the pains with which Father Girard sought to bring the theories of Pestalozzi into harmony with those of Bell it is perhaps unwise to speak too conclusively of movements in education. Inspiration, it would appear, can blow with too wild a breath for its consequences readily to be calculated and a particular teacher's predilections can easily frustrate any attempt to explain him as an example of a rule or to claim him as a representative of this or that party. Yet, if Father Girard be regarded as an unusually advanced exponent of the monitorial method and if attention be directed to those among his contemporaries who likewise furthered the cause of popular enlightenment, it is possible to see that, broadly speaking, primary education in Europe was promoted by representatives of three entirely independent schools of thought.

The first and historically the oldest of these was the Catholic Brothers of the Christian Schools. During the period under review they began to prosper not only in France and Italy but also in Canada and the United States of America. In 1825, for example, with 950 Brothers, they conducted 210 houses and offered instruction free of charge to no less than 60,000 pupils. About half-way through the nineteenth century this number grew to 8,385 Brothers running 986 houses and catering for the needs of 335,000 pupils.[1] Wherever they founded schools, moreover, they adhered to the principle of simultaneous instruction and insisted that all teaching be conducted in the vernacular. Thus they extended their influence whilst all the time remaining faithful to the wishes of their founder: the Christian education of youth, the cultivation of letters and the diffusion of knowledge.

The second body of thinkers who had both a conscious purpose and an agreed philosophy was the Nature School of teachers and administrators. They owed a special debt of gratitude to Rousseau who, in *Emile* (1762), propounded with great eloquence his theory that Nature was the wisest of all preceptors, and to Basedow, Salzmann, von Rochow and Richter, who first showed that this doctrine was capable of practical application. But it was to Pestalozzi, the man who more than any other erected a metaphysic to explain the new revelation, that they were principally beholden. Indeed when we speak of the Nature School of teachers it is of him primarily that we think, his ideas that we remember. Pestalozzi attempted to ascertain what scheme of natural development lay concealed behind or within the appearances of natural phenomena and to systematize educational theory and practice in the light of his discoveries. Such a formidable task proved a lifetime's work, and the resultant method, which was never fully understood by anyone save its originator, presented many grave difficulties. Not least among these was the question of 'Anschauung'—a recondite doctrine which provoked animated discussion in intellectual circles and prompted investigations by such eminent educational philosophers as Herbart and Froebel.

Even so, with the publication of *How Gertrude Teaches Her Children* (1801), it was quickly recognized that Pestalozzi had given to the Nature School a body of theory, a source of inspiration and a programme of action. He had, in fact, perfected a wonderful tool and was ready to devote the remainder of his days to the instruction of others in the use of it. Within a short time, therefore, many teachers arose who were prepared to admit the truth of his basic contentions.

Perhaps the greatest of Pestalozzi's contributions, however, was the way in which he showed both by precept and example that his

[1] See article on 'Brothers of the Christian Schools' by Brother Constantius, published in *A Cyclopedia of Education* edited by P. Munroe

method of teaching was capable of helping 'the raw, unkindled masses of humanity'. Previous to his six months' stay in Stanz the Nature School had been distinctly patrician in its bias; thenceforth it became a most powerful agency in spreading popular enlightenment. Thus two of Pestalozzi's compatriots—de Fellenberg, a rich nobleman, and Wehrli, a poor schoolmaster—were able to demonstrate, by virtue of several noteworthy experiments at Hofwyl, that the new education could cater for the needs not merely of young aristocrats but likewise of farm labourers, bailiffs and even juvenile delinquents.

This extension of educational privilege to embrace the poorer classes had, of course, long been a cherished ideal—particularly in France. Around 1750 such men as Turgot, Condillac, Helvétius, d'Alembert, La Chalotais and Diderot had given detailed consideration to the most effective means by which it could be secured. And when they died, others—notably Mirabeau, Talleyrand and Condorcet—had carried on their work so that, by 1792, it had become generally recognized by advanced thinkers that education for all would be a definite outcome of the revolution and the first responsibility of a newly elected government. That so bold a scheme of social amelioration never materialized was owing primarily to the fact that Napoleon succeeded the revolutionary leaders. Yet, where France failed, others were prepared to implement her carefully conceived plans and so, within a few years, Holland and Prussia were busy attempting to lay the foundations of state systems of education.

Undoubtedly the most interesting feature of this new development was the way in which, thanks to such enthusiastic propagandists as van Wapperen, Scholten and van den Ende in Holland and Fichte, Nicolovius and Süvern in Prussia, the zeal for popular enlightenment in both these countries became fused with a desire to further Pestalozzi's educative principles. This, of course, meant a great deal of expense since so complicated and personal a system of instruction demanded many highly trained teachers for its operation. Nevertheless, within a short time, both nations established themselves as champions of educational reform—a fact that we may appreciate the more readily if we recall that, by 1837, Prussia had built no less than fifty Normal Schools and Holland had introduced such far-reaching schemes as the training of pupil-teachers, the provision of child nurseries and the inspection of all publicly and privately owned schools. That these reforms were at all possible was in large measure owing to such advanced legislation as was contained in the 1806 Code of Popular Education in Holland and the 1819 Law of Public Instruction in Prussia—two efficient enactments which demonstrated both meticulous planning and amazing foresight. Thus these two countries, both of which in the early years of the nineteenth century lay under a conqueror's yoke, eventually triumphed over their difficulties and added great lustre not only to their own educational systems but likewise to the ideas and ideals of the Nature School.

The third body of thinkers consisted of those who followed the Bell-Lancaster method of instruction by monitors which, in 1814, spread from England to the Continent and within a few years enjoyed considerable success in France, Spain, Italy, Greece, Denmark, Sweden and Norway. This system was intended to furnish the teacher with an effective means of multiplying his personal influence over hundreds of children by soliciting the co-operation of his best pupils. Its great merit was that it was inexpensive, and it played its tremendous rôle in instructing the children of the masses only so long as funds were lacking to provide some more profitable means of education. Nevertheless it was not without important results. In France it was solely responsible for bringing about a great revival of choral music under the baton of Guillaume Wilhem, and in Switzerland it was used by so eminent a scholar as Father Girard.

Thus, in studying the evolution of educational consciousness during the period under review, it is impossible to escape the conclusion that primary instruction was largely promoted by representatives of three essentially different movements. There were, of course, exceptions to this rule such as Wilhem, who effected a partial reconciliation between the monitorial and simultaneous methods of instruction, and Father Girard, who devised an interesting compromise between the competitive systems of Pestalozzi and Bell. On the whole, however, most teachers and administrators were prepared to select one of the three movements as their ideal means of spreading popular enlightenment and violently to defend it against its rivals. The Christian Brothers, for example, were constantly engaged in fierce contentions with such men as de Lasteyrie and de Laborde, who advocated the adoption of the mutual method, whilst van den Ende, a staunch supporter of Pestalozzi, could see no merit whatsoever in the use of monitors.

In presenting the different teachers and administrators, therefore, an attempt has been made to show them both as individuals and as representatives of one or other of the three prevailing schools of thought. Only by so doing are we able to see them in their rightful setting and to appraise their outstanding merits. Yet, in the last resort, it has to be remembered that the intellectual emancipation of the poorer classes was effected by men rather than movements, by philanthropists rather than theorists. It has also to be borne in mind that these great humanitarian thinkers, no matter what their outward differences, were inwardly agreed on at least two important points—that the victims of want would have to be helped if a more reasonable future were to be opened up for Europe, and that it paid better to have intelligent human beings than ignorant beasts of burden.

This identity of purpose cannot be emphasized too strongly for it is the principal means of explaining the results that were achieved in primary education during the years succeeding the French Revolution. In 1789, it will be remembered, the majority of European peasants were, in effect, serfs. They could not learn a trade without their lord's consent, were forbidden to leave their villages or to marry without his authorization and were often called upon to give him so much of their time that they had perforce to cultivate their own strips of land by moonlight. As a result their sons and daughters grew up in ignorance and penury, frequently deprived of comfort, care, tuition and domestic tenderness. Yet, within a few years, thanks largely to the efforts of these able teachers and administrators, this dismal scene began to change and a brighter future dawned for the offspring of the poor.

In reflecting on these years of progress, therefore, and on the speedy alteration in attitude which they produced, it is perhaps wise, in addition to the work of prominent individuals, to take into consideration certain other factors which likewise helped to determine the struggle against ignorance.

In the first place there would seem to be little doubt that one of the chief influences in promoting a better understanding of humanity's responsibilities towards indigent children was a deep faith in Christian principles. This does not mean that the source whence the era of enlightenment sprang was primarily religious. It was not, as any glance at the writings of the Encyclopaedists will testify. What it does indicate, however, is that many of the people who interested themselves in the possibilities of education, even those among them who played minor rôles, were frequently devout Christians. Salzmann, for example, was the pastor of a church in a remote village of Thuringia; Richter, a theological student at the University of Leipzig; the Abbé Gaultier, at one time a parish priest in Paris; and Nieuwenhuysen, a Mennonite clergyman in North Holland.

A second thought which immediately strikes the mind is the almost incalculable debt of gratitude that every country in Europe owed to Swiss initiative. In this respect one need only mention such pioneers as Rousseau, the discoverer of Nature as an educative force; Pestalozzi, the initiator of a body of doctrine to justify this revelation; Stapfer, the architect of the first state system of education; de Fellenberg, the founder of the foremost educational estate of his time; Wehrli, perhaps the greatest of all teachers of poor children; and Father Girard, the most distinguished exponent of the mutual method of instruction.

And a third consideration which must not be ignored is the influence that war exerted. Strange to relate, in almost every instance, it acted as a spur to educational reform. It would seem indeed that wanton destruction caused many fine spirits to cherish learning as the only rewarding thing in a world of confusion and to strive with all their might to ensure its survival. The French Revolution, for example, gave birth to the reports of Mirabeau, Talleyrand and Condorcet; the atrocities of the Swiss Revolution materially affected the lives and careers of Pestalozzi, de Fellenberg, Stapfer and Father Girard; Napoleon's invasion of the Low Countries had a powerful influence on 'The Society for the Public Good'; his subsequent victories at Jena and Auerstadt awakened an unparalleled zest for learning in Prussia; and the mere fact that Abrahamson served with the forces of occupation in Northern France changed the educational future of Denmark.

Thus a variety of influences, some of them of a most unexpected nature, contributed to the expansion of popular enlightenment in Western Europe.

The purpose of this study has been not only to show these influences at work but also to trace the gradual development of educational activity during the late eighteenth and early nineteenth centuries, to demonstrate how it was canalized into three main streams as far as primary education was concerned, and to bring into full relief the individual efforts of such labourers in the field of popular enlightenment as the Brothers of the Christian Doctrine, Pestalozzi, de Fellenberg, Wehrli, Wilhem, Father Girard and the architects of the state systems in Holland and Prussia. These particular exponents of educational enterprise have been selected from the many distinguished teachers and legislators who flourished at the time because they represent the main sources whence Britain and, in particular, England gained inspiration for the training of her own youth during the first half of the nineteenth century.

It would seem to be impossible to study the careers of these men without realizing, if only to a limited degree, the earnestness of their beliefs. Individually, and in strife with great odds, they contributed to a more enlightened view of humanity's responsibilities towards the poor, and from their joint endeavours came a new conception of education. The debt of gratitude which teachers of subsequent generations owed to their devotion was immeasurable, and it is perhaps no exaggeration to say that much that we treasure as valuable in present-day educational thought was first conceived and enunciated by these pioneers whose mission, quite simply, was to dispel the clouds of ignorance and whose faith gave them the will to do so.

PART TWO

Great Britain

12

PRIMARY EDUCATION IN GREAT BRITAIN AT THE OUTSET OF THE NINETEENTH CENTURY

'Tandis pourtant que la Suisse et la Hollande avançaient rapidement dans la voie des réformes scolaires et que l'Allemagne elle-même, forcée de devenir liberale pour lutter contre Napoléon, favorisait le développement de l'instruction, il semblait que l'Angleterre, isolée par sa position, son antagonisme contre la France et la puissance de son aristocratie, voulût se soustraire à ce mouvement continental.'

L. ARMAGNAC—*Mémoire sur l'enseignement en Angleterre.* 1887

AFTER discussing in some detail the educational forces at work in Switzerland, Holland and Prussia during the first half of the nineteenth century, it is necessarily depressing to turn one's gaze from the mainland of Europe and take stock of the meagre efforts which were being made at the same time to check the growth of illiteracy in these islands. So different a scene is presented as to be barely credible. Instead of the ferment of ideas we have educational stagnation; instead of activity, inertia; instead of hope, despair. Only Scotland held promise of brighter days and even there the prospect was not unclouded.

We must remember, however, that the nineteenth century opened darkly for the inhabitants of Great Britain. We were a small, impoverished and gravely harassed nation; our country folk, for the most part, dwelt in poverty; our town dwellers often eked out a subsistence in scenes of squalor; criminal activity and gross ignorance were prevalent; food was by no means plentiful; prices were high; we bore with fortitude a vast burden of taxation; we were engaged in a life and death struggle with Napoleon; invasion threatened us closely and our very survival appeared in jeopardy. In brief the times were troubled, and few appeared anxious to concern themselves with the intricacies of social, intellectual and political reform.

Perhaps we realize the gravity of this situation the better if we examine such educational facilities as existed for the benefit of poor children. First and foremost, for example, there were the dame schools where elderly women, armed with birch-rod and cane, 'received and minded pupils for a small weekly fee'. In such institutions boys and girls might be instructed in the three R's and, under rather exceptional circumstances, in 'the use of the globes' also. More than this, however, they could not learn. Indeed it is open to question whether, in the majority of dame schools, the curriculum extended even to these lengths. Certainly if we are to believe descriptions of them written in 1834—and there is no reason to suppose they were any better or worse at the outset of the century— they were excessively noisome institutions where young children were assembled not so much to receive formal instruction as to be kept out of harm's way whilst their parents worked. 'With few exceptions,' says a report of the Manchester Statistical Society, 'the dame schools are dark and confined; many are damp and dirty; and more than one half of them are used as dwelling, dormitory and schoolroom, accommodating in many cases families of seven or eight persons.' [1]

Such were the main characteristics of the dame schools. It remains to be noted, however, that, though thousands of them lay scattered about the country, they were by no means the only places where poor children could acquire the rudiments of knowledge. In addition there were the common day schools, usually somewhat larger in size and presided over by men instead of women—points of difference which, according to the most reliable records, rendered them no whit the better or more efficient. 'In a garret, up three pairs of dark, broken stairs,' we read in one account, 'was a common day school with forty children in a compass of ten feet by nine. On a perch forming a triangle with the corner of the room sat a cock and two hens; under a stump bed, immediately beneath, was a dog-kennel in the occupation of three black terriers, whose barking, added to the voices of the children and the cackling of the fowls on

[1] See 'Analysis of the Reports of the Committee of the Manchester Statistical Society' as given in the first volume of *The Publications of the Central Society of Education*, pp. 292 and 293

the approach of a stranger, were almost deafening; there was only one small window, at which sat the master, obstructing three-fourths of the light it was capable of admitting.' [2] This particular school which existed in Liverpool may well have been an extreme case, but it is generally conceded that even the best of them left much to be desired.

The two places of instruction already mentioned were, it is important to realize, private schools: that is to say they charged fees, however small, for such tuition as they gave. In addition, however, for completely indigent children, there existed other kinds of institution. And foremost among these were the Charity Schools which, as their name implies, were religious foundations, having originally been started in 1698 by the Society for Promoting Christian Knowledge and influenced to a large extent by Hermann Franke, the initiator of the powerful Pietist movement in Germany.[3] The masters of these schools had to be members of the Established Church, to have passed certain religious examinations and to have reached the age of twenty-three. They were also required to possess some knowledge of the art of teaching, to be able to write in a good, clear hand and to have attained a reasonable proficiency in Arithmetic. And finally they were expected 'to be of meek tempers and humble behaviour; to have a good government of themselves and their passions; and to keep good order'. As may be imagined, then, the Charity Schools, soon acquiring fame for their earnestness of purpose, began to spread rapidly. In 1743, for example, there were 132 in the London area and 1,329 in the provinces, catering altogether for some 25,000 children. Indeed, during the first half of the eighteenth century, they were clearly a most useful means of combating illiteracy. Certainly they taught 'Reading, Writing and Elementary Accounts' to large numbers of boys and girls who would otherwise have remained without any formal instruction, and some even went so far as to include Sewing, Carpentry, Gardening and Spinning in their curricula. Furthermore, being under one governing body, they acquired a certain uniformity of outlook. All, for instance, laid particular stress on religious and moral training, and almost all dressed their scholars in distinctive uniforms of blue, orange or green,

[2] Quoted by Thomas Adkins in his introductory chapter to *The History of St. John's College, Battersea* (1906), p. 9
[3] See p. 38 of *The Charity School Movement in the XVIII Century* by M. G. Jones

reminiscent of such famous foundations as Christ's Hospital. Unfortunately, however, once the burst of philanthropy in which they were born began to wane, they lost much of their influence. Indeed, though large numbers of them still existed at the start of the nineteenth century, for the most part they had sunk to a low level of efficiency; their methods were mechanical, their buildings squalid and their results negligible.

And what was true of the Charity Schools was equally true of another means of providing basic instruction for poor children—the Schools of Industry. These dated from 1675 when Thomas Firmin set up a spinning factory in Little Britain where he employed children from the age of five, taught them to read and to say the catechism. So successful was his venture, moreover, that within a short time it was imitated in various parts of the country and many infants were thereby enabled to acquire the rudiments of knowledge. Yet, as the eighteenth century progressed and as the schools of industry multiplied, they began to reveal serious defects, not least of which was the appalling length of time the pupils were expected to work. Indeed by 1800 they had become a byword for cruelty and oppression. At Fincham in Norfolk, for instance, some sixty children had to plait straw for seven hours daily before starting their lessons; and at Lewisham, in a knitting factory, the reading lessons began after the boys and girls had been standing almost continuously for twelve hours. Similar defects characterized the schools of industry in Cheshire and Lincolnshire. In fact it was the same story throughout the country—a story for the most part of hardship and oppression far worse than that told by the dame schools and the common day schools.

One of the principal reasons why the Industrial Schools sank to such appalling depths was, of course, the high premium on child labour. A journeyman or artisan might well be out of work indefinitely but his sons and daughters could always secure employment. So great was the demand for their services, in fact, that some were compelled to work as many as fourteen hours daily for six days a week. On the seventh, however, in strict accordance with the fourth commandment, they were permitted to rest, and so, in 1780, Robert Raikes, the editor of a West Country newspaper, conceived the idea of collecting together a group of such children from the slums of Gloucester and teaching them to read. After a period of trial, moreover, so encouraged was he by the results that he added to his original plan by engaging assistants and, two years later, inaugurated 'The Society for the Establishment and Supply of Sunday Schools' which soon attracted nation-wide attention. Thus by 1787 there were some 250,000 pupils in weekly attendance at Sunday Schools, and, by 1801, the London area alone could boast no fewer than 1,516 such institutions catering altogether for 156,500 indigent boys and girls.[4]

The history of this important movement is perhaps too well known to require further elaboration. Suffice it to say, therefore, that thousands of children, who would otherwise have remained unlettered throughout life, were first taught to read by this means and that at least one reformer, whose activities were radically to alter the nature of English primary education, expressly recognized this fact. 'The Sunday School was the root from which sprang our system of day schools . . .' commented Sir James Kay-Shuttleworth in a letter written in October 1867 to the old scholars of the Bamford Sunday School. 'The force which makes religious training the chief aim in the elementary day school was derived from this root.'[5]

Such, in brief, were the main institutions where poor children could acquire the rudiments of knowledge—institutions which, for the most part, were inefficient, squalid, unknown in number and unrecognized by the State. Little wonder, then, that Britain at that time was dubbed 'the worst educated nation in Europe'. Indeed so intense an atmosphere of frustration, almost of futility, surrounded her educational endeavours that, to discover a parallel, we have to turn to Prussia between 1768 and 1797 or Holland in the 1780's before Nieuwenhuysen founded 'The Society for the Public Good'. There, too, it will be recalled, the lot of the pauper child was exceedingly bleak and there, too, primary institutions were everywhere in a state of neglect.

The movement of ideas which opened up the way to general intellectual progress on the Continent has already been discussed in detail. Granted the fact that Prussia, Holland and Britain were ripe for educational reform towards the close of the eighteenth century, therefore, we may wonder how it came about that the first two

---

[4] See p. 19 of *History of Elementary Education in England and Wales from 1800 to the Present Day* by B. Birchenough

[5] See p. 8 of *The Life of Sir James Kay-Shuttleworth* by Frank Smith

countries were able so shortly afterwards to introduce schemes of social amelioration whilst the third remained powerless to effect any change for the better. And, in endeavouring to explain this curious situation, we might be driven to the conclusion that Prussia and Holland were able to rouse themselves from a state of intellectual inertia because, for a large number of years, their philosophers had paid close attention to the views of Rousseau, La Chalotais, Diderot, d'Alembert, Helvétius, Turgot, Mirabeau and Condorcet, whereas Britain remained indifferent to the advantages of systematic instruction because she lay outside the orbit of French influence. Such, however, was by no means the case. The Encyclopaedists and Revolutionary thinkers had a spiritual following on this side of the Channel just as they had on the Continent.

As evidence of this we may point to some of the outstanding social, political and economic treatises which appeared in Britain during the latter half of the eighteenth century. In 1765, for example, Sir William Blackstone, the noted jurist, published his *Commentaries on the Laws of England* in which he declared that the majority of European nations were steeped in ignorance for the simple reason that they did not compel parents to give their offspring an adequate mental and moral training. Yet that such should be the case was in itself both a serious charge of neglect and a weighty deterrent to progress. As Continental reformers were well aware, he said, 'a parent conferred no considerable benefit on his child by bringing him into the world, if he afterwards entirely neglected his culture and education, and suffered him to grow up like a mere beast, to lead a life useless to others and shameful to himself'.[6] Blackstone expressed the hope, therefore, that all countries would turn their attention to the enlightenment of the masses and, as a preliminary measure, insist upon compulsory schooling—the one safeguard for freedom and democracy.

Similarly, in his *Inquiry into the Nature and Causes of the Wealth of Nations* (1776), Adam Smith, largely influenced by the views of Turgot, asserted boldly that the intellectual, spiritual and physical condition of the labouring poor was beginning rapidly to degenerate and would continue so to do unless the State set itself to devise an adequate means of protection. As an incentive to progress, therefore,

---

[6] See p. 450 of Book I, *Commentaries on the Laws of England* by Sir William Blackstone (Tenth Edition)

he suggested that two reforms be introduced: first that some sort of military training be made available to ensure a higher standard of physical fitness among the menfolk, and secondly that a system of compulsory, if not of free, education be introduced for the benefit of the children. Indeed he advocated that all children, whatever their rank or station, be given some form of instruction because he was convinced that systematic mental training was the only thing which eventually would rid them of 'delusions of enthusiasm and superstition'. He trusted, too, that once they had savoured the delights of learning, they would look upon it as a valuable acquisition and continue to derive benefit from it long after they left school.

Such were the views expressed by Sir William Blackstone and Adam Smith. Nor were they the only people at that time to stress the importance of a widespread extension of educational privilege. Thomas Paine, for example, in *Rights of Man* (1792) not only denounced those who, like Burke, raised objections to the principles underlying the French Revolution but even extended the claims of Condorcet by suggesting that the Government, instead of granting poor relief, advance the sum of £4 yearly in respect of all indigent children under the age of fourteen and compel them to attend school. Likewise the Revd. Robert Malthus in his highly controversial *Essay on the Principles of Population* (1798) proclaimed that pauperism could be rooted out if only the poorer classes were taught to exercise moral control, that illiteracy could be banished were the State to accept the responsibility for instructing all its citizens and that the welfare of the greatest percentage of the population could effectively be secured provided political economy classes were introduced into the common day schools. 'It is surely a great national disgrace,' he wrote, 'that the education of the lowest classes in England should be left entirely to a few Sunday Schools, supported by a subscription from individuals, who can give to the course of instruction in them any kind of bias which they please.' [7]

And finally that great lover of French culture Jeremy Bentham, in his *Principles of Penal Law* (1802), asserted that education was one of the greatest sources of happiness that mankind had yet devised. Indeed it was more than this: it was both an efficacious method of promoting the well-being of the community and an

[7] See *An Essay on the Principles of Population*, Vol. III, Book 4, chapter 9 (Fifth Edition, London, 1817), pp. 203–205

indirect means of stopping crime. In a very real sense, then, it could be compared with the work of a domestic magistrate whose duty it was to safeguard public morals, control violent conduct and administer an equitable system of rewards and punishments. Viewed in such a light, moreover, education clearly possessed far-reaching social implications. Yet among the majority of European nations it stood sadly in need of reform and nowhere more so than in England which seemed loth to adopt even the most rudimentary measures to ensure its success. He also pointed out, and this is of particular interest in view of what happened in this country, that instruction in day schools could be greatly improved provided pupil-teachers, drawn from the ranks of the scholars, were afforded extra tuition and rendered thoroughly conversant with sound educative principles— an idea which occurred to him when, prior to the Revolution, he visited Paris and inspected a school for two hundred children conducted by the Chevalier Paulet.[8]

As may be appreciated, then, the Encyclopaedists and Revolutionary thinkers had their supporters and admirers in this country just as they had among France's immediate neighbours. Unfortunately, however, there were to be found amongst them no reformers of such commanding stature as Pestalozzi, Stapfer, van der Palm, van den Ende, Basedow, von Stein and von Humboldt. In other words Blackstone, Adam Smith, Paine, Malthus and Bentham, anxiously though they strove to secure improved educational facilities for poor children, were writers rather than teachers, theorists rather than administrators. Indeed Great Britain at that time could boast so few practical reformers with an intimate knowledge of the contemporary scene abroad that it is small wonder she became both apathetic in her attitude towards educational advancement and, once the international situation deteriorated, deeply suspicious of foreign pedagogical ideas and ideals. Yet before we can appreciate how such a state of affairs arose we must first note how European political developments towards the close of the eighteenth century completely disrupted the harmonious cultural relations that had existed between England and France for almost a hundred years.

When describing the debt which this country owed to the specu-

---

[8] See *The Works of Jeremy Bentham*, Vol. I, p. 570 (William Tait, Edinburgh, 1859)

lations of such men as Turgot, Condorcet and Talleyrand the impression may well have been given that the flow of ideas was entirely in one direction and that France for the most part remained ignorant of the contribution that British philosophers, scientists and political theorists had given to the advancement of knowledge. But this was by no means the case. Montesquieu, Voltaire and Rousseau, for example, were greatly indebted to political and philosophical ideas engendered in this country and so, too, were many other important writers and thinkers who, in 1751, rallied around Diderot and d'Alembert. Indeed, as Professor Cazamian has pointed out, it is a matter of some difficulty from 1730 onwards to study the development of French culture without reference to Britain or, for that matter, the development of British culture without reference to France. 'The cult of Voltaire and Rousseau among the English', he wrote, 'has its counterpart in the anglomania of the French. Innumerable are the facts connected with the full history of this reciprocal action which becomes in the middle of the century a more alive exchange, a closer intercourse than ever before.' [9] Nor did this happy 'entente' break down after 1750. It developed until the outbreak of the Revolution—an event to which many in this country, conscious of the extent to which French politicians were indebted to British concepts of social justice, responded with the same degree of enthusiasm as Wordsworth and Coleridge.[10]

Once France was proclaimed a Republic, however, and the September massacres were followed by the Reign of Terror, many of those who, in 1789, were overjoyed at the success of the revolutionaries

[9] See *A History of English Literature* by Emile Legouis and Louis Cazamian, p. 923

[10] Wordsworth, it will be recalled, was transported with joy as he proclaimed:

> 'Not favoured spots alone, but the whole earth
> The beauty wore of promise'

(See 'French Revolution as it appeared to enthusiasts at its commencement')

and Coleridge, according to Hazlitt, 'sang for joy when the towers of the Bastille and the proud places of the insolent and oppressor fell'. (See *The Spirit of the Age*, Everyman Edition, p. 200.) We may also remember, in this connection, how those two remarkable youths at Merchant Taylors'—Richard Hayward and John Grose —became so elated at the turn of events in France that they decorated the walls of the alleys leading to the school with treasonable remarks and later hung a large tricolour from the Tower of London. (See *The Old Public Schools of England* by John Rodgers, p. 84)

turned in revulsion from their former sympathies. The outcome of events was totally different from what they had anticipated and never more so than when the struggle for Liberty, Equality and Fraternity ended not in a reign of freedom but in the rule of a single soldier. Indeed few in our midst, when Napoleon assumed charge of France's destiny, would have been prepared to echo Fox's famous pronouncement in 1789: 'How much is this the greatest event that ever happened in the world, and how much the best!' In other words Britain, shaken by the storm of events abroad, was suddenly forced to look to her own safety. And France, instead of being the pole of attraction around which her intellectual life had centred for generations, suddenly became an object of repulsion.

Between 1789 and 1815, therefore, the drift of European thought can in certain respects be determined in relation to France, whose violent destiny inspired amongst neighbouring governments and nations differing reactions of fear and hostility. In Switzerland, Holland and Prussia, for example, a strong dislike of Napoleon, reinforced by a horror of occupation, caused an uprush of patriotic fervour which stimulated an already urgent demand for popular enlightenment. In Britain, however, whose fate was entirely different, an active hatred of the French helped rather to stiffen national self-consciousness. Thus, to add to her other educational difficulties, she now held herself aloof from the enlightening influence of cultural movements abroad. Furthermore, unlike her Continental neighbours, she had never seriously considered so ambitious a scheme of social welfare as a state system of schools and was certainly disinclined to do so when struggling for her survival.

As may be seen, then, the years 1789 to 1815 present a bleak period in this country's educational history—a period in which practically the only new developments as far as primary instruction was concerned were the monitorial institutions of Bell and Lancaster. And these, though certainly a slight improvement on existing educational facilities, left so much to be desired as to stand no comparison whatsoever with the various kinds of elementary school then being planned and erected in Switzerland, Holland and Prussia. In complete contrast to our Continental neighbours, therefore, we were blind to the value of pedagogical experiment and indifferent to the welfare of youth. Indeed it is no exaggeration to say that we, the one nation which successfully defied Napoleon and brought hope to thousands of subjugated people in Europe, did so, to some extent at least, at the expense of our own children, omitting either to watch over them in the factories or to provide them with any satisfactory means of instruction.

13

THE FOREIGN EDUCATIONAL TOURS OF ANDREW BELL AND ROBERT OWEN

'The eye only sees what it brings with it, the power of seeing.'
GOETHE

THE year 1815 is usually taken to mark an event in British history of greater significance even than the defeat of Napoleon. It is held to signal the beginning of a new epoch and the dividing line between the eighteenth and nineteenth centuries. That there is much justification for this point of view, moreover, may be judged from the fact that, when the expeditionary force of 300,000 soldiers which fought the battle of Waterloo returned home, they found a country in many ways unfamiliar to them—a country whose attitude to commerce was rapidly changing, whose cotton imports already amounted to eighty-two million pounds a year, whose woollen trade was slowly being transformed, whose heavy industries were enjoying a boom and whose roads were being altered beyond recognition by Telford and McAdam.

Unfortunately, however, as regards primary education, no new era was in sight. Had the returning soldiers decided to visit anew the miserable institutions where some of them, at least, must have learnt to read, write and cipher, they might, at a superficial glance, have thought that everything was much as they remembered it. Had they looked more closely, however, they would have detected a noteworthy difference—that the classrooms were not so densely crowded as aforetime. In other words fewer and fewer children were in daily attendance at schools because of the increased demands on their labour; and the educational position, already bad towards the close of the eighteenth century, was beginning rapidly to deteriorate.

Granted this sad state of affairs, therefore—a state of affairs which, we do well to note, the majority of people accepted without question—there is perhaps a peculiar interest in studying the views of a few individuals who, during the first half of the nineteenth century, not only ventured from these shores to study the educational programmes of more enlightened peoples but thereafter lost few opportunities either of describing what they saw to their fellow-countrymen or of exposing evils they considered to be a national disgrace. Indeed, as the present work endeavours to illustrate, it was largely because of such enterprising men and women that Britain eventually awoke to the peril of her educational position and sought ways and means of bringing herself more closely into touch with Continental educational thought and practice.

Before we can appreciate the importance of their activities, however, we have perforce to take into consideration yet another weighty deterrent to educational advancement in this country—the extent of our pedagogical ignorance. For, in 1815, few had ever heard of such men as Pestalozzi, de Fellenberg and Father Girard, or, indeed, of the ambitious schemes of social amelioration then being implemented by Holland and Prussia. Furthermore to such as were interested in the dissemination of learning amongst the poorer classes it appeared that the monitorial system was not merely an inexpensive means of combating illiteracy but a happy issue out of present difficulties.

And as proof of this we need only cite the conspicuous success of Bell whose activities have already been mentioned in chapter 9. At the conclusion of the French wars, it will be remembered, he was in the happy position of knowing that his advice on educational matters was constantly sought both in this country and abroad. Indeed by that date his self-esteem knew no bounds. So certain was he of the rightness of his system that he bitterly resented any departure from it—especially such deviations from the normal routine as were put into practice by Lancaster. In other words his method was sacrosanct and he the sole arbiter of what was right and wrong —hardly the type of person, one would suppose, to derive much benefit from a sojourn abroad or from contact with foreign educational thinkers. And such proved to be the case. Indeed, if a flagrant example of insularity be required, no better illustration can be provided than this remarkable clergyman's tour through France and Switzerland in the summer of 1816.

It was on the 18th June in that year that Bell, then at the height of his powers and confident that his pedagogical discoveries would revolutionize primary instruction throughout the world, set out for the Continent. And, as might be expected from one who held so exalted an idea of his importance, he speedily sought out a number of people abroad who, he considered, would appreciate his ministrations and interest themselves in the virtues of the Madras system. In Paris, for example, he established contact with the Society for Elementary Instruction and, from the Abbé Gaultier, learnt of such progress as had been made. But the account must have proved singularly disappointing to him as the following comment in his journal testifies: 'I might indulge in the most enthusiastic view in regard to the propagation of the new system of education in France, and over the world through France, if I did not know that the beautiful simplicity of the new system is ill adapted to the genius of the French nation.' [1] Considering the powerful influence which the Society for Elementary Instruction was already exerting upon France one can only surmise that something transpired at this interview which displeased the British visitor. Perhaps one of its members was unwise enough to mention the name of Lancaster. Certainly thereafter Bell found little to commend in France and the name of his bitter rival was ever close to his lips. The monitorial school of the Duchess de Duras, for example, disappointed him greatly because its seventy pupils indulged in 'all the Lancasterian nonsense—loss of time and dreadful clattering of hands and slates'.[2] And the well-known school of Saint-Jean-de-Beauvais, whence originated the 'fixed doh' system of teaching singing, disgusted him for the same reason. Indeed it was the same story wherever he went. He found nothing to satisfy him and nobody who seemed capable of understanding the finer points of the Madras system.

It must have been with relief, therefore, that, on 17th July, Bell quitted France for Switzerland. Yet, even there, the first teacher he met disquieted him. He was a certain Dr. de Roche, who had been educated in Edinburgh and who, at that time, was acting as principal of one of the largest academies in Geneva. Yet to Bell he appeared self-opinionated and stubborn, 'arguing and disputing every point' connected with the benefits of mutual instruction. Were the

[1] See *The Life of the Revd. Andrew Bell* (Vol. III) by Robert Southey, p. 84
[2] *Ibid.* p. 85

Swiss, then, going to prove as refractory and unappreciative as the French? Such a thought must have crossed Bell's mind for he concluded that Continental teachers in general were jealous of him and were one and all striving to re-make a discovery which had been vouchsafed to him alone and that after the world had been in existence some six thousand years! [3]

It was clearly a disgruntled man, therefore, who turned up at Yverdun on 30th July ready to offer his advice and cast a critical eye over the institute. Yet whether Pestalozzi appreciated these ministrations is open to question. We know only that Bell expounded his educative principles to the students, watched them at their work and discussed topics of educational import with their director. The latter, he concluded, had 'much that was original and much that was excellent in him' but unfortunately spoiled a great deal of his work by surrounding himself with a 'multitude of masters' not all of whom were capable of understanding what was required of them. Would it not be better, in consequence, to get rid of them? Economy, after all, was an important factor in Bell's life and to increase over-head expenses by employing a large number of assistants naturally struck him as senseless. It is perhaps hardly surprising, then, that his final comment on Pestalozzi should have laboured this very point: 'If he had a course of study——he were to dismiss four-fifths of his masters, retaining three, and to adopt the monitorial system and the classification of a Madras school, with the emulation, he would be superexcellent.' [4]

From Yverdun Bell proceeded to Hofwyl where he immediately sought out de Fellenberg—'a man of much ingenuity and, like his master, Pestalozzi, a determined enemy to emulation',[5]—and together they visited 'The School for the Poor' whose pupils, Bell

---

[3] See *The Life of the Revd. Andrew Bell* (Vol. III) by Robert Southey, p. 86

[4] *Ibid.* p. 94

[5] In view of the fact that Bell criticized both Pestalozzi and de Fellenberg for their dislike of 'emulation' it is perhaps of interest to give the latter's ideas on this subject as reported by Robert Dale Owen: 'Emulation was limited among us to that which naturally arises among young men prosecuting the same studies. It was never artificially excited. There were no prizes or college honours, no "double-firsts" to be won; there was no acknowledged position, marked by numbers, giving precedence and conferring name and fame; there was not even the excitement of public examinations; we had no Commencement exercises that might have assembled the magnates of Switzerland to criticize or to applaud.'

(See *Threading My Way*, pp. 125 and 126)

commented, though chiefly employed in mechanical work, nevertheless managed to acquire the rudiments of Reading, Writing, Ciphering, Drawing, Music and Geometry together with an expert knowledge of Gymnastics. Indeed this tiny institution struck him as an interesting venture whose worth could clearly be attributed to the fact that one master had control of it—the indefatigable Wehrli 'who was constantly at the side of his pupils whether at study, work or play'. About the remainder of the estate, however, about 'The Academy for Young Gentlemen', 'The Advanced Institute of Agronomy', the agricultural classes for farm labourers or the seminary for schoolmasters—nothing was said. One wonders, in fact, if Bell visited them, for his final comment on Hofwyl was: 'How slow improvements travel!' [6]

Such sentiments give a clear idea of Bell's attitude to Continental schools and educational reformers in general. Indeed there can be no doubt that the whole of his tour would have proved exceedingly disappointing had it not been for the fact that, towards its conclusion, he visited Fribourg. There, however, much to his delight, he met Father Girard whose educational methods immediately impressed him as superior to any that he had yet discovered. 'From Hofwyl,' he wrote in his journal, 'I was invited to Fribourg—the capital of the Roman Catholic canton of that name. There I found the new schools in a most flourishing state: and Père Girard, a priest, who deserves to be recorded in history as an amiable, benevolent and indefatigable friend of humanity and of youth, has the superintendence of these schools. Where one expects least, is often found most. This liberal father felt the true spirit of the Madras system and has introduced none of the fooleries, absurdities, noise and nonsense, which are found in the other schools or in the [Lancasterian] models from which they are chiefly taken. . . . He imbibed with eagerness the instructions which I gave and pledged himself to follow them.' [7]

In the last sentence we have perhaps the secret of Father Girard's popularity—he had been willing to learn of the virtues of the Madras system from the only man alive capable of expounding them. It is pleasing, therefore, to think that Bell's journey was not undertaken in vain and that he found at least one convert who appreciated his worth.

[6] See *The Life of the Revd. Andrew Bell* (Vol. III) by Robert Southey, p. 98
[7] *Ibid*. pp. 96 and 97

So ended a tour of the Continent undertaken by a famous British teacher and educational reformer—a journey which was largely induced by a desire for self-advertisement and which, even on that slender basis, proved a dismal failure. Indeed in the annals of educational tours it deserves to rank as a classic example of bad taste and flagrant insularity. It shows, nevertheless, how utterly blind one British traveller could remain to the ambitious schemes of social amelioration inaugurated by such men as Pestalozzi and de Fellenberg and how much had yet to be done if, by virtue of her natives travelling abroad, the United Kingdom were to awaken to the peril of her educational position.

In contradistinction to Andrew Bell's foreign tour in 1816, therefore, we may turn with satisfaction to that made by Robert Owen in 1818—a journey wholly different both in conception and purpose. Indeed it may well be argued that whereas the one went abroad to teach, the other went to learn; whereas the one set forth desirous solely of expatiating on his own beliefs, the other set forth equally determined to listen to those of others. The contrast, in fine, was marked and so were the results.

Before discussing Robert Owen's tour in detail, however, it is perhaps important to note that, by 1816, he had acquired great fame both as a social reformer and educational pioneer.[8] So hotly were his ideas on co-operation and socialism discussed, in fact, that during the course of that year and the next an almost continuous procession of visitors made its way to his home in New Lanark—visitors amongst whom were sometimes educationists of great importance such as Jullien de Paris, the foremost disciple of Pestalozzi in France, and Charles Pictet, Professor of Pedagogics in Geneva.[9] But there was nothing unusual about this. So many

[8] For a full description of the New Lanark Infant School, see *Robert Owen—A Biography* by Frank Podmore

[9] On p. 121 of *Threading My Way* Robert Dale Owen passes the following comments on Professor Pictet and the 1818 tour: 'An enlightened agriculturist and firm friend of distinguished scientists; one of the editors of the "Bibliothèque Britannique'; a diplomatist, too, trusted by his countrymen—Pictet had been sent by the Swiss Republic as Envoy Extraordinary to the Congress of Vienna in 1814, and to that of Paris in 1815. In 1817 he visited New Lanark; and he and my father contracted a warm and lasting friendship. They agreed to travel together to London, Paris and Geneva; and afterwards to visit in Switzerland a certain Institution, the most remarkable of its kind in the world. . . . It embraced the various establishments of M. de Fellenberg on his estate of Hofwyl, two leagues from Berne. . . . The journey had an important influence on all my after life'

eminent people came to the small Scottish village from distant parts that the natives grew accustomed to the babble of foreign tongues.

It so happened, however, that one of these visitors—Professor Pictet—became so enamoured of Owen's school that, after a short interval, he decided to inspect it a second time. At the conclusion of this visit, moreover, and as a token of appreciation for the kindness with which he had been received, he begged Owen to accompany him to the Continent, assuring him of 'a kind and warm reception from the first men of the day in France, Switzerland and Germany'.[10] And so, in the summer of 1818, the two of them set forth for Paris where they encountered such eminent figures of the contemporary scene as the Duke of Orleans, La Place, Alexander von Humboldt, Camille Jourdain and the Duke de la Rochefoucauld and were soon caught up in a social whirl the like of which Owen had never previously encountered. 'For six weeks did the Professor and myself luxuriate amongst the élite of the most distinguished men then in Paris'; he commented, 'and I lost no opportunity of obtaining the best thoughts of these superior characters. . . . In this manner was the inexperienced cotton-spinner initiated into the so-called great ways of the world.' [11]

From France the travellers next proceeded to Switzerland and there the same life continued—the notables of the country taking great pleasure in meeting Owen and discussing with him his 'New Views of Society'. What was far more significant than this, however, was the fact that, when staying in Geneva, Owen decided to visit the 'three most noted schools for poor children' then in existence in Switzerland—Fribourg, Yverdun and Hofwyl. And, as might be expected of one who was himself so keenly interested in the welfare of youth, he was not satisfied until he had examined them closely and availed himself of the opportunity of discussing topics of general educational import with their directors.

Before turning to Owen's appraisal of these famous schools, however, it is perhaps important to remind ourselves of the fact that he was, on his own admission, incapable of understanding a word of any language save English. And an unfortunate example of this deficiency occurs in his autobiography for, when treating of his

---

[10] See *The Life of Robert Owen, written by himself*, Vol. I, p. 166
[11] *Ibid.* p. 168

interview with Father Girard, he inadvertently refers to him as Oberlin—an error which at first causes some confusion to the reader and which his biographers unfortunately have perpetuated. Indeed it is remarkable to find in so authoritative a work as Professor Cole's *Robert Owen* the curious statement: 'Oberlin's Catholic school seemed to have impressed him more than Pestalozzi's.' [12] That there can be no doubt at all that it was Father Girard with whom Owen conversed, however, is obvious if we recall that the latter's journey took him nowhere near the Ban-de-la-Roche where Oberlin lived; that the man whom he encountered was a Roman Catholic priest and not a Lutheran pastor; that the said priest lived in Fribourg; and that Owen urged him above all to found Infant Schools —the very thing which Oberlin had done some forty years previously.[13] It is possible, indeed, that this particular topic of conversation occasioned the error in the first place for Father Girard could scarcely have discussed nursery education for any length of time without referring at some point to Oberlin's famous 'conductrices de la tendre jeunesse'—an allusion which may well have caused Owen to confuse their names.

Having noted this slip, then, we may turn to the Fribourg school. It was, so Owen stated, a large institution consisting entirely of boys between the ages of seven and fourteen and run chiefly along monitorial lines. What was particularly noteworthy about it, however, was its truly Catholic spirit—a spirit as tolerant as it was profound. In this respect, of course, and in the high standard of learning which it maintained, the school did but reflect its director's personality. Indeed it was immediately obvious to Owen not only that 'this industrious curé' had 'laboured hard and long' to bring his institution to such a state of excellence but also that his pioneer efforts had had a profound effect upon the poorer element of the town's population.

Yet one thing rather puzzled the British visitor. Why was it, he debated, that so worthy an educational establishment, which strove so valiantly to mould the characters of indigent boys in conformity with Christian standards, should neglect to receive pupils until they

[12] See *Robert Owen* by G. D. H. Cole, p. 162. (We may note that, on pp. 88 and 129 of her *Robert Owen of New Lanark* (1953) Margaret Cole is guilty of the same error)

[13] See *Memoirs of John Frederic Oberlin, Pastor of Waldbach in the Ban-de-la-Roche* (Third Edition), p. 87

were seven years of age? 'I see by your school,' he said to the Franciscan, 'that it is after that age that you, like other masters of schools, receive your pupils. But to a great extent the character is made or marred before children enter the usual school room.' The answer, however, was readily forthcoming. 'I have no means,' said Father Girard; 'and it is with great difficulty I can procure funds to maintain what I have, and to do so has cost me many sleepless nights.' [14]

Perhaps this statement was not wholly satisfactory to Owen who had encountered even more formidable barriers when starting his own educational experiment and so, by way of encouragement, he gave a lengthy description of the New Lanark Infant School, adding that such institutions would be commonplace as soon as society sloughed off its attitude of self-seeking and money-grabbing. 'But do you think that change can ever be effected?' enquired the Catholic priest; and Owen, launching himself on his favourite topic—the vision of a world at peace knowing nothing of distinctions of rank and class—said that he was certain that it could. 'But', continued Father Girard, 'you will be opposed by all religions and governments, and by the people whom they govern, and whose educated prejudices in favour of existing practices will be a difficulty insurmountable in your way.' 'So I am told,' replied Owen, 'by men of all parties. But my knowledge of human nature leads me to know that conviction does not depend upon the will of the individual; but that it depends upon the strongest impression which can be made upon his mind; and I hope by degrees to create new impressions upon the most advanced minds, and that they will gradually make similar impressions upon the general public mind.' [15]

There is something rather moving in this conversation as recorded by the British traveller for both parties were agreed that to help suffering humanity was their first concern and that to spread popular enlightenment the most effective way of so doing. It was simply in their conception of the millennium that they differed, for whereas the one looked forward to a new world state where justice and equality would reign supreme, the other had little thought save for the coming of Christ's kingdom upon earth. That no trace of rancour entered their minds despite this cleavage of opinion, however, may be judged from Father Girard's parting words to his

[14] See *The Life of Robert Owen, written by himself*, Vol. I, p. 176
[15] *Ibid.* pp. 176 and 177

guest: 'You must have great faith in the truth of your principles to resolve upon such a course of conduct, against such obstacles as you must meet by the way. I, however, wish you all the success you desire, without much expectation that it is possible for any one to overcome the prejudices and apparent interests to be encountered from all sects and parties in all countries.' [16]

So ended an interchange of views as urbane as it was amicable and Owen next proceeded to Yverdun to see Pestalozzi. Unluckily, however, Professor Pictet, who acted as his guide and interpreter, experienced such difficulty with the latter's 'confused patios' that not a great deal of conversation was possible—an eventuality which doubtless accounts for the fact that the two travellers did not linger at the celebrated institute. Perhaps, too, Pestalozzi was in no fit state to entertain them for at that time he was ill and experiencing much difficulty with his assistants. Yet Owen spent sufficient time with him to form a good opinion both of his methods of sense-training and his lessons on mental arithmetic—educational features which, we do well to note, he subsequently copied at New Lanark. Apart from that, however, he was not greatly impressed by what he saw. Indeed it struck him that Pestalozzi's 'means and experience were very limited' and that, as a result, his seminary was 'but one step in advance of ordinary schools'. One can only regret, therefore, that the language difficulty presented so formidable a barrier that these two eminent teachers were prevented from enjoying each other's company—the more so as Owen took kindly to the aged Swiss reformer, speaking warmly of his 'goodness of heart', 'benevolence of intention' and 'honest and homely simplicity'.[17]

After Yverdun the two travellers then ventured to Hofwyl where they were most cordially received by de Fellenberg, an old friend of Professor Pictet, who immediately asked them to share his home—an honour, be it noted, accorded very few and those usually the heads of European states. Once there, moreover, Owen was treated with every kindness and allowed to inspect at his leisure such interesting features of the estate as Wehrli's 'School for the Poor', 'The Advanced Institute of Agronomy' and 'The Academy for Young Gentlemen'—all of which he found in excellent order 'and the schools two or three steps in advance of anything of the kind either in England or on the Continent'.[18]

[16] *Ibid.* p. 177   [17] *Ibid.* p. 177   [18] *Ibid.* p. 178

What chiefly impressed him, however, was the character of de
Fellenberg himself—a man 'possessing rare administrative talent
and a good knowledge of human nature' who was clearly 'very
superior in talent and attainment to his former partner, Pestalozzi'.
Indeed it was not long before the two of them were engaged in a
lengthy discussion concerning the best methods of spreading popular
enlightenment—Owen openly advocating that Hofwyl extend the
scope of its educational facilities by creating infant schools and de
Fellenberg promising to give the suggestion careful consideration.
More than this, as the two warmed to their discussion, they discovered they shared many ideas in common—that both, for example, held 'strong liberal, not to say democratic principles' and
were keen to proceed with the democratization of society 'as fast
and as far as their surroundings permitted'.[19]

Thus two men whose ideas at first blush one might imagine to be
irreconcilable, succeeded not only in having an amicable discussion
but in reaching agreement on several important issues. Yet, in reflecting on their conversation, one cannot help wondering if de
Fellenberg did not so oversimplify his political ideas as to render
himself liable to misunderstanding. In other words, since there is
nothing either in his theory or practice to suggest that he genuinely
subscribed to egalitarian principles, one can only conclude that by
the democratization of society or perhaps by the rather ambiguous
phrase 'as fast and as far as surroundings permitted' he meant
something very different from what Owen imagined.

Whatever construction one may put on their talk, however, it is
impossible to deny the fact that these two reformers found much in
common or that Owen regarded his visit to Hofwyl as the highlight
of his foreign tour. Furthermore so impressed was he with the
'Academy for Young Gentlemen' that, despite its enormous fees,
he decided to send his two sons—Robert Dale and William—to study
there. 'I had seen nothing to equal the existing and projected
arrangements or surroundings of the establishment,' he confessed;
'and accordingly I agreed to place my sons under M. de Fellenberg's especial care and direction.' [20]

So ended a tour of the Continent in the summer of 1818 undertaken by a wise traveller—a tour which, it would be foolish to

[19] See *The Life of Robert Owen, written by himself*, Vol. I, p. 178
[20] *Ibid.* p. 179, and *Threading My Way* by Robert Dale Owen, p. 122

assume, had any dramatic results as far as the importation of foreign ideas into this country was concerned, but one which, nevertheless, was clearly by no means valueless. For it was in large measure because of such excursions as these and the expansion of ideas that they brought about that Britain eventually realized the extent of her insularity and sought ways and means of improving her educational status.

14

LORD BROUGHAM'S STRUGGLE FOR A STATE SYSTEM OF EDUCATION

'The science of education is an essential branch of moral and political philosophy. Like all other departments of science, worthy of that name, it has need of being surrounded by the light of experience; and to avoid the danger of being misled by fantastic theories, we must lose no opportunity of obtaining an accurate acquaintance with the various systems of education that are followed by all great civilized nations.'

VICTOR COUSIN

In treating of the importance of foreign educational tours and of the extension of intellectual frontiers which they helped to secure, one factor has constantly to be borne in mind—the strength of character of those who made them. Indeed, with few exceptions, those who set forth to visit Yverdun and Hofwyl were men and women of great tenacity—a fact that becomes increasingly apparent the closer we examine their activities. Certainly this was true of Robert Owen, and it was also true of his one-time associate Henry Peter Brougham, later Lord Brougham and Vaux, the foremost statesman of his generation to draw attention to the necessity of popular education and the earliest reformer to devise means for its attainment.

To consider Brougham as an educationist, however, it is important to recognize, first and foremost, that he was 'a citizen of the world'. Indeed, as the famous *Punch* cartoon of 1848 made abundantly clear, he was a man whose sympathies were too cosmopolitan for the majority of his contemporaries and, as such, liable to ridicule.[1] That he himself regarded isolationism as an evil and placed reliance on contact with other peoples, however, cannot be questioned. It is apparent both in his public utterances on the state of

[1] This cartoon, showing Brougham in an assortment of national costumes, bears the title of 'The Citizen of the World; or Lord Brougham Naturalized Everywhere'

education in England and Wales and in the numerous journeys he undertook to foreign parts. As early as 1799, for instance, he spent several months wandering through Scandinavia, studying the living conditions of the poor and forming, amongst other impressions, an unfavourable estimate of Swedish morals; in 1804—the year following Britain's renewal of the struggle against France—he set out alone for Holland and Germany to examine Europe in the throes of occupation, passed himself off as an American, sailed up the Rhine in a passenger boat, caught a glimpse of Napoleon in Cologne, escaped detection by a hair's breadth and eventually crossed, unmolested, into Italy; between 1815 and 1836 he journeyed each summer to France, Holland, Switzerland or Italy, rarely returning without having examined some seat of learning or encountered some foreign educationist; in 1850 he visited the United States of America; and, from 1835 until his death in 1868, he spent a large part of every year at his villa in Cannes where he frequently entertained distinguished guests and speedily won for himself the affection of the local residents because of the interest he took in their welfare. In addition he was an accomplished linguist, speaking French, according to Wilberforce, 'as well as English, besides several other languages'.[2] And finally he was a man with an undoubted flair for getting to know 'the right people'. Indeed, in the fashion of his day, he did not indulge in foreign travel to gratify any love of scenic beauty but to broaden his mind. 'Switzerland', he wrote to Creevey, 'is a country to be in for two hours or two and a half if the weather is fine, and no longer. Ennui comes on the third hour, and suicide attacks you before night. There is *no* resource whatever for passing the time, except looking at lakes and hills, which is over immediately.'[3]

The cosmopolitan nature of Brougham's interests has been stressed in order to illustrate the truth that, to all intents and purposes, he was devoid of national attachments and prejudices. Indeed, since the main concern of his life was 'to elevate the views and refine the character of the great mass of mankind',[4] he thought it only natural that he should draw on the accumulated experience— scientific, economic and educational—of all nations. Furthermore,

---

[2] See *The Correspondence of William Wilberforce*—letter from Wilberforce to Pitt dated 25th October, 1805. Vol. 2, p. 51

[3] See letter to Creevey dated 25th August, 1816. *The Creevey Papers*, Vol. I, p. 258

[4] See *Practical Observations Upon the Education of the People* (1825), p. 117

so intimately acquainted was he with contemporary cultural and intellectual movements in Western Europe that he rarely thought it worth while to expatiate either upon them or those who initiated them—in the way, for example, of Bell or Owen. He merely worked on the assumption that all well-informed people would understand what he was talking about when he made oblique references to the Prussian state system of education, that everyone interested in the diffusion of learning had read Cuvier's *Rapport sur les établissements d'instruction publique en Hollande* and that the work of the 'Frères Ignorantins' was universally acknowledged for its benevolence of intention. In other words he tended to assume too wide a range of information on the part of those who listened to or read his speeches, and the task of summarizing his debt to foreign educational thinkers thus becomes difficult for it is sometimes impossible to state categorically that he derived this idea from France and that from Switzerland, especially so since he himself was usually satisfied with the brief reflection that such and such a course of action was recommended in order to bring this country more closely into touch with its Continental neighbours.

Such were the attributes of one who may with justice be regarded as the pioneer of a state system of education for this country. In order to search out the sources whence sprang his interest in popular enlightenment, however, we have to turn to the early years of the nineteenth century and, in particular, to the work of Joseph Lancaster. By 1810, it will be remembered, the latter's educational endeavours had not only won him considerable renown but had received the blessing of the king with the result that the Royal Lancasterian Association had been formed whose aim it was 'to afford education, procure employment and, as far as possible, to furnish clothing to the children of the poorer subjects of George III'.[5] As members of its executive committee, moreover, it numbered James Mill, Samuel Rogers, several Quaker philanthropists and Brougham himself, at that time a young enterprising lawyer, who worked with such ardour that, within three years, he was elected to succeed Lancaster as President. It was quite simply as an advocate of mutual instruction, therefore, that he began his educational career. Yet, even at this early date, his sympathies were far too liberal to be bounded by so narrow an objective. Indeed, in the

[5] See *A History of English Elementary Education* by Frank Smith, p. 81

course of 1813, when conducting an enquiry on behalf of the West London Lancasterian Association into areas of the metropolis that demanded increased attention, he found such 'scenes of misery and vice' confronting him that he conceived the idea that what was primarily needed, both for London and the country as a whole, was a network of primary schools.

It was not until 1816, however, that he was able effectively to begin his crusade. Before that date the deadweight of opinion against a measure designed primarily to help the poor was too considerable, and few indeed would have supported it. In that year, however, Brougham, judging that the times were more propitious, made his first move and, after a great deal of agitation inside and outside Parliament, was able to convince members of the necessity of appointing a 'Select Committee to Enquire into the Education of the Lower Orders of the Metropolis'. In view of his past experience with the West London Lancasterian Association, moreover, he volunteered to act as its chairman and, within a matter of months, was able to place before the House a mass of educational statistics which showed just how necessary the enquiry had been. In Spitalfields, for example, only 2,100 children received regular instruction and of those more than seventy-five per cent never attended any institution other than a Sunday School; in Shoreditch only 160 children were in daily attendance at school, the remainder wandering helplessly on the streets or, when old enough, working in factories, shops, etc.; in St. Giles there were less than 4,865 children who had any possibility of learning to read and write; in the East Union 30,500 children were completely illiterate; and, in the metropolis as a whole, no less than 120,000 boys and girls remained destitute of any means of education whatsoever. It was, of course, the London of Dickens' boyhood—the London of dark alleys and unpoliced slums whence half-starved children and miserable cripples emerged only to gather such sustenance as the day might bring. 'The poor', said the Report, 'were in general anxious for education, yet in some cases they objected to sending their children to school, preferring rather to let them out to common beggars, and out of this number came most of the juvenile depredates who swelled the calendar of Newgate.' [6]

[6] See *Hansard Parliamentary Debates*, Vol. XXXIV, p. 635—Speech of Henry Brougham in the House of Commons of 21st May, 1816

Having assembled these statistics—the first of their kind to be collected in this country—Brougham naturally hoped that some sort of action might be forthcoming from the Government. In this, however, he was disappointed for the apathy both inside and outside the House of Commons was far greater than even he deemed possible. No satisfactory results may be said to have come of his investigations, therefore, save that his committee was allowed to continue in operation and to extend its field of enquiry from London to the rest of England.

Such was the position which confronted Brougham in 1818—a position as dispiriting as any that he faced. One would underestimate his resilience, however, if one were to imagine that because of it he was prepared for one instant to abandon his faith in popular education. Indeed, as the work of his committee progressed and as it was gradually revealed that the rural areas of England were in an even worse state of neglect than the towns, the realization was born in him that nothing save a supreme effort on his behalf would ever convince those in authority that it paid better to have intelligent human beings than ignorant artisans. He recognized, too, that the successful outcome of his struggle depended to a tremendous degree on supplying his fellow-countrymen with accurate information concerning pedagogical discoveries abroad which would stimulate educational endeavour at home.[7]

Accordingly, in March of that year, he wrote, 'from personal observation of minute particulars', a lengthy description of the Hofwyl Academy for Young Gentlemen, the Advanced Institute of Agronomy, the Training College for Teachers and the Wehrli Poor School—a description which was at once a tribute to de Fellenberg's foresight and a cogent plea to the British public to give increased attention to the important subject of popular instruction. He showed, for example, how every branch of the Swiss institute was intimately connected with manual labour; how the life the students led, because it was constantly associated with Nature, never failed to quicken their senses and improve their morals; how all ranks of society, by the mere fact that they worked together in the same community, became united by ties of sympathy; and how, in the face of opposition, de Fellenberg himself maintained confidence

[7] See *Reports from Committees: Education of the Lower Orders*, Third Report, Vol. 4, p. 194

both in the importance of his project and the regenerative powers of education. Brougham also showed, and this proved the most significant part of his account, that the branch of Hofwyl which was most deserving of visitors' attention was the Poor School —for there an interesting exposition was given of the doctrine that 'to make poor people better it was necessary first to make them comfortable'. Indeed it struck him that the Wehrlischule, which was constituted entirely of 'destitute boys from the most degraded of the mendicant poor in Berne and other Swiss towns', was 'one of the most extraordinary and affecting sights' that could be seen. And for that reason he debated whether others might not profit, as he had done, from a prolonged sojourn in Berne.[8]

By way of encouraging would-be reformers in this country to interest themselves in the welfare of poor children, therefore, Brougham finally summarized what he considered to be the main points of de Fellenberg's educational creed. It was, so he asserted, a sustained effort on the part of the Swiss reformer to show pupils 'gentleness and kindness, so as to win their affections'; to treat them as rational creatures; to watch over their lives with 'a constant and even minute superintendence'; to show them that 'manual labour, in cultivating the ground, was the paramount care upon which their existence depended; to impress upon them 'the necessity of industrious and virtuous conduct'; and to inspire them with 'a deep sense of religion'.

Brougham recognized, of course, that the prime difficulty with regard to founding schools of similar nature in this country would be 'to find such admirable superintendents as Wehrli', but he thought that nothing but good would result if teachers from Britain were sent to study at Hofwyl or, failing that, if such famous reports on de Fellenberg as those written by Albert Rengger and Count Capo d'Istria were translated into English.[9]

Such were the views expressed by Brougham in his *Third Report on the Education of the Lowest Orders*—views which afford evidence both of his interest in foreign educational endeavour and of his concern that this country should take steps to check the incidence of illiteracy. We do well, therefore, to emphasize the influence

[8] *Ibid.* pp. 195 and 196
[9] *Ibid.* pp. 195 and 196

which Hofwyl exerted upon him at this period for there can be little doubt that he regarded it not only as an incentive to intellectual progress but a successful means of harmonizing the most disparate elements of society. In fact so certain was he that England had a vital lesson to learn from this unusual project that, within a year, he described it anew in a special article for *The Edinburgh Review*. Accordingly, as on a previous occasion, he drew public attention to such interesting features of the Swiss estate as the Academy for Young Gentlemen, where scrupulous care was taken 'to mould the character, the temper and the habits of young people' in conformity with Christian standards; the Advanced Institute of Agronomy, where students were taught scientific methods of husbandry; and the Poor School, where children 'taken from the worst classes of society were thoroughly reformed and brought to an eminent degree of excellence'. Nor was this all for he described in detail the extensive curricula of the various establishments showing, for example, what a large part of the students' lives was spent in contact with Nature and what benefit they derived from the Pestalozzian method of instruction. And finally, after praising de Fellenberg's foresight, he expressed the hope that those in the United Kingdom 'whose public spirit was proportionate to their means of serving the community would devote a season or two of recreation from other employments to the important and not uninteresting business of visiting Hofwyl'.[10]

Thus Brougham continued his struggle for a widespread extension of educational privilege—a struggle which, it cannot be emphasized too strongly, he undertook because 'England, in this most essential particular, was so far behind other countries'. Indeed it seemed to him that part at any rate of our indifference to the welfare of poor children could be attributed to the fact that we knew nothing whatsoever of the ambitious schemes of social amelioration then being implemented by France, Switzerland and Holland. And so, in 1820, in a speech characterized by great restraint, he introduced a new proposal—his Parish Schools Bill, which was as cogent a piece of reasoning as any he made and which, had it found acceptance at the time, would have changed the entire history of primary educa-

---

[10] *The Edinburgh Review, or Critical Journal* (December 1818 to March 1819), Vol. XXXI

tion in this land.[11] Brougham showed how his committee, if it had served no other purpose, had at least revealed both the inadequacy of existing educational facilities and the amount of absenteeism then prevalent in English schools. 'It appeared', he stated, 'that there were educated in unendowed schools 490,000 children, and that to those were to be added about 11,000 for 150 parishes from which no returns had yet been made. In the endowed schools 165,432 children were educated; making a total (exclusive of the 11,000) of 655,432. In England it appeared that on the average one-fourteenth or one-fifteenth of the whole population was placed in the way of receiving education. Another deduction ought also to be made for the dame schools, where 53,000 were educated—or rather not educated, for it amounted to no education at all. . . . The average means of mere education, therefore, was only in fact one-sixteenth in England.' [12] Yet how different, Brougham continued, was the position in such countries as France, Switzerland and Holland where for some time past enlightened men had subscribed to the theory 'that the education of the poor was the best security of morals and the peace of nations'. Between 1817 and 1820, for instance, France had built no less than 7,120 new primary schools catering for some 204,000 pupils —'an example well worthy of our admiration and imitation'. Nor was she the only country to have sought new ways and means of spreading popular enlightenment. Switzerland, also, had long realized the importance of good primary institutions and had taken elaborate precautions to promote the welfare and happiness of her citizens by giving them systematic instruction at a low cost, with the result that the percentage of her population that could read and write was roughly ten times that of England. And Holland, too, had not been slow in realizing the value of an educated proletariat. Between 1806 and 1811 she had built as many as 4,451 primary schools educating 190,000 children—a truly remarkable accomplishment on any account.[13]

In view of these facts, therefore, Brougham made the following recommendations: that primary schools be established throughout England and Wales 'wherever needed'—the power of allocation to be left to the Quarter Sessions; that schoolmasters be given a minimum salary of between £20 and £30 per annum—the money to

[11] Printed in full in J. E. G. de Montmorency's *State Intervention in English Education*, Appendix III   [12] *Ibid.* p. 258   [13] *Ibid.* pp. 258–260

come from a tax on the landed gentry; that new schools be built from funds obtained from the manufacturers 'who, while they increased the objects of the poor rates, contributed but little towards them'; and that additional expenses be covered both by parish officers levying a rate twice yearly and by parents, save those in extreme poverty, paying between 2d. and 4d. a week for their children's tuition. Altogether, Brougham estimated, £500,000 would be required to build all the institutions he deemed necessary and some £150,000 a year to support them—a vast amount of money on any account. Odd as it may seem, however, the financial clauses of his bill proved the least controversial. What chiefly distressed his fellow parliamentarians was not the thought of providing more than half a million pounds for the instruction of the 'lower orders' but the suggestion that all children, regardless of religion, be taught in state schools. Brougham had, needless to say, foreseen that this issue would prove extremely contentious and taken precautions to obviate it by devising a compromise similar in many respects to that which the Dutch had adopted in 1806. He advocated, for example, that all teachers be members of the Established Church and that the vicar of each parish be given the authority not merely to examine all schools under his jurisdiction but likewise to determine the type of instruction they gave. And he also recommended, so as not to alienate the sympathy of Dissenters, that no form of worship be allowed in school save the Lord's Prayer and that religious teaching be confined to passages of Holy Writ. Thus, he trusted, sectarianism would be avoided and, if parents desired their offspring to learn the tenets of a particular faith, they could do so by taking them to church or chapel on Sundays. Such was the compromise Brougham suggested —a compromise not unlike that which van der Palm worked out for Holland, but one which, nevertheless, proved displeasing to all parties of Englishmen. In fact so strongly was it resented not only by Roman Catholics and Nonconformists but also by members of the Church of England that, when the bill came up for its second reading on 21st June, 1820, Brougham was compelled to withdraw it. And by so doing, of course, he unfortunately had to abandon what was his boldest attempt to date to bring this country into line with her Continental neighbours.

By this time, it would seem, Brougham must have realized that his ambitious plan to erect hundreds of new primary schools throughout England and Wales had small chance of winning public support. It was typical of his perseverance, however, that he allowed no such thought to daunt him. Instead defeat seemed only to stir him to further activity and so, between 1820 and 1830, though temporarily compelled to abandon his scheme for a state system of schools, he nevertheless made three attempts to show his contemporaries how unambitious were their educational plans in comparison with those of their neighbours.

The first of these dated from about 1820. At that time Brougham was taking renewed interest in the work of the British and Foreign Schools Society, spending a great deal of his leisure time at the Borough Road Society and visiting numerous monitorial institutions in various parts of the country. The wider his experience of them grew, moreover, the surer he became that one and all were seriously lacking in what he termed 'moral discipline'.[14] Indeed, so greatly did this defect worry him that he took the opportunity of discussing it with his friend, de Fellenberg, who assured him that the basic trouble with the Bell-Lancaster system of instruction was that 'it taught too fast, making mere machines of its scholars'—an objection which, according to his own admission, Brougham had been at a loss to refute.[15] Pondering this criticism, therefore, he came to the conclusion that 'If a child was neglected till six years of age, no subsequent education could recover it. If to that age it was brought up in dissipation and ignorance . . . it was in vain to attempt to reclaim it by teaching it reading and writing.' [16] And so he began to search diligently for experimental methods of teaching which would give to young children the 'moral discipline' that he deemed so essential. As might be expected, moreover, it was not long before his attention was directed to Robert Owen's Infant School in New Lanark, which so impressed him that he straightway borrowed a member of its staff and proceeded to found similar institutions first at Westminster and later at Banbury. And so well did these new schools prosper that, within a short time, they, too, acted as a spur to educational reform with the result that, in 1824, the Infant School Society came into being whose object was to promote

[14] See 'The Speech of Mr. Henry Brougham in the House of Commons, on Wednesday, June 28th, 1820, on the Education of the Poor'. Reprinted in J. E. G. de Montmorency's *State Intervention in English Education*, p. 284
[15] *Ibid.* p. 284   [16] *Ibid.* p. 283

the establishment of 'asylums for children of the poor' throughout the London area. Thus Brougham helped to initiate what was, in
effect, an entirely new movement in English elementary education
—a movement from which he derived the utmost satisfaction. Indeed, as he himself admitted, he attached particular importance to
it—first, because it gave promise of correcting what de Fellenberg
justly censured as the fundamental weakness of the monitorial
schools; and secondly, because it afforded evidence of vastly improved methods of instruction from which those responsible for
training youth could derive immeasurable benefit.

As may be seen, then, Brougham, in his desire to promote the
welfare of mankind and to banish the stumbling-block of ignorance,
was prepared to support almost any philanthropic effort which
aimed at helping the needy—a truth that perhaps becomes more
obvious when we consider his next undertaking. In 1824 he took the
initiative, along with Dr. Birkbeck, in founding the first Mechanics'
Institute in London—a new departure in this country's educational
practice designed to supply lectures on scientific and other subjects
to the growing class of artisans. Anxious to forward this movement,
Brougham, in 1825, drew up his *Practical Observations Upon the
Education of the People*—a plea that all classes unite in an effort to
improve both themselves and their country. Furthermore, to those
who protested that such an ideal was impossible of realization, he
pointed to Hofwyl where students from all walks of life lived together in amity, and where even the humblest peasants took delight
in forwarding their knowledge of agriculture. Indeed Brougham
gave it as his opinion 'that a high degree of intellectual refinement,
and a taste for the pleasure of speculation, without any view to a
particular employment, may be united with a life of hard labour,
even in its most humble branches, and may prove its solace and its
guide'.[17] In view of this fact, therefore, he wished to see circulating
libraries, book clubs and reading societies established throughout
the country and, above all, cheap editions of worth-while publications. 'The first method which suggests itself for promoting knowledge among the poor', he said, 'is the encouragement of cheap
publications; and in no country is this more wanted than in Great
Britain, where . . . we have never succeeded in printing books at
so little as double the price required by our neighbours on the

---

[17] See *Practical Observations Upon the Education of the People* (1825), p. 143

Continent.' [18] Thus, once again, Brougham emphasized the fact that Britain should turn to such countries as Holland and Switzerland where inexpensive editions of important literary and scientific works had long been the order of the day. To hasten progress in this direction, moreover, he founded, in 1826, the 'Society for the Diffusion of Useful Knowledge', which not only popularized scientific investigation very effectively but led to the appearance of such well-known periodicals as the *Penny Magazine* (1832) and the *Penny Cyclopaedia* (1833).

And another object which Brougham set himself to achieve at this time was the creation of a university free from religious tests. In 1825, therefore, he and Thomas Campbell, the poet, initiated a scheme which led some three years later to the opening in Gower Street, London, of University College—soon to be popularly known, in view of its motto 'Patens Omnibus Scientia', as 'Brougham's Patent Omnibus'. So often has the early history of this famous foundation been recorded, however, and so far removed is it from the subject of the present enquiry, that there would seem to be little point in repeating it here save to comment on the fact that this new college proved a complete innovation as far as seats of learning in England were concerned and that, as both its founders testified, it was originally inspired by the newly created University of Bonn.[19] In yet another way, then, did Brougham demonstrate his indebtedness to Continental educational thought and practice.

Such were the main reforms introduced between 1820 and 1830 by one of the ablest parliamentarians of the first half of the nineteenth century—reforms which may be said to have given new hope to the common people of England and to have persuaded at least some members of the House of Commons that the future well-being of this country lay with an educated democracy. Indeed if we recollect what happened so shortly afterwards when, on 17th August, 1833, Lord Althorp's suggestion to vote £20,000 for the purposes of education was carried by 56 votes to 26, the significance of Brougham's work becomes increasingly apparent. Little wonder, then, that, as the public demand for information of all kinds began to grow, he was inspired anew to take up his campaign for a state system of schools. Thus, on 23rd May, 1835, and on 1st December, 1837, he delivered two lengthy addresses in the Upper House which,

[18] *Ibid.* p. 105   [19] See *An Outline of English Education* by J. W. Adamson, p. 30

if not entirely new in their suggestions, were nevertheless clear indications that his desire to 'enlighten the people' had in no sense abated. He began, for example, by reaffirming his belief in the efficacy of early training. 'I consider the establishment of Infant Schools', he said, 'one of the most important improvements—I was going to say in the education, but I ought rather to say in the civil polity of this country—that have for centuries been made.'[20] But he went on to censure this country for having failed to staff such institutions with adequately trained teachers. Indeed it seemed to him that, in far too many cases, the 'effects of the old system of instruction' were being flagrantly perpetuated, with the undesirable effect that a large number of pupils were acquiring 'the most mischievous habits and becoming listless, indolent and inattentive'.[21] Not all countries, however, subscribed to so short-sighted a policy. France, for example, had recently given striking proof of her concern for the welfare of her youngest citizens by establishing progressive 'salles d'asyle' both in Paris and the provinces. Were we, then, in all matters educational, constantly to remain in the wake of the Continent? 'It would seem', Brougham said, 'that our insular prejudices had spell-bound us . . . and made us believe that a school means useful instruction, and that when we had covered the land with such buildings, whatever was done within them, or left undone, we had finished the work of instructing the people.' [22]

Warning his hearers against insularity, therefore, Brougham next censured what he considered an equally undesirable trait of responsible people in this country—their indifference to educational improvement. Indeed it seemed to him that many of them subscribed to the theory that England had latterly made great strides in combating illiteracy. Yet anyone who had travelled abroad knew how false such a supposition was. Holland, for example, with its highly organized system of elementary education put us completely to shame. And so, too, did Sweden, Denmark, Würtemberg, Bavaria and Saxony, all of which possessed large numbers of state-aided primary institutions.[23] Reflecting on these facts, then, was it not reasonable to suppose that our educational indifference was in some way connected with our insularity? How else could one

---

[20] See 'Speech on the Education of the People' (1835) reprinted in Vol. III of *Speeches of Henry Lord Brougham* (Edinburgh, Adam and Charles Black, 1838), p. 233
[21] *Ibid.* p. 236   [22] *Ibid.* pp. 250 and 251   [23] *Ibid.* p. 249

account for the fact that Holland, France, Prussia and Switzerland, none of which was in any degree narrow in its educational outlook, possessed so many Normal Schools whilst this country could claim but one—the monitorial training centre in the Borough Road? [24] Apparently so apathetic were we with regard to the diffusion of knowledge that we thought we had every reason to congratulate ourselves when we had dealt out 'a niggard dole of mental sustenance' to those responsible for training our youth.

As a means of correcting these two serious faults, therefore, Brougham made the following suggestions: first that enlightened schoolmasters in this country turn for guidance to his 'old and venerated friend' de Fellenberg; [25] and secondly that those interested in the well-being of this land speedily set to work to create what was known on the Continent as a 'Department of Public Instruction', complete with a minister of Education, school inspectors and other responsible officials. [26] Only by so doing could England be cured of her insularity and made to take her place alongside Switzerland, Holland and Prussia as a champion of educational reform.

As may be appreciated, then, Brougham was incalculably indebted to Continental educational enterprise. Indeed it is only when we assemble the various sources whence he drew inspiration—sources, be it noted, as disparate as Hofwyl, the Prussian and Dutch state system of schools, the University of Bonn, the 'salles d'asyle' in France and the primary institutions in Sweden, Saxony and Bavaria—that we realize the extent both of his cultural experience and pedagogical knowledge. Of him, accordingly, almost more than any other reformer of his time, it would be true to say he realized to what extent the apathy of the English public towards social and intellectual reform was attributable to ignorance of happenings abroad. And so he directed attention to the Continent, not because he was enamoured of all things foreign, but because he found there the best means of promoting human welfare and the most satisfactory antidote to misery and ignorance.

By way of conclusion, however, we do well to remind ourselves that Brougham was first and foremost a politician and not an educationist. To search for immediate results of his policy, therefore, would be pointless. He merely mapped out the way for others to

[24] *Ibid.* p. 254   [25] *Ibid.* pp. 251 and 252   [26] *Ibid.* p. 288

follow and indicated the lines along which general progress lay. Yet the fact remains that, by dogged determination and by constantly reminding successive Governments of the necessity of educational reform, he succeeded more effectively than any other person of his generation in drawing attention to the misery and ignorance in which the majority of Englishmen lived. And that this proved a spur to progress may be judged from the fact that, when eventually he abandoned his campaign for popular enlightenment, others were prompted to take it up and to devote their energies towards securing for this country what Holland, Switzerland and Prussia had long possessed—improved methods of teaching in primary schools and a state system of education, cheap and universal.

15

FOUR EARLY PIONEERS OF PESTALOZZI'S METHODS IN THE UNITED KINGDOM

'La plus grande difficulté de l'humaine science semble estre en cest
endroit où il se traicte de la nourriture et instruction des enfants.'
MICHEL DE MONTAIGNE à MADAME DIANE DE FOIX

IN treating of Lord Brougham's efforts to secure a nation-wide network of primary institutions for this country and of his repeated
assurances to those interested in the diffusion of learning that no
lasting progress would be theirs unless they turned for guidance to
the Continent, the impression may well have been given that he was
a lone voice crying in the wilderness. Such, however, was not the
case. Among his contemporaries there existed several individuals
who were not only determined to combat illiteracy but just as
anxious as he that careful consideration be given to improved
methods of instruction. And of their number special mention must
be made of a small but effective group of philanthropists who studied
at Yverdun and thereafter determined that one of the most important
ways in which they could benefit Britain was to convert unbelievers
to a faith in Pestalozzi's pedagogical ideals.

Before attempting to pass judgment on their activities, however, it
is perhaps wise to remind ourselves of two salient facts connected
with the growth of Pestalozzianism in the United Kingdom: first
that the great Swiss reformer himself made no attempts to win
proselytes here until well advanced in years, and secondly that those
interested in his theories and eager to apply them in British schools
had to brook much opposition. Such considerations have constantly
to be remembered when assessing the debt which this country owed
to foreign educational reformers during the first half of the nineteenth century for, though they in no way excuse her indifference to

the welfare of poor children, they nevertheless go far towards explaining why she placed reliance on the mutual method of instruction long after it had served its distinctly limited purposes. Indeed it may well be argued that, for at least twenty years, she clung to the outmoded traditions of Bell and Lancaster because she was aware of no effective substitute.

The new gospel of enlightenment which revolutionized primary teaching in Switzerland, Holland and Prussia was, therefore, slow to arrive in this country. And the main cause of this, as has already been shown, was the vexed international situation. For a variety of reasons, chief among which was the protracted struggle with Napoleon, the inhabitants of Great Britain were prevented from travelling on the Continent and widening their outlook by contact with other peoples and other cultures. It is hardly surprising, in consequence, that no British visitors appeared at Burgdorf or Yverdun when those institutes were at the height of their fame.

A turning point was reached in 1814, however, when, with the apparent end of the Napoleonic wars, an Irish traveller named Synge from Glanmore Castle, County Wicklow, set out on a prolonged tour of Switzerland. It so happened, moreover, that, during a period of residence in the canton of Berne, a number of friends prevailed upon him to visit Yverdun—an idea which, according to his own admission, he at first resisted because he thought he was merely being asked to view 'an object of curiosity pointed out to all travellers'. Indeed he could not conceive what possible benefit he might derive from such a visit since, 'from the little he had seen of the mechanical systems practised at home, he felt no small degree of prejudice against schemes of education'. Once he had entered the establishment, however, he was immediately struck by 'the intelligent countenances of the children and the energetic interest which they appeared to take in their studies'. Nor was this all for, after observing an arithmetic lesson conducted in French, he straightway recognized the 'admirable principles on which the instruction was given'. And so, 'having his time entirely at his own disposal', he decided to remain at Yverdun in order to render himself thoroughly familiar with Pestalozzi's educative principles and 'to bring home as much as possible of what appeared to be so intrinsically valuable'.[1]

[1] See Preface to *A Biographical Sketch of the Struggles of Pestalozzi to establish his System* (1815)

Such, in brief, is the story of Synge's conversion to Pestalozzianism —a conversion as sudden as it was dramatic and one which surprisingly had important repercussions not only in Britain but likewise in Switzerland. Yet, before we can see how this happened, we must first note how Synge, during his three months' stay at Yverdun, made a 'peculiar study' of 'those important principles of instruction derived from a close investigation of Nature which are applicable to every branch of knowledge which can be acquired by the human mind' [2] and, whilst so doing, conceived the idea that what was primarily needed to rescue his fellow-countrymen from the depths of ignorance in which they dwelt was a knowledge of improved methods of instruction that had long enjoyed popularity on the Continent. Indeed so sure was he that both Ireland and England had a valuable lesson to learn from Yverdun that, shortly after his return to Wicklow, he set to work to prepare an account in English of what he had learnt. And it was thus that *A Biographical Sketch of the Struggles of Pestalozzi to establish his System* (1815), *A Sketch of Pestalozzi's Intuitive System of Calculation* (1815) and *The Relations and Description of Forms, according to the Principles of Pestalozzi* (1817) first saw the light of day—publications of considerable importance when estimating Britain's debt to Continental educational thought and practice during the first half of the nineteenth century.

As may be appreciated, then, Synge, by virtue of being the first native of Great Britain to study at Yverdun, acquired a certain educational significance. Yet he was not, as he took care to point out in the preface to *A Biographical Sketch*, a man possessed of a wide knowledge of schools, nor yet one who could say that he had given prolonged thought to the subject of education since finishing his own 'painful labours' at the university. He was simply an Irish traveller who had become impressed by the Yverdun experiment and subsequently determined that one of the most profitable tasks he could perform was to publicize Pestalozzi's educative principles.

Thus, having confessed his limitations as an educationist, Synge proceeded to examine those aspects of Pestalozzi's thought which struck him as peculiarly significant. And, as might be expected of one who had lived in daily contact with the great Swiss reformer, he began by stressing the importance of a mother's love. This, he

---

[2] See *Reports from Committees: Education of the Lower Orders*, Third Report, 1818, by Lord Brougham

asserted, more than any other agency was capable of rectifying the errors of ignorance and of calling the intellect into action. Indeed it was the basic factor in all true education, and for that reason it behoved teachers above everything else to study the way in which a good mother trained her children. 'The great point in which Pestalozzi appears to have surpassed all his predecessors', commented Synge, 'is the removal of all that misery and compulsion which, till now, has clouded the acquirements of our juvenile years. He insists on the master never losing sight of his responsible situation—viz. that he has undertaken to represent the parent to his pupil and that, as a parent, he must watch over his morals, as well as his literary acquirements.' [3]

These and other truths of a like nature, the majority of which are to be found in *How Gertrude Teaches Her Children*, Synge elaborated in great detail in order, as he said, 'to make his readers acquainted with the noble heart of Pestalozzi' and 'to remove a large portion of that prejudice with which any theory for the betterment of mankind emanating from the Continent was received by his fellow-countrymen'. Nor was this all for, in 1815, 'prompted by personal friends', he opened a fund in London to prevent the 'evening of Pestalozzi's well-spent life from being spent in pecuniary difficulty', arranging that subscriptions be received by James Digges La Touche, Esq., at the Bank of the Right Honourable David La Touche and Co., and by Messrs. Puget, Bainbridge and Co., Warwick Lane, 'one half of the sum contributed to be remitted to the venerable Pestalozzi as a testimony of esteem; the other moiety to be expended in the translation of his elementary works'. [4]

That Synge's efforts had at least some effect in stimulating British interest in Pestalozzi's educational work may be judged from the fact that, from 1815 onwards, a small but ever-increasing number of pupils made its way from these shores to Yverdun—an event which naturally gladdened the heart of the aged Swiss reformer who was pleased to welcome pupils from the United Kingdom to his 'family' of 180 children from the majority of the nations in Western Europe. [5]

And it was thus, during a period of financial embarrassment, that

---

[3] See Preface to Synge's *A Biographical Sketch*, p. 15

[4] See Synge's *A Biographical Sketch*, p. 117

[5] See 'Student Life at Yverdun under Pestalozzi. Reminiscences of a Westminster Boy' reprinted in *Pestalozzi and His Educational System* by Henry Barnard, pp. 131–143

Pestalozzi came to look on Britain as the one means of ensuring his survival. Indeed so anxious was he that this country should realize the importance of his pedagogical discoveries that, in 1817, he announced through the press that he had purchased a modest house at Clindy, about a quarter of a league from his main institute, which he hoped eventually to turn into an 'Armenanstalt' for poor children from Britain but which, until such time as they arrived, he purposed to fill with destitute boys and girls from the neighbourhood. On the 14th September, 1818, moreover—the day after the official opening of the establishment—he issued a pamphlet from Yverdun which bore the following curious title: *An Address of Pestalozzi to the British public, soliciting them to aid by subscriptions his plan of preparing school masters and mistresses, that mankind may receive the first principles of intellectual instruction from their mothers.*[6]

At that time, it must be realized, Pestalozzi was under the impression that an English edition of his works would shortly appear in print. Anticipating great pecuniary benefit from this source, therefore, he further announced by way of his address—an address which unfortunately no longer exists among his personal papers—that, provided sufficient funds were forthcoming from the United Kingdom to cover the expense of transporting a number of indigent British boys and girls to Clindy, he would willingly devote whatever revenue he obtained from the English translation of his writings to training such children both as respectable citizens and effective exponents of 'the synthetical method of instruction'.[7]

Such were the noble sentiments that Pestalozzi cherished towards the people of this country for having subscribed to a fund on his behalf in London. As it happened, however, no English version of his works appeared at that time nor, so far as we are able to ascertain, were any poor children sent to Clindy. But what did occur was that a number of well-to-do people, possibly inspired by Synge's tracts, became interested in Yverdun and sent their sons to be educated there. And the upshot was that, in the autumn of 1819, Pestalozzi was able to realize one of his most cherished ambitions—to create a special department of his college known as the 'colonie Britannique' where he assembled all the pupils who had been sent to him from the United Kingdom and arranged that they be given special

[6] See article on Pestalozzi in *Dictionnaire de Pédagogie et d'Instruction Primaire*, p. 2344   [7] *Ibid.* p. 2344

tuition in their native tongue. Nor was this all for, to assist him in this venture, he enlisted the services of three Englishmen—two of whom subsequently exercised a profound influence on the development of infant and primary education in this country.[8]

The first was James Pierrepont Greaves, a native of Merton, Surrey, forty years of age, a disciple of Swedenborg and Boehme, and a great student of the occult. Previous to 1817, so he later declared, he had taken no particular interest in education and for a number of years had lived the life of a recluse. But in that year, after reading Synge's *A Biographical Sketch of the Struggles of Pestalozzi to establish his System*, he had found himself unable to rest until he visited Yverdun. Indeed, as he subsequently wrote to his American friend Alcott: 'In the year 1817 . . . I was prompted to investigate the work of the venerable Pestalozzi . . . and so great was the interest quickened in my mind that I straightway left for Switzerland where I lived for four years in holy companionship with this inspired being.' [9]

As may be appreciated, then, it was rather an unusual type of person who suddenly presented himself at Yverdun towards the close of 1817, unable to speak a word of German and totally ignorant of pedagogical theory. Yet, according to all accounts, he settled in his new surroundings without difficulty and was soon happily engaged giving English lessons to the children. Unfortunately, however, he proved so poor a linguist himself and had to rely so heavily on the services of an interpreter that Pestalozzi became worried lest his theories be misinterpreted and accordingly, between 1st October, 1818, and the 12th May, 1819, wrote for the benefit of his assistant a series of thirty-four letters giving a straightforward account in German of the educational truths by which he set greatest store. And these Greaves presumably mastered at the time by means of a rough translation. Certainly he came to prize them greatly for, when eventually he returned to this country, he brought the original documents with him and had them translated anew by a German named Worms—a man who, doubtless experiencing some difficulty with Pestalozzi's involved style, decided to touch up the contents. When, therefore, they were finally published in 1827 under the title of

---

[8] The third member of staff was a clergyman named Brown about whom nothing is known save that he came from Worcester

[9] From a letter written in 1837 by Greaves to Alcott quoted in the article on Greaves in the *Dictionnaire de Pédagogie*, Vol. II, p. 3028

Letters on Early Education addressed to J. P. Greaves, Esq. they were by no means a faithful rendering of the original. It is said, however, that, shortly before his death, Pestalozzi had the Worms' version read back to him in German and gave it his blessing.[10]

Such, in brief, is the history of *Letters on Early Education*—a book of which the only available text is in English. And since it was clearly designed by its author to serve a twofold purpose—first to give a succinct statement of his views for the benefit of Greaves, and secondly to speak through the latter's voice to 'the mothers of Great Britain'—we do well to note its contents with care. It showed, for example, how education really began from the moment the newborn infant first turned to his mother for succour; how it depended to a great degree on the training of the senses; how it prospered better in an atmosphere of love and freedom than in one of fear and constraint; how it was the art of leading an infant from the known to the unknown by way of several carefully graduated steps; and how its ultimate aim was to foster the harmonious development of a child's physical, mental and moral attributes, thus giving him the true dignity of a spiritual being.

Truths of this nature, of course, had constantly been emphasized by Pestalozzi. To search in the Greaves letters for novel ideas, in consequence, would be to misinterpret their purpose. They were not intended to herald further pedagogical discoveries but to give the reflections of an experienced teacher on subjects which might prove of interest to a comparative beginner. And if anything new occurred in them it was simply a newness of emphasis rather than of idea. Thus, in letter XXIII, Pestalozzi wrote a most effective plea for the inclusion of music in the school curriculum, pointing out, as Luther had done before him, that it was 'one of the most efficient means of elevating and purifying genuine feelings of devotion'. In letter XXX he issued a series of admonitions concerning the 'play-way' method of instruction, stating frankly that too great an emphasis on amusement often precluded 'solidity of learning'. In the same letter he added a number of wise reflections on the use of corporal punishment confessing that, though he did not hold it inadmissible under all circumstances, he objected to it most strongly when it was used by a master to cover his inefficiency; and in letter XXXIV, taking

[10] *Ibid.* p. 3028
See also article on Greaves in *Dictionary of National Biography*

the second verse of the eighteenth chapter of St. Matthew as his text and dwelling on his favourite theme—the importance of a mother's love—he gave one of the finest homilies on Christian charity that ever came from his pen.

To return to Greaves, however, we learn that, after leaving Yverdun in 1822, he spent a certain amount of time in Basle and rounded off his sojourn abroad by visiting Tübingen where he stayed until 1825, in which year he fell foul of the Würtemberg authorities for spreading subversive political doctrines among the students. Forced to flee the country, therefore, he returned to England and, having settled on the outskirts of London, devoted the remainder of his days to propagating the doctrines of Pestalozzi. As an earnest of his desire to see them more widely applied, moreover, he started a nursery school at Ham, near Richmond, which, though it excited little interest in this country, was not without influence abroad. Indeed, according to Professor Vulliemin, it was this very establishment which first prompted Swiss educational reformers to interest themselves in the training of tiny children. 'Clindy fell,' he wrote in his *Reminiscences*, 'but there was a man there who had taken part in the short-lived enterprise, a man of Christian spirit and enlightened understanding. This man, who was an Englishman, by name Greaves, carried the ideas he had gathered at Clindy back to England, where they took root and became the origin of nursery schools. From England these schools returned to us, first to Geneva, then to Nyon, then everywhere. We had not understood Pestalozzi, but when his methods came back from England, though they had lost something of their original spirit, their meaning and application were clear.' [11]

As may be seen, then, Greaves was in several respects an important pioneer—the first native of Great Britain to be employed at Yverdun, the first person in this country effectively to demonstrate how Pestalozzi's pedagogical principles could benefit very young children, and one of the first teachers to start an experimental school in direct imitation of what he had learnt abroad. Among those who helped to quicken British interest in foreign educational ideals during the first half of the nineteenth century, therefore, he deserves special mention. And what was true of him was no less true of his one-

[11] See Introduction (p. xxviii) to *How Gertrude Teaches Her Children* edited by Ebenezer Cooke (1907)

time friend and colleague, the Revd. Charles Mayo, LL.D., whose activities may likewise be summarized under two main headings—study at Yverdun and subsequent work as a practical educator in England. There exists, indeed, a curious parallelism between the careers of these two schoolmasters—the more so since both were led to visit Pestalozzi after reading Synge's pamphlets.[12]

Yet, in dealing with Mayo, one senses a mental stability which was lacking in Greaves. He, in truth, was no visionary with advanced political sympathies but a level-headed Protestant clergyman who debated long before, in July 1819, he resigned his position as headmaster of Bridgnorth School, Shropshire, and, together with fifteen of his pupils, set out for Yverdun.[13] Furthermore he was a man of high principle who, once he had undertaken a task, endeavoured to discharge it to the utmost of his capability. Indeed, according to his own admission, he admired 'moral earnestness' and 'fixity of purpose' more highly than any other virtues,[14] and it is hardly surprising, in consequence, that, soon after arriving at Yverdun, he accepted an appointment as chaplain to the 'colonie Britannique' and became Classics and Divinity Master to the senior class.

Perhaps the most interesting feature of Mayo's sojourn abroad, however, was the way in which he set himself to master Pestalozzi's educational theories, studying such expositions of them as were contained in *How Gertrude Teaches Her Children* and attending, alongside the students, courses on 'Pädagogik', 'Didaktik' and 'Methodik'. It was, as a result, a very different type of person who returned to England in 1822 from the one who set out thence in 1819—a man well versed in educational theory and one who, like Greaves, had developed a particular interest in young children. This period of intimate association with Pestalozzi remained, in fact, a constant source of inspiration to Mayo and he invariably recalled it with pleasure. 'Could I convey to others', he told an audience when lecturing at the Royal Institute in Albemarle Street, London, in 1826, 'the sentiments I feel for him, Pestalozzi would be loved and honoured as he deserves. Three years of intimate connection with

[12] See *Dictionary of National Biography*—article on Charles Mayo. See also pp. 143 and 144 of *Pestalozzi and His Educational System* by Henry Barnard

[13] See article on Pestalozzi in *Dictionnaire de Pédagogie et d'Instruction Primaire*, Vol. II, p. 2344; also article on Greaves, p. 3028

[14] See *Observations on the Establishment and Direction of Infants' Schools* by the Revd. Charles Mayo, LL.D., Fellow of St. John's College, Oxford, pp. 7 and 8

him, every day marked with some proof of his affection, may well have knit my heart to his; and among the most cherished recollections of the past is, that Pestalozzi honoured me with his friendship and thanked me for cheering his decline.' [15]

It was not alone by means of lecturing, however, that Mayo strove to interest his fellow-countrymen in the work of Pestalozzi. In addition, soon after his return to England, he opened an experimental school at Epsom which, though primarily designed to educate the sons of a few wealthy families in the neighbourhood, soon proved so successful that, in 1826, larger premises had to be sought in Cheam. Nor was this all for, within a few years, so numerous were the requests he received to admit new pupils that he had perforce to restrict entry to such as had had their names entered at birth. Indeed there can be no doubt that, by virtue of his experiment, Mayo gave a lively demonstration of Pestalozzi's pedagogical principles and established himself as a highly successful educational reformer. His insistence, for example, that History, Geography, Nature Study, Gymnastics, Music and Drawing be given their rightful place in the school curriculum immediately distinguished his ideas on formal instruction from those of his contemporaries. And his teaching methods, which aimed above all else at 'strengthening and directing the affections of his pupils' hearts' and 'quickening their powers of observation', likewise proclaimed his independence of thought. But it was in his very definite views on moral training that he gave the clearest proof of his originality for, as he was ever ready to admit, 'early impressions often sink deeper than is suspected; they form a kind of under current in the character which, though sometimes overborne by the violence of the upper tide, is yet felt at particular seasons and under particular circumstances'.[16]

Such were the noble aims that this Protestant clergyman set himself to defend—aims which demonstrate with what zeal and application he had studied at Yverdun. Small wonder, then, that the Cheam school not only enjoyed a remarkable reputation but became the cynosure of all who were interested in progressive teaching methods. Indeed so great was the interest it kindled that both Mayo and his sister Elizabeth determined that one of the best ways in which they could hasten educational reform in this country was to

[15] See Barnard *Pestalozzi and His Educational System*, p. 144
[16] See *Observations on the Establishment and Direction of Infants' Schools*, p. 11

prepare a series of text books, suitable for adoption in infant schools, which would describe in as exact a manner as possible the way in which object lessons should be given. And so it was that *Lessons on Objects* (1831), *Lessons on Shells* (1832) and *Model Lessons for Infant School Teachers and Nursery Governesses* (1838) first appeared in print—text books which,, within a few years, were in constant demand in many parts of the United Kingdom. In view of this fact, therefore, we do well to take a typical extract from one of them and note the detailed manner in which a pupil was trained to exercise his visual, gustatory and olfactory capacities—aspects of his development which, until then, but few British teachers had recognized as even remotely connected with the process of education. Thus, in a lesson entitled 'The Nutmeg', we read as follows:

1. *The teacher supplies the following information to the class.*

'The Nutmeg is the kernel of a fruit, the produce of a tree resembling our cherry-tree, both in size and growth. It is found in the West Indies. The external covering of the fruit is a husk: this opens when ripe and displays a thin scarlet membrane called mace: this being carefully removed, there still remains a woody shell which surrounds the nutmeg. The nuts are first dried in the sun and then placed on a frame of bamboos over a slow fire, until the kernels, on being shaken, rattle in their shells.'

2. *The teacher, with a specimen nutmeg before him, then solicits the following information from the class.*

Qualities.

It is sapid, hard, oval, dingy, brown, dull, opaque and dry. Its surface is uneven. It is vegetable, natural, inanimate, foreign, pungent, conservative, pulverable, agreeable to the taste, aromatic, odorous.

3. *The teacher, recognizing the importance of sense training and the necessity of giving his pupils exact impressions, endeavours to establish the distinction between 'odorous' and 'aromatic'.*

TEACHER: Why is nutmeg said to be odorous?
PUPIL: Because it has a smell.
TEACHER: Why aromatic?
PUPIL: Because it has that pungent smell distinguished by the name aromatic.

TEACHER: Are all things that are aromatic also odorous?
PUPIL: Yes.
TEACHER: Are all things that are odorous also aromatic?
PUPIL: No.
TEACHER: Is an onion odorous?
PUPIL: Yes.
TEACHER: Are these smells alike?
PUPIL: No.
TEACHER: Does the term odorous include every kind of smell?
PUPIL: Yes.

TEACHER: A term which includes all the varieties of one kind of quality or substance is called a generic term, whilst that which marks one of the species is called a specific term. Odorous is a generic term, because it includes every kind of smell; aromatic is a specific term, because it applies only to one particular smell. Give examples of generic terms and of a specific term applicable to each of them.

PUPIL: Odorous, fragrant; coloured, red; foreign, Chinese.

The pupils should determine in succeeding lessons what terms are generic and what specific.[17]

Such skeleton lessons, of which *Lessons on Objects* contains no less than a hundred examples, were bold attempts on the part of the Mayos to convince British teachers of two fundamental truths—first that they should present new subject matter to children in a logical sequence, and secondly that they should at all times give full scope to sense-training. But that, we do well to emphasize, was the extent of their purpose. They strove neither to set up an easy procedure for conducting classes nor yet to produce a simplified version of the Pestalozzian method of instruction. Indeed nothing could have been further from the Mayos' intention than to encourage laziness on the part of those entrusted with 'the sacred task of educating youth'. 'It is not easy thus to teach,' they stated; 'it requires much skill in adapting the question so as to draw out the right answer, much previous thought to determine what points will be most profitable to dwell upon, and, above all, much study to determine how the said points can best be presented to excite attention.' [18]

As may be seen, then, the Mayos were emphatic that Pestalozzi's pedagogical principles were by no means susceptible of facile inter-

[17] See *Lessons on Objects*, pp. 70–72
[18] See Preface to *Lessons on the Miracles of our Blessed Lord*, p. 5

pretation—a fact that becomes increasingly obvious when we consider their next undertaking. For in 1836, spurred on by the apathetic attitude of British teachers towards improved methods of teaching, they were instrumental in founding the Home and Colonial Infant School Society—an institution in the Gray's Inn Road, London, which proved both a radical departure in this country's educational practice and a much-needed incentive to reform at a time when the inherent weaknesses of the monitorial system were becoming daily more obvious. Its original object was 'the improvement and general extension of the Infant School system on Christian principles as such principles are set forth and embodied in the doctrinal Articles of the Church of England' but, as time passed, it extended the scope of its activities by embracing the following additional aims in its grand design—'to obtain individuals of character and piety, and to qualify them, by appropriate instruction, for masters and mistresses; to afford existing teachers the means of improvement, and to recommend them to schools as occasions might offer; to appoint inspectors to visit existing schools; to circulate information on the Infant School system; to print and publish proper lessons; to provide school materials; and to correspond with the friends of infant tuition in different parts of the world'.[19] With such an extended programme of action, moreover, it is perhaps hardly surprising that the Home and Colonial Infant·School Society soon attracted attention far beyond the confines of London—especially so when, in an effort to make its aims more widely known, it established a 'Model School' for children between the ages of two and ten and a 'Training Establishment' for such as wished to qualify as Infant Teachers.

The first of these establishments, which was the responsibility of Elizabeth, was designed primarily 'to counteract the cold, lifeless style of teaching and ineffective moral influence then visible in the majority of schools'.[20] That it had another and more positive end in view, however, may be judged from the fact that it accepted as its guiding principle the oft-repeated maxim from *How Gertrude Teaches Her Children* : 'the first faculty of the infant mind to be developed is the faculty of observation'. Indeed this experimental venture, by reason of being the first attempt on the part of a British reformer to show how effectively Pestalozzi's pedagogical principles could help

---

[19] See *The Quarterly Educational Magazine and Record of the Home and Colonial School Society* (1848), Vol. I, pp. 3 and 4   [20] *Ibid.* p. 46

poor children, clearly marked a step forward in the history of infant education. In contradistinction to the monitorial institutions of its day, moreover, it strove at all times to show that the acquisition of knowledge was an agreeable, fascinating and stimulating occupation. Thus, during the initial stages, its pupils spent much of their time learning letters from cards, practising sounds from various combinations of syllables, listening to stories (usually simple anecdotes from the Bible) and playing with wooden blocks of various colours. Gradually, too, they learnt to draw, to form letters, to read and to write. And, whilst all this was in progress, they exercised their senses by handling flowers, vegetables, shells, stones, etc., until they were able to distinguish with facility not merely the size and weight of the said objects but likewise their shape, colour and smell. Then, proceeding from the known to the unknown in the approved manner, they learnt to add, subtract, multiply and divide. Later still they began Nature Study and Geography—starting, needless to say, by investigating the immediate neighbourhood. And finally they studied History, Gymnastics and Singing.

When one considers this curriculum which, far from limiting itself to Reading, Writing and Ciphering, strove to give the pupils a wide range of interests, one can realize, albeit to but a limited degree, the extent of Elizabeth Mayo's contribution to educational progress. To denigrate her venture, therefore, to compare it unfavourably with a modern nursery school and to censure it because it lacked 'spontaneity, freedom, games and practical occupations', would seem to be slightly unjust.[21] What, indeed, it should be compared with is a typical dame school or common day school of its time. And against such a background it stands out clearly as an interesting example of educational initiative.

What was true of the Model School, moreover, was no less true of the Training Establishment which was opened on 1st June, 1836, and was a bold attempt on the part of Charles Mayo 'to prepare men and women of all religious denominations for the important office of

[21] See *A History of Elementary Education* by C. Birchenough, p. 334
In view of this criticism it is perhaps of interest to quote a testimony to the worth of the Model School by E. Carleton Tufnell—a man who, after all, was in a far better position to judge: 'I have visited many schools where the pupils acquire more extensive knowledge, but I have never seen children of this class whose minds appeared to have been more thoroughly opened or who exhibited a more lively intelligence.' (See *The Quarterly Educational Magazine*, Vol. I, p. 54)

teachers'. Unfortunately, however, this particular enterprise en-countered many initial set-backs—not least among which was the standard of learning of those who enrolled as students. In fact so woefully ignorant were the majority of the candidates that, in the early part of 1837, it was decided to extend the course of training from twelve weeks to six months and to restrict entry to such persons as possessed 'at least some familiarity with the usual branches of knowledge'.

Yet, once these and other reformatory measures had been adopted, there can be little doubt that the Training Establishment speedily acquired fame both as an efficient college for infant teachers and an excellent means of publicizing Pestalozzi's work. By 1838, for example, so great was the interest it aroused that enquiries as to its guiding principles were constantly being received—sometimes from countries as far distant as Belgium, Malta, Russia and the United States of America.[22] And, in view of this fact, it is perhaps advisable briefly to consider the six rules which Dr. Mayo followed when devising a suitable programme of studies for his students.

In the first place he stipulated that they should have a course on the English language so that they might 'not merely learn to speak and write it correctly but likewise to use it as a means of calling out their minds and exercising their thoughts'; secondly, a course on the Pestalozzian concepts of Number and Form in order to aid 'their mental development and render them capable of teaching small children'; thirdly, a course on Geography 'which would embrace a general view of the earth, especially in its physical characters, to-gether with a more particular study of England and the Holy Land'; fourthly, two courses on Drawing—'the first using it as a method of developing invention, the second as an imitative art'; fifthly, a simple course on Singing which 'by its elementary exercises would cultivate both the ear and the voice'; and finally a full course on Biblical Instruction 'which would thoroughly inform the students in Scripture history, doctrine and principles'.[23]

Such, in brief, were the six main branches of study which Dr. Mayo included in his curriculum. It remains to be noted, however, that, as additional means of extending his students' experience, he arranged that they attend lectures on child guidance by Hermann Krüsi, the son of one of Pestalozzi's associates, and that they conduct

[22] See *The Quarterly Educational Magazine*, Vol. I, p. 48   [23] *Ibid.* p. 57

practice teaching in the Model School under the guidance of his sister. Small wonder, then, that E. Carleton Tufnell, a frequent visitor to the Gray's Inn Road and himself an important educational pioneer, commended the Training Establishment for its inspired efforts not only to advance 'the science of pedagogy' but also to train teachers 'both as sound practical instructors and matured, established Christians'.[24]

It is clear, therefore, that much credit must be ascribed to the handful of reformers who, during the first half of the nineteenth century, strove to draw public attention to the importance of Pestalozzi's methods. In fact there can be little doubt that these pioneers helped in more ways than is generally suspected to persuade Britain of a vital but exceedingly unpleasant truth—that her overall scheme for promoting the welfare of poor children was both hopelessly outmoded and utterly inadequate. And by so doing, of course, they not only presented a challenge to those who upheld the monitorial system of instruction but likewise—and this was even more important —supplied unmistakable evidence of superior and highly individualistic methods of teaching which had long enjoyed popularity in Switzerland, Holland and Prussia.

[24] See *The Quarterly Educational Magazine*, Vol. I, p. 56

16

THE INFLUENCE OF THREE MAJOR PUBLICATIONS CONCERNING EDUCATIONAL ACTIVITIES ABROAD (1830–40)

'Our consciousness rarely registers the beginning of a growth within
us any more than without us: there have been many circulations of
the sap before we detect the smallest sign of the bud.'

GEORGE ELIOT—*Silas Marner*. 1861

IN view of what has been stated in the preceding chapter it must not
be assumed that about 1830 a large number of teachers in this country chose to become disciples of Pestalozzi and to abandon their ideas
on formal instruction. Such was far from being the case as the following comment in *The Edinburgh Review* of July 1833 makes clear—'The
difficulty of all educational improvement in Britain lies less in the
amount, however enormous, of work to be performed, than in the
notion that not a great deal is requisite. Our pedagogical ignorance
is only equalled by our pedagogical conceit; and where few are competent to understand, all believe themselves qualified to decide.' [1]
Nothing like a general appreciation of Continental educational
theory and practice was, therefore, apparent among us at the time.
Indeed, since no legislative enactment corresponding to the Dutch
decree of 1806 or the Prussian edict of 1819 had come into being or
seemed likely to do so, it becomes a matter of difficulty to decide
when first we awakened to the challenge of improved methods of
instruction. All that can be said with certainty is that such pioneers
as Brougham, Synge, Greaves and the Mayos provided those who
were interested in educational reform with new standards of comparison and that, by 1834, there existed a number of intelligent
people in this country who were anxious both that consideration be
given to improved methods of teaching and that Britain, following

[1] Vol. 57, p. 541

the example of Switzerland, Holland, Prussia and France, inaugurate a state system of schools.

Among their number was Sarah Austin who, in 1834, translated into English the famous *Report on the State of Public Instruction in Prussia* by Victor Cousin which has already been noted in chapter 8. She was prompted to undertake this task, so she affirmed, because the Factory Commission, the Poor Law Commission and other public and private bodies had tended of late years to reveal the extent of our intellectual and moral wants. Furthermore she was aware that there existed in the public mind 'cheering symptoms of a general tendency towards the subject of National Education'—a tendency which she was determined to encourage by laying before the British people 'the harmonious picture of a system of public instruction in full activity among another people'.

As may be appreciated, then, Mrs. Austin's translation was one of considerable importance for it was undertaken with a specific aim in view—to convince the people of this land that great benefits were to be obtained from a national system of schools. In Great Britain, she maintained, the strife was keener and the curiosity more awake than perhaps in any other country in Europe. Furthermore society was no longer a calm current but a tossing sea, whilst reverence for tradition and authority was waning. In such a state of affairs who could deny that a state system of education, similar to that which existed in Prussia, would be a national benefit? Nevertheless, as anyone with an understanding of racial consciousness was bound to admit, there existed a fundamental cleavage of opinion between Prussia and Great Britain with regard to the theory of government. The former country, for example, believed that the welfare of its people could best be secured by means of a well-devised code of regulations, whereas the latter was convinced that the prime excellence of government lay in letting well alone. Given this basic difference of attitude, therefore, many people tended to the opinion that Britain, educationally speaking, had little to learn from Prussia for the sole reason that the latter's state system was based upon compulsion. Yet such a conception was surely mistaken for there were clearly two kinds of constraint—the one salutary, the other pernicious—and the necessity of sending children to school seemed unquestionably to her to belong in the former category.

The obligation of parents to have their sons and daughters educated was, therefore, the first point which Mrs. Austin stressed. Indeed she maintained that nothing save systematic instruction could enlarge and stimulate the human understanding and turn the offspring of the peasants into useful members of society. People who really desired an extension of educational privilege, therefore, should resist criticizing the 'military and despotic government of Prussia' with its doctrine of 'Schulpflichtigkeit' for, if interpreted aright, 'the latter was no form of tyranny but a sacred Christian trust which all countries should accept'.[2]

A second point which Mrs. Austin strove to make clear was that, under an ideal state system of education, parents need not forego their right to select the type of school which they wished their children to attend. Some might be contemptuous of all existing institutions and prefer to employ a family tutor, whilst others might elect for private academies and others again for schools provided by the state. In any case a reasonable degree of liberty should be allowed them—a liberty which, contrary to popular opinion, Prussia likewise encouraged.

It is obvious, therefore, that, in discussing the whole issue of national education, Mrs. Austin was anxious that individual freedom be safeguarded—a truth that becomes even more apparent when we consider her attitude towards other issues. She advocated, for instance, that conferences of headmasters take place at regular intervals for the purpose of comparing notes and discussing modern tendencies in educational theory and practice. She was concerned, too, that the choice of text books for state schools should not be relegated to government inspectors but to headmasters working in close co-operation with local committees—committees on which a number of parents might well be represented. And finally, she stressed the fact that a sound system of education could not afford to be divorced from religion. The last point, indeed, seemed to her the most important of all and one which von Altenstein, Nicolovius and Süvern had wisely insisted upon when framing the edict of 1819. Yet, in spite of this, she was constantly hearing criticisms of Prussia's anti-religious attitude. Such ill-considered judgments, however, were misleading and, as proof thereof, she instanced the small Normal School at Lastadie, near Stettin, where such sterling work

---

[2] 'Schulpflichtigkeit' literally means 'school duty'—i.e. the obligation of parents to send their children to school

was done in providing teachers for the offspring of humble cottagers. Not all its students belonged to one Church or accepted the same religious tenets. Yet, once their training was completed they were more than efficient instructors; they were servants of God who had been educated above their poor neighbours only that they might be the servants of all and give to the lowliest children a real sense of human dignity. To affirm that Prussia had founded her state system on anti-Christian principles, in consequence, was thoroughly unjust. As anyone familiar with that country would readily attest, there existed a 'spirit of veneration' and an 'unworldly tone of feeling' therein which far surpassed anything of the kind in Great Britain.

This led Mrs. Austin to consider a grave inconsistency with regard to the nature of education which was then prevalent in this country. Too often did men in authority here impress upon the poorer sections of the community that knowledge was power and that learning alone could help them to better themselves. Yet, ironically enough, these same men were the first to express dissatisfaction when their advice was followed. On discovering, for example, that some poor man was reaping benefit from systematic instruction they complained that education was setting him above his station and making him unwilling to work. It was high time, in consequence, that a more consistent attitude prevailed. Either, as a nation, we had to place our faith in the efficacy of education for all or we had to state frankly that learning and the means of acquiring it were the prerogatives of the privileged classes. To nurture expectations which could not be fulfilled was cruel. In fact, the sooner the country adopted a definite policy with regard to the enlightenment of the masses, the quicker would reforms follow.

As a final comment on Mrs. Austin's remarkable plea for the establishment of a state system of schools in Britain, therefore, it is perhaps wise to examine the kind of policy she had in mind. First she was opposed to the use of monitors. Time and experience had convinced her, she asserted, that mutual instruction was at best a poor substitute for real teaching and that more wisdom than was conceded lay behind the Prussian maxim : 'As is the master; so is the school.' Secondly, she asserted that no system of education, which was worthy of the name, would ever achieve success without an unfailing supply of teachers. She was anxious to obtain the latter, moreover, as much for the adults as for the children. And thirdly, she

advocated the establishment of a number of first-rate Normal
Schools. In this country, she affirmed, the greatest ignorance prevailed concerning them and yet, in the long run, the people's education was almost wholly dependent upon them. Could it be that
the work of Pestalozzi, de Fellenberg and a host of German reformers had been lost on us? She hoped not and begged those who were
opposed to the importation of foreign ideas into Britain to remember
the wise words of Victor Cousin—'I am as great an enemy as anyone
of artificial imitations; but it is mere pusillanimity to reject a thing
for no other reason than that it has been thought good by others.' [3]

Such were the main recommendations which Mrs. Austin made
in the preface to her work—recommendations which were important
and needed to be stated but which, one cannot help feeling, gave too
flattering a picture of the Prussian state system of education. Her
over-enthusiastic attitude was clearly to be pardoned, however, for
she knew the appalling state of primary instruction in this country
and had a definite cause to plead. Furthermore, by putting into the
hands of the public a most able and scholarly translation of Cousin's
report, she rendered an invaluable service to education in general.
Indeed she ensured thereby that many people, totally ignorant of
French and German, were able not only to study Prussia's remarkable enactment of 1819 but also to appraise its worth—a point upon
which she was expressly complimented when, in July 1834, her
translation was reviewed in the leading periodicals of the day.

It was not long, moreover, before the results of Mrs. Austin's
labours began to show themselves. In 1838 Leonard Horner, encouraged by the success of *On the State of Public Instruction in Prussia*,
offered to the British public his translation of two well-known reports
on Dutch education : Cuvier's *On the Establishments for Public Instruction in the Netherlands*, the result of a detailed enquiry undertaken in
1811, and Cousin's *Narrative of my journey in Holland*, written in 1836.[4]
And he did so for two definite reasons. In the first place he was convinced that nothing but good could result if the wise observations of
these French philosophers were more widely known in this country,
and secondly he was anxious to refute once and for all the baseless
allegations that some people had made after studying Cousin's *On the
State of Public Instruction in Prussia*, namely that a national system of
schools might well appeal to a race habituated to military rule from

[3] Austin Translation, p. 292   [4] See present work, chapter 7

infancy but that it would never function successfully amongst a free-dom-loving people such as the British.[5]

As may be seen, then, the motive behind his endeavours was pre-cisely the same as that which had inspired Mrs. Austin—to convince the people of this land that the only satisfactory means of ensuring educational progress was to establish a state system of schools. Accordingly he kept this object in view throughout, restricting his canvas to those parts of the Cuvier and Cousin reports that were ger-mane to the discussion and dwelling lovingly on Holland's battle against illiteracy, the pioneer work of such men as van der Palm and van den Ende, the reforms which followed the edict of 1806 and the degree to which Pestalozzi influenced the new educational pro-gramme—facts which have already been noted in chapter 7. Furthermore, in the preface to his work and in a long supplementary essay entitled *Preliminary Observations*, he gave a diagnosis of the ills attending primary instruction in this country and suggested various ways of curing them. The whole book thus became a convincing plea to the British public to give consideration to reforms which had been initiated by a nation whose political sympathies were closely akin to their own.

Before examining its recommendations in detail, however, it is perhaps wise to recall how peculiarly fitted Leonard Horner was to prepare a work of this kind. In the first place, from 1827 to 1831, he had served as Warden of University College, London, and, from 1831 onwards, as one of the four chief inspectors who came into being following the successful passage of the Factories' Regulation Act; and secondly he was on familiar terms with both Cousin and Baron Falck. It was no mere amateur, in consequence, who reviewed Holland's achievements and strove to ascertain the best way in which this country could profit by them. It was a scholar of some dis-tinction whose personal knowledge of Dutch schools dated back some twenty-four years.[6]

Turning first to the preface, then, we may note with what earnest-ness Horner strove to convince his fellow-countrymen that their slothful attitude towards educational reform was inexcusable. 'It is a national reproach', he asserted, 'that so admirable a system should have been going on for so long a period in a neighbouring Protestant country without our profiting by the example.'[7] In addition he com-

---

[5] See Horner's Preface, pp. lxv and lxvi   [6] Preface, p. lxiii   [7] *Ibid.* p. lxv

plained bitterly that 'in this great work of national concernment' Britain was loth to take any step towards improvement whilst other countries, whose economic resources were as nothing compared with ours, daily devoted more and more energy to furthering popular enlightenment.

The same sentiments were echoed in his *Preliminary Observations* where he treated of legislative measures that were necessary to extend and improve educational facilities in this country. To anyone who took the trouble to study authentic records, he pointed out, it would soon become obvious that the proportion of schools per head of the population in England, Wales and even Scotland was totally inadequate. Furthermore, since such institutions as existed were almost invariably squalid, it was high time that the whole question of public instruction became the concern of parliament. The day was mercifully past, he added, when it was necessary to debate whether or not the poorer classes should be educated: the immediate issue was how best they could be elevated from a state of mere existence to one of intellectual refinement. If, therefore, any alarmists still lingered in this country who were hostile to the education of the proletariat, they should direct their attention to Holland—a country which had long enjoyed the advantages of a state system of schools.

Having, as he hoped, silenced the opposition of those who resisted educational reform, Horner animadverted next upon those who clung to the stultifying traditions of Bell and Lancaster. For too many years, he said, Great Britain had placed reliance on the monitorial method with the result that teaching was relegated for the most part to badly trained assistants who made 'a mere mockery of education'. Indeed few children left the primary schools capable either of reasoning for themselves or of understanding even a simple passage of prose. Of what avail, then, to read the Bible or repeat the catechism, if the meaning of the phrases was by no means clear? Holland, of course, had long foreseen this danger and, since 1808, had made strenuous efforts to avert it by introducing the more personal methods of teaching advocated by Pestalozzi.

If Great Britain were seriously to tackle the problem of illiteracy, therefore, it was obvious that some central authority would have to be constituted in order to examine the whole question of primary instruction. This, for want of a better term, Horner called a 'Board of Commissioners' and suggested that it be composed of prominent men from various walks of life who were interested in the elevation of the masses. Only such men, he declared, would be able to rescue Britain from its backward state and ensure that it kept abreast of such countries as Holland, Germany, France and the United States of America. As a means of guiding their activities, moreover, he made bold to suggest six subjects to which they should direct attention: (1) religious instruction; (2) normal schools, including the subjects taught there, the methods of teaching and the text books required; (3) additional types of school which should be founded; (4) general inspection and local superintendence; (5) the appointment and provision of teachers; and (6) the means of obtaining the requisite funds.

He placed religious instruction first, so he asserted, because it presented a challenge to all thinking people. Indeed so serious an obstacle was it likely to prove to the establishment of a state system of education in this country that he warned all would-be reformers against trying to draw up some ingenious plan of teaching Scripture which would prove equally acceptable to members of all religious persuasions—a task beyond the capabilities of man to devise. Yet, despite this hindrance, there was no reason why some satisfactory compromise could not be reached, for more people than was generally suspected subscribed to the theory that education and religion were inseparable and should never be forced asunder.

In Holland such a compromise had been possible because of the spirit of toleration which existed among her people. Was it not possible, therefore, for Britain to profit by her example and to allow Jews and Roman Catholics complete freedom of choice as to the kind of education they wished their children to receive? And if this necessarily led to their forming schools of their own was not that a concession which should readily be granted? Certainly nothing was more distasteful to Horner than discrimination against minorities, as evidenced in Prussia, and he would be mightily aggrieved if Britain were to adopt a similar attitude of intransigence.[8]

As may be appreciated, then, Horner approached the question of religious instruction with an open mind, refusing to lay down hard and fast rules which would set one section of the community at variance with the rest. He adopted this attitude, moreover, for two definite reasons: first, so that those who already accepted the tenets

[8] *Preliminary Observations*, p. lix

of Christianity should be encouraged to greater efforts in alleviating the condition of the poorer classes; and secondly, so that those 'who had never heard the voice of God or anything connected with it' should realize the value of a 'sober practical religion' working in their midst.

From religious instruction Horner turned next to Normal Schools, giving it as his considered opinion that 'all other improvements in primary institutions would be of little avail unless a systematic plan of training teachers were established'.[9] He emphasized this fact, moreover, because seminaries for schoolmasters had for several years past formed a branch of public instruction in Holland and Prussia and done much good in training the minds of those on whom the characters of the rising generation depended. Indeed if Great Britain were completely to revolutionize the methods of instruction prevalent in her primary schools, it was clear that she, too, would have to found Training Colleges.

As Mrs. Austin before him, then, Horner was insistent that one of the best ways in which Britain could profit by Continental experience was to found and equip a number of new educational establishments. In fact he looked forward to the day when this country, fully provided with primary and secondary institutions and such additional necessities as nursery schools and domestic science colleges, would insist not only upon compulsory education but also on the licensing of teachers. In addition he made a forceful plea for the creation of an inspectorate, pointing to Holland's remarkable achievements in this field and emphasizing the wisdom that lay behind van den Ende's comment to Cousin—'Take care whom you choose as inspectors; they are a class of men who ought to be searched for with a lantern in one's hand.' [10] And finally he stressed the fact that none of these reforms would ever come to pass unless parliament made public instruction one of its first responsibilities and secured the future of all worthwhile educational enterprises by means of adequate grants.

Such were the main recommendations advanced by Leonard Horner in the preface to his translation of the Cuvier and Cousin reports—recommendations which had great value for the simple reason that they were inspired by the reforms of a country whose political sympathies were closely in harmony with those of Britain.

[9] *Ibid.* p. xxxix   [10] Cousin Report (Horner Translation), p. 31

That thought, indeed, has constantly to be remembered when assessing their value, for they were, above all else, designed to show how advanced educational legislation was not only possible but already in existence amongst a freedom-loving people. In one sense, therefore, the purposes of Mrs. Austin and Horner may be said to have differed for, whereas the former was clearly anxious to awaken interest in the educational programme of a nation only too well known for its despotic tendencies, the latter had a completely contrary objective in view. In another and far more important sense, however, their work was complementary, for both offered remarkably similar suggestions and both were inspired by a common ideal—to convince the people of this land that great benefits were to be obtained from a state system of schools.

This ideal, needless to say, was not shared alone by Sarah Austin and Leonard Horner. Indeed there were a number of individuals who, between 1830 and 1840, gave consideration to the subject of national education and advanced reasons why the United Kingdom should avail itself of so striking a means of elevating the masses,[11] though few among them possessed that knowledge of reforms abroad which was shared by the translators of the Cousin reports. Brief mention, nevertheless, must be made of the Central Society of Education which came into being in 1836 with Lord Denman, Chief Justice of the King's Bench, as its President, and Baldwin Francis Duppa, barrister of Lincoln's Inn, as its Secretary.

Before scrutinizing its activities, however, it is important to realize that, among the advocates of a state system of education in this country, there existed two factions : those who were of the opinion that religious communities should have a say in the manner in which Scripture was taught in elementary schools; and those who were diametrically opposed to any interference by the Church in what they considered to be primarily a concern of the state. In the vanguard of the latter, moreover, stood the Central Society of Education —an august body of men, numbering no less than eighteen members of Parliament on its committee—which argued that national edu-

---

[11] Three notable examples were (1) Lord Brougham; (2) J. A. Roebuck, M.P., who, on July 30th, 1833, moved that 'the House proceed to devise a means for the universal and national education of the people', quoting France and Prussia for Britain's guidance; and (3) William Lovett who stressed the necessity of a national system of education in his address to the London Working Men's Association in 1837

cation could only succeed if the peculiarities of religious belief were ignored in schools. It also asserted, and this was perhaps the point about which it felt strongest, that a state system of education could never be secured, let alone made to function, if it were left in the hands of those who demanded religious interference by the clergy, for the obvious reason that no compromise could possibly be devised which would prove equally acceptable to members of all denominations.[12]

Having clarified its position with regard to religious instruction, the Central Society proceeded to offer reasons why education alone could determine what this nation should become. In truth so convinced was it that systematic instruction could go far towards curing the misery of poor children that it expressed the sanguine hope that 'all good, learned and noble-minded people' would lend a helping hand in furthering its grand design. And, lest they should be under a misapprehension as to what this 'grand design' embraced, it set out four objectives which it hoped to achieve : first, the establishment of a state system of education; secondly, compulsory attendance at schools; thirdly, the replacement of the monitorial system by more personal methods of teaching; and fourthly, the development of a saner attitude towards educational reform.

Thus, apart from matters of religion, there was nothing particularly new about the recommendations of the Central Society. The majority of them were identical with those which Mrs. Austin had advanced in the preface to her translation of Cousin's report on Prussia—a fact that is readily discernible if we consult the annual publications of the society which appeared in 1837 and 1838. There would seem to be little point, then, in discussing anew suggestions covering the formation of a Ministry of Public Instruction, the creation of an inspectorate and the establishment of Normal Schools which have already been noted at length. What is of interest to record, however, is the way in which the society, by means of its publications, strove to keep its members abreast of current developments in educational theory and practice and to convince them that nothing short of a sustained effort on their behalf would help to reform the primary schools of Great Britain. Thus we discover an illuminating study entitled *Education in the United Kingdom, its Progress and Prospects* by Thomas Wyse, M.P., himself an experienced traveller,

[12] See pp. 37 and 38 of *Public Education* by J. P. Kay-Shuttleworth

which was a direct challenge to those who resisted improved methods of teaching; two articles on primary and Normal schools in Prussia by W. Wittich, which were obviously intended to supplement the discoveries of Cousin;[13] a report on a visit to the Model School of the British and Foreign School Society in the Borough Road by Thomas Coates demonstrating the inadequacy of the monitorial method; and a study of agricultural establishments calculated to show the importance and influence of Hofwyl by B. F. Duppa. Indeed it was largely owing to the latter's influence that a number of Continental reformers became interested in the Central Society and wrote descriptions for its members of educational enterprises with which they were intimately associated. Thus the Prince de Chimay contributed an account of his experimental school at Menars, near Blois, and de Fellenberg not only submitted an essay entitled *The Connection between the welfare of a country and the education of the mass of its citizens* but likewise, in 1838, consented to become an honorary president of the society.

More is the pity, therefore, that these interesting articles, which supplied such a wealth of information concerning educational experiments at home and abroad, were not allowed to continue and multiply. In 1838, however, the Central Society unfortunately fell foul of a number of prominent Anglicans, headed by the Bishop of London, who charged it with planning to enforce upon the nation a compulsory system of secular education which was inimical to the true cause of Christianity. So influential were they, moreover, that within a short time, despite a spirited defence put up by Lord Denman, the society ceased to exist. Its efforts, nevertheless, did not go entirely unrewarded, for it served to awaken many people to the sad state of primary instruction in this land and to collect together a number of distinguished individuals who were united in their determination to check illiteracy.

If, then, we are to see how a further educational link was forged between Britain and the Continent we must turn from theory to practice and examine the work of such prominent social reformers as Lady Noel Byron, Lord Chichester, Lord Lovelace and E. Carleton Tufnell—all of whom were members of the Central Society of Education and all of whom subscribed to its basic contention that nothing save systematic instruction could secure the happiness and well-being of mankind.

[13] See present work, chapter 8

17

THE INFLUENCE OF LADY NOEL BYRON
AND HER IMITATORS (1834–40)

'Le travail est le grand moralisateur de l'homme, mais le travail des
champs a des avantages qui lui sont particuliers. La propriété acquise
par le travail inspire les respects des droits d'autrui.'

Revue Encyclopédique. 1834

In tracing the evolution of educational consciousness in Great
Britain during the first half of the nineteenth century it is extraordinary to discover how many of those who strove to foster among
their fellow-countrymen an increased awareness of the value of
foreign pedagogical discoveries were people whom normally one
would associate neither with teaching nor schools. Synge, for example, was a landowner in Ireland; Brougham and Roebuck, politicians; Duppa, a barrister; and Sarah Austin, the wife of a distinguished jurist. And what was true of them was no less true of a small
group of philanthropists who suddenly achieved educational prom-
inence between 1830 and 1840 and who, by virtue of their endeavours, succeeded more effectively than any other reformers of their
generation not only in publicizing the work of de Fellenberg but
also in demonstrating the truth of his oft-repeated maxim—that
nothing but a life closely associated with Nature would secure the
happiness of mankind.

Before attempting to describe their activities, however, it is perhaps wise to remind ourselves first of the career of Henry Brougham
and, in particular, of the description of Hofwyl which he wrote for
The Edinburgh Review of December 1818—a description wherein, it
will be recalled, he begged those of his compatriots 'whose public
spirit was proportionate to their means of serving the community'
to devote 'a season or two of recreation from other employments to
the important and not uninteresting business of visiting Hofwyl'.[1]

---

[1] See present work, chapter 14

And among those who read and pondered his words with care was Lady Noel Byron, the estranged wife of George Gordon Byron, the poet, and herself a person of high intellectual calibre and fine literary sensitivity.[2] Indeed so greatly did Brougham's account interest her that she determined, once a suitable opportunity arose, to visit Hofwyl and make a study of the way in which delinquent children were rescued from a life of vagabondage by means of agricultural work.

Unfortunately, however, the next few years of Lady Byron's life were fraught with difficulties—not least among which were her husband's erratic behaviour abroad, the scandals that continued to mount concerning his private life and finally the tragic news of his death at Missolonghi on 19th April, 1824. In fact, as she herself admitted, one thought 'ran through, through, yes through' her mind during the whole of this time—the tragic memory of her ruined marriage.[3] And, under such circumstances, it is perhaps hardly surprising that she temporarily shelved all thoughts concerning education.

In 1827, however, she set out on a tour of the Continent—a journey which took her by easy stages to Rotterdam, Heidelberg, Baden, Milan, Genoa and eventually, in the autumn of the following year, to Berne. And thus it was that she finally came to Hofwyl—an estate whose size truly amazed her and whose educational worth struck her so forcibly that she straightway conceived the idea that one of the greatest benefits she could render to the indigent children of her native land was to found an institution closely modelled on the 'Wehrlischule'. Nor was this all, for in de Fellenberg she found a wise counsellor whose moral earnestness and profound pedagogical knowledge struck her as in every way remarkable. Indeed, after her return home, she began regularly to consult him on educational matters; and so great was her admiration for his qualities that she not only placed two young cousins in his 'Academy for Young Gentlemen' but likewise despatched a teacher from England to learn the system of training which prevailed in his 'School for the Poor'.

As may be appreciated, then, Lady Byron derived much benefit

[2] It is perhaps important to note that Frank Smith in his *The Life and Work of Sir James Kay-Shuttleworth* invents an imaginary husband for Lady Byron whom he calls 'Noel Byron'—see pp. 52 and 112

[3] See p. 313 of *The Life and Letters of Anne Isabella, Lady Noel Byron* by Ethel Colburn Mayne

from her period of residence in Berne—the more so when, in 1834, she started her school for vagrant boys. Yet, before discussing this undertaking, it is perhaps wise, in view of the fact that it served as a model for other institutions of a like nature, first to give a brief account of its founder's views on the formal training of children— views which she fortunately sorted out and collected in the introductory remarks to her book *What de Fellenberg Has Done for Education* (1839). She began, for example, by stating that 'school' and 'education' were thought by many people to be synonymous terms and that ideally they ought to be so, but that unfortunately such was not the case in England at that time. In fact too many people were prepared to accept Dr. Johnson's bald statement in his Dictionary that education was, quite simply, 'the instruction of children' whereas it envisaged something far more important than this—the training of a child's senses, the discipline of his mind through application and study, the correction of his faults, the strengthening of his physical powers and, above all, the cultivation of his moral principles.[4]

Such a conception of education, Lady Byron continued, was only slowly beginning to take root in England though it had long been viewed with favour on the Continent. Basedow, Salzmann, von Rochow, Pestalozzi and de Fellenberg had all, in their different ways, helped to inaugurate a new era of mental and moral training for children.[5] If their ideas were to survive, in consequence, it was clearly the duty of all who were shocked at the ignorance of the poorer classes to familiarize themselves with what these great Continental teachers had done and said. And if they did so, she maintained, then they would probably discover, as she had done, that their interest was particularly engaged by the work of de Fellenberg because he and his assistant Wehrli, more than any of the others, had directed their attention to 'rescuing juvenile offenders from the path of ruin and restoring them to society'.

The remainder of Lady Byron's essay was an able exposition of de Fellenberg's doctrines and an eloquent plea to her readers to afford them earnest consideration. Anyone who visited Hofwyl, she promised, would find 'a great scheme in action of schools, workshops and agriculture; new things taught, and old things taught in a new way;

[4] See p. xxvi of Introductory Remarks to *What de Fellenberg Has Done for Education*
[5] *Ibid.* p. xlii

and schools for all classes, the lowest and highest, carried on under one superintendence'.[6]

Turning from theory to practice, then, we may examine the way in which Lady Byron interpreted her ideas. In 1833 she acquired in Ealing Grove a large stable situated in its own grounds which, once the horse stalls had been removed and the interior remodelled, provided a spacious school complete with two airy classrooms, a dormitory, a workshop, a kitchen and a schoolmaster's house. And there, in the summer of the following year, she assembled some twenty destitute boys and placed them under the charge of a master whom she had sent to Hofwyl for special training. Unfortunately, however, he proved totally incapable of coping either with the rough pioneer work that was demanded of him or with the difficult children under his care. And the upshot was that, within six months, he had to be replaced and a new master engaged—a man named Atlee who previously had been accustomed only to teaching in a village school. In other words he was totally ignorant either of de Fellenberg's theories or Lady Byron's aims. Yet so patiently did she instruct him and so apt a pupil was he that soon the school achieved quite remarkable results. Indeed, by 1839, Lady Byron was able to write exultantly to her friend Mrs. de Morgan that Atlee had so far gained in confidence that he was able to maintain excellent discipline without resorting to the cane.[7]

In view of these facts, therefore, we do well to note several characteristics of the Ealing Grove experiment which not merely contributed to its success but likewise distinguished it boldly from the monitorial institutions of the day. And of these perhaps the most important was the emphasis which it placed upon horticulture. Thus, on entering the school, all pupils were assigned individual patches of ground which they were required to cultivate for at least three hours daily under the watchful eye of an experienced gardener. And from him they learnt not merely when to sow their seeds, prune their trees and harvest their vegetables but at what time they should sell their produce so as to make the maximum profit. Indeed so eagerly did the pupils strive to capitalize on their labour that Lady Byron soon decided that they should pay monthly rental for their

[6] See *What de Fellenberg Has Done for Education*, p. xxxix
[7] See *The Life and Letters of Anne Isabella, Lady Noel Byron* by Ethel Colburn Mayne, p. 330

allotments and enter all their business transactions in specially prepared ledgers. By so doing, she said, they learnt a lesson of importance to all whose livelihood depended on the soil—that good
husbandry and prudent economy could not easily be divorced.

Yet it must not be imagined that the Ealing Grove boys spent an
undue amount of time in their gardens. Such was by no means the
case for, on several afternoons a week, they betook themselves to the
workshop where, under expert tuition, they learnt the trades of
glaziers, carpenters, metal-workers and cobblers. And it was thus,
we understand, that they slowly acquired those 'habits of patient
industry' and 'feelings of self-reliance' which de Fellenberg deemed
so essential for those 'destined to earn their living by the sweat of
their brows'.[8]

It was not alone by means of horticulture and manual labour,
however, that Lady Byron strove to aid her pupils' development. In
addition she devised for their benefit a programme of studies which
was similar to that used in the Hofwyl Poor School. Thus, besides
Reading, Writing and Ciphering, the boys learnt Nature Study,
History, Geography, Music, Drawing and Scripture—in all of
which, according to an impartial witness, they reached a high
standard of attainment. Certainly Seymour Tremenheere considered
this to be the case for, as one of the three inspectors appointed by the
Committee of Council in 1840, he paid several visits to Ealing Grove
and became very impressed by the alertness and industry of its
pupils. On one occasion, for instance, he heard a language lesson
which struck him forcibly because the boys were able not only to
analyse difficult sentences with ease but also to give the etymology of
every compound word they met. And, on another occasion, he discovered to his amazement when questioning a class on the staple
manufactures of the United Kingdom that their knowledge extended
also to Europe and that they were able to supply him with detailed
information concerning important articles of export and import
from the principal rivers of the Baltic, Atlantic and Mediterranean.
Indeed the further he pursued his enquiries the more impressed he
became for, in Mathematics, the pupils had attained a standard
'quite sufficient for ordinary purposes'; in Singing, they could exe-
cute difficult intervals with facility; and, in History, they were able

[8] See *The Edinburgh Review* (December 1818 to March 1819), Vol. XXXI,
p. 158

to boast an exact knowledge of events 'as far as the reign of Henry the First'.[9]

As may be seen, then, the Ealing Grove School was soon acclaimed as much for its academic results as for its agricultural activities. And the main reason for this was, of course, the highly individualistic methods of teaching used by Atlee and his assistant. Indeed so patiently did they strive to cultivate their pupils' powers of observation and memory that Pestalozzi himself could hardly have failed to be impressed by the thoroughness with which his theories were interpreted.[10]

We may note in this connection the great attention to detail which was characteristic of the lessons on Drawing—a subject which was stressed, we understand, for two reasons. In the first place it interested boys in a useful activity, and secondly it helped them to obtain and retain precise notions about the forms of objects. Thus, to instance a common occurrence, it was found that, when a pupil became interested in an agricultural implement and wished to describe it in detail, he had perforce to inspect it on several occasions before he was ready to supply precise information concerning the way in which it worked to others. If he learnt accurately to transfer to paper his visual impression of the said object, however, the case was otherwise. For then every detail of the implement stamped itself indelibly on his mind. Indeed, at Ealing Grove as at Hofwyl, it was early discovered that drawing was not merely an excellent means of amusing children but likewise a powerful agency in fortifying their intellectual powers.

With regard to music, however, different benefits accrued—benefits such as the growth of tender sentiments, the cultivation of a hunger for things beyond the merely material and the uplifting of the mind towards God. For these and other reasons, then, the pupils were encouraged to sing both during their leisure hours and whenever they worked out of doors—a feature of their life upon which B. F. Duppa commented with approval in 1837. 'There is a considerable gaiety and alacrity in all this,' he observed; 'the boys learn to sing many cheerful and merry songs; they strike up a

[9] See *Minutes of the Committee of Council on Education* (1842–43), pp. 559 and 560

[10] See p. 26 of *The Education of the Peasantry: what it is and what it ought to be* by B. F. Duppa

tune as they go in bands to work, and as they return they do the same.' [11]

And a final characteristic of the Ealing Grove curriculum which calls for comment was the amount of time which it set aside for silent reading. So anxious, indeed, was Lady Byron that her charges should have access to 'books of an improving nature' that, early in 1835, she fitted up a library—a library which, far from limiting itself to the standard classics for children, included interesting publications concerning horticultural and agricultural development. Thus the boys soon acquired the habit of 'patient study' and, what is perhaps equally impressive, so, too, did a number of their parents who were never so happy as when Lady Byron allowed them to borrow library books.[12]

It is obvious, therefore, that the Ealing Grove School helped in more ways than is generally acknowledged to stimulate intellectual endeavour and foster new interests. Yet we should completely misinterpret its aims if we were to imagine that, by so doing, it fulfilled the whole of its purpose. Nothing could be further from the truth for, as Lady Byron was ever ready to point out, the mere development of the intellect was as nothing compared with the fostering of religious instincts. And for this reason she insisted, however brilliant a pupil might be, that he learn first and foremost to respect moral principles. Thus, on entering the school in the morning, he was given a 'white badge' which betokened 'average conduct'. As the day proceeded and as it was discovered that his behaviour was in every way exemplary, then he was allowed to substitute a 'red badge'. But if, by any chance, the reverse were the case and it was shown that he had been guilty of lying, disobedience, dishonesty or unkindness, then he was made to wear a 'black badge'. Nor was this all for, to keep alive a sense of responsibility, 'a register was kept of the number of red and black badges given to each boy and, at certain periods, the sum total was made public'. And in this way, we learn,

---

[11] See p. 186 of *Publications of the Central Society of Education*, Vol. I. Article on 'Industrial Schools for the Peasantry' by B. F. Duppa

[12] This desire for learning, which evinced itself among the parents, induced Atlee in 1838 to open a room near the school for the systematic instruction of adults during two evenings of the week. In the course of one month, we learn, fifty labouring men and artisans asked to be enrolled as readers and were prepared to subscribe two shillings a quarter for the privilege. See p. 561 of *Minutes of the Committee of Council on Education* (1842–43)

every pupil quickly acquired a clear idea of 'what was right and wrong'.[13]

Such were the main features of one of the earliest schools in England to apply de Fellenberg's theories—a school which continued in existence until 1852 and eventually exercised considerable influence in various parts of the country. Great credit, in consequence, is due to Lady Byron as a pioneer. Yet, before concluding this review of her educational activities, it is perhaps important to remind ourselves that her original intention in forming an agricultural institution at Ealing Grove was not merely to create a model school for indigent boys but also to induce others to form 'a society for the purpose of demonstrating the value of work closely associated with the cultivation of the land'. And if such a society were formed, she promised, then she would undertake to support it financially and supply it with premises rent free. In yet another way, therefore, did Lady Byron strive to promote educational progress, and the only conditions she imposed were as follows:

(1) that gardening, and other kinds of manual labour, be considered an essential part of the employment and instruction of children;

(2) that all Christians, no matter what their denomination, be admitted into such schools as the Society might found;

(3) that the Bible never be used as a lesson or spelling book, and that such passages in it as a master considered necessary for his pupils to study be free of all suspicion of having been chosen to forward the tenets of a particular sect.[14]

Unfortunately there is no evidence to suggest that Lady Byron's offer created any response in educational circles or that a society such as she contemplated came into being. But what is evident is that her experiment at Ealing Grove proved a challenge to those who resisted improved methods of teaching and stimulated an interest in de Fellenberg's theories which produced several noteworthy results. Thus, between 1835 and 1840, largely inspired by her example, other benefactors came forward who were likewise anxious to

---

[13] See *The Training of Pauper Children* by James Phillips Kay, p. 31 (Norwich Report, 1838)

[14] See pp. 188 and 189 of B. F. Duppa's article on 'Industrial Schools for the Peasantry'

prove that a life closely associated with the soil could benefit poor children.

Amongst the earliest of these was James Cropper, a wealthy land-owner in the North of England and a member of the Society of Friends, who, in 1835, assembled some thirty orphans on his estate at Fearnhead, near Warrington, Lancashire, and devised a system of training them which, to quote Lady Byron, 'could clearly be traced to his acquaintance with Hofwyl'.[15]

The difficulties that confronted him at the outset of his venture, however, were particularly formidable. Several pupils proved so unmanageable that they had to be sent away; two members of staff found themselves incapable of doing the rough work that was de-manded of them and resigned; and theft and absenteeism were so prevalent that, some three months after its inception, the school was threatened with collapse. But in 1836 a new master was appointed who soon showed that he was able not merely to control the pupils but also to stimulate their desire for learning. From that time for-ward, then, the character of the institution changed and a number of reforms were adopted which previously would have been impossible. Early in 1837, for example, agricultural work of a scientific nature was started and a new programme of studies introduced which included Reading, Writing, Arithmetic, Geometry, Algebra, Gram-mar, Geography, History, Natural Science and Religion. In the course of the following year, moreover, Cropper decided that those among his charges who showed the greatest intellectual promise should not merely remain with him until they were eighteen but be given extra tuition in Music, Art and Pedagogy. In this way he strove to prove to his fellow-countrymen that, in England as in Switzerland, indigent boys could be taken from the streets and trained to become efficient gardeners, nursery-men, farmers and even schoolmasters. Nor was this all; for he also took pains to show, however refractory his pupils, that, by means of a sound education based upon Christian principles, they could ultimately be made to take their places in the world as respectable members of society. 'I consider religion', he said, 'to be the basis and foundation of edu-cation and, next to this, habits of order and steady industry.'[16]

It was, we learn, principally by means of work on the land that Cropper strove to rescue his charges from 'habits of vice and

---

[15] See p. 101 of *What de Fellenberg Has Done for Education*   [16] *Ibid.* p. 102

ignorance'. Yet, as de Fellenberg before him, he soon discovered that 'such neglected and untutored minds' as came under his care 'required cogent and self-interested motives to induce them to labour'.[17] Accordingly, as a preliminary measure, he made over to them nine acres of land and arranged that they be given regular instruction in horticulture. Then, at a later date, he assigned to them individual patches of ground and, in accordance with Lady Byron's practice at Ealing Grove, allowed them to sell their produce—a move on his part which had a most stimulating effect upon the boys who were soon working hard to take advantage of the high prices paid for early vegetables in the markets of Bolton and Manchester. And, later still, he added a small holding of fifty acres to the school grounds and started an experimental farm—a venture which proved so lucrative that, by 1839, he was able to feed, clothe and house his pupils from the profits.

These and other reformatory measures of a similar nature were described by Cropper in a pamphlet he wrote for private circulation in June 1839 entitled *A letter to a friend. Some Account of an Agricultural School for Orphans at Fearnhead, near Warrington*—a pamphlet in which, after urging others to follow his example, he gave it as his considered opinion that England as yet had scarcely begun to realize the tremendous advantages that poor children were able to derive from agricultural labour.

As may be seen, then, Cropper, by virtue of his school at Fearnhead, not only gave a much-needed spur to educational reform but also afforded striking evidence of the superiority of de Fellenberg's theories with regard to the training of indigent youth. And what was true of him was no less true of the Earl of Chichester who was likewise a wealthy landowner and 'a most earnest-minded Christian gentleman'.[18] Unlike Cropper, however, he was a man 'of great influence'[19] whose fame extended throughout the land and who, for many years, had been intimately concerned with questions affecting the moral welfare of the nation. It is perhaps scarcely to be wondered at, therefore, that, as a result of visiting Lady Byron in 1835, he developed a keen interest in her singularly successful means of helping poor boys. Indeed so impressed was he with her undertaking

[17] See p. 102 of *What de Fellenberg Has Done for Education*
[18] See p. 191 of *The Life and Work of Sir James Kay-Shuttleworth* by Frank Smith
[19] *Ibid.* pp. 112 and 128

that he straightway determined to imitate it on his estate near Brighton. And it was thus that yet another agricultural school came into being—a school which closely followed the 'Wehrlischule' and which, after a tentative beginning, gradually gained in recognition until in 1838 it catered for upwards of sixty poor boys varying in age between eight and fourteen.

Before examining this institution more closely, however, it is perhaps important to remind ourselves that the majority of the pupils did not come from East Sussex as one might imagine but from the London suburbs—boys, in other words, just as undisciplined and unmanageable as those assembled by Lady Byron at Ealing Grove or Cropper at Fearnhead. Indeed so refractory were they at the outset and so profane in their language that Lord Chichester decided, first and foremost, they should be given a respect for religious principles. Accordingly he insisted that each day begin and end with prayers and that Sunday be set aside for the study of the Scriptures, when he himself was at liberty to visit the school and instruct the boys in their duties as Christians.

In this respect and in the arrangement of the time-table there was, of course, a striking similarity between the Brighton experiment and the Hofwyl Poor School. Thus, from 8.0 a.m. until 11.0, the boys worked in the fields; from 11.0 to 1.0 p.m. they received instruction in their classrooms; from 1.0 to 1.30 they had their mid-day meal; from 1.30 to 4.0 they worked either in their gardens or on the estate; and from 4.0 until 6.0 they had further lessons indoors. Every school day save Sunday, therefore, was divided roughly into four and a half hours of manual labour and four of instruction.

Further information suggests an even closer link with Hofwyl. On admission the boys were strictly limited to the most elementary kinds of horticulture. Then, in proportion as their skill increased, they were given greater responsibilities until at length they were able not merely to tend the livestock on Lord Chichester's farms but also to perform any number of tasks connected with arable farming. In other words they were trained whilst at school to do the work which many of them would be called upon to undertake later in life. Nor was this all, for Lord Chichester also arranged that his boys receive regular instruction in History, Geography, Natural Science and Scripture as well as Reading, Writing and Ciphering.

Such, then, were the main features of three important agricultural

schools inaugurated between 1834 and 1840 by reformers who in no
sense could be classed either as trained teachers or professional educators. Nor were they the only people at that time to realize the
importance of de Fellenberg's pedagogical discoveries and the value
of a life closely associated with the cultivation of the land. Indeed,
from 1835 onwards, more and more British reformers turned their
thoughts in that direction—as may be judged from the agricultural
schools inaugurated by Lord Lovelace at Oakham in Surrey,[20] by
Smith at Southam in Warwickshire, by Pearson at Baterbury in
Essex and by Rham at Winkfield in Bucks.[21] So similar were these
institutions both in design and performance to the ones already discussed, however, that there would seem to be little point in dealing
with them individually. Suffice it to say that, thanks to Lady Byron,
a number of reformers felt themselves impelled to challenge current
educational methods and to try to make the instruction of poor children more interesting. 'I had often remarked that the result of the
common system of teaching was not always advantageous to the
future progress of the pupils,' commented the Rev. W. L. Rham,
'and failed in giving them a *taste* for acquiring general information.
The duration of school hours was too long and tedious, and the idea
of *ennui* was associated with every kind of instruction. . . . The first
object I had in view, therefore, was to teach my pupils something
which they should like to do; and I always found boys fond of working
in a garden.' [22]

In this passage we find a simple statement of the noble aims which
the founders of the agricultural schools kept in mind : to banish the
curse of ignorance by making lessons attractive, to inculcate habits
of industry by means of manual labour and, above all, to bring children into direct contact with Nature. Such ideals, it must be remembered, were new to the majority of English teachers even at so late
a date as 1830. But they had, of course, long been recognized as
important on the Continent. In France one could instance the
Prince de Chimay's establishment at Menars, near Blois, and the

[20] In 1839 we find that Lady Byron was in the habit of sending her 'rejected
Boarders' to Oakham. See p. 331 of *The Life and Letters of Lady Noel Byron* by Ethel
Colburn Mayne

[21] See 'Industrial Schools for the Peasantry', p. 172. *Publications of the Central
Society of Education*, Vol. I

[22] See pp. 189 and 190 of B. F. Duppa's article 'Industrial Schools for the
Peasantry'

'Colonie Agricole' at Mettray, near Tours; in Denmark the experimental schools at Kathrinelyst, Boggildgaard, Holsteinsminde and Flakkeberg; and in Italy the 'Instituto di Agricoltura' of Cosimo Ridolfi at Meleto, near Florence.

The English agricultural schools, we do well to realize, were part of this European movement and may, in consequence, be regarded both as something new in this country's educational practice and as proof positive that the routine methods of Bell and Lancaster were losing favour. Yet, in comparison with their Continental counterparts, they were diminutive and limited in scope. They never, for instance, achieved such notable academic results or entertained such advanced schemes of social amelioration as were evident at Menars or Meleto. But we render them an injustice if, on that account, we deny them a rightful place in the evolution of social consciousness in Europe or fail to appreciate the valuable contribution they made to educational progress in England. Indeed one of their number—Lady Noel Byron's establishment at Ealing Grove—was not without influence upon a young man who, within a few years, wrought drastic changes in almost every elementary school throughout the kingdom. To trace the next development in English primary education, therefore, is to turn to the work of Dr. James Phillips Kay, who, together with his friend Edward Carleton Tufnell, not only perpetuated much that was of value in the agricultural institutions but also, by creating the first Normal School at Battersea, strove to provide better trained teachers and so to remedy what was undoubtedly their weakest feature.

18

JAMES PHILLIPS KAY (JULY 1835 TO JULY 1838)—EARLY EDUCATIONAL WORK IN NORFOLK AND SUFFOLK

'Sir James Kay-Shuttleworth was a great official because he had the mind of a statesman; a great reformer because he was stern as well as tender in his judgment of men; a great administrator of education because he was himself a teacher; a great teacher because he set himself to learn from others whether in humble station or highly placed, and whether their work lay in Britain or abroad.'

SIR MICHAEL SADLER

So far in this enquiry into the numerous influences from abroad that served to quicken in this land an increased awareness of foreign educational theory and practice during the first half of the nineteenth century reference has been made to a number of prominent men and women who, after travelling on the Continent, devoted their energies either to publicizing the work of Pestalozzi, Father Girard, de Fellenberg and Wehrli or to describing in detail the state systems of education then functioning in Holland and Prussia. Yet no account has so far been given of the one person who successfully gathered together these various threads of foreign influence and, by some mysterious process, wove them into the very fabric of British primary education—James Phillips Kay (afterwards Kay-Shuttleworth and later Sir James Kay-Shuttleworth, Bart.). Indeed had it not been for him and his close associate, E. Carleton Tufnell, there can be little doubt that the pioneer efforts of such notable reformers as Lord Brougham, Leonard Horner, the Mayos, Lady Byron and Lord Chichester would, to a large extent, have gone unrewarded.

Before attempting to discuss so prominent a personality of nineteenth-century life, however, it is perhaps important to remark that Kay-Shuttleworth has invariably been considered in the past more as an official or administrator than as a teacher or educational philosopher—a viewpoint which is usual and legitimate, for it was as such that he primarily regarded himself. But if, for the purpose of obtaining additional information, the emphasis be changed and an attempt made to piece together his views on the formal training of children and teachers, it is possible to demonstrate not only that he possessed an abundant knowledge of pedagogical theory but also that he was a keen student of comparative education. The task, therefore, would seem to be worth attempting if only for the reason that, as his ideas clearly exercised a profound influence on this country's educational destiny, we ought to know what they were, whence they sprang and what results they produced.

We do well to remember in this connection, however, that Kay-Shuttleworth, unlike many of those who wrought far-reaching socia changes on the Continent, was not destined by his training to become an educationist. He had, in fact, to discover for himself, slowly, clumsily and painfully, everything that he eventually held dear about the duties of teachers, the purpose of schools and the nature of education itself. And, therefore, it would be futile to look in his early career for a set of well-defined pedagogical principles to which at all times he instinctively responded. Such was far from being the case for, though he worked unbelievably hard, he was quite literally a tyro in a vast and complicated field of research and, as a result, spent much of his time considering theories on child guidance which were often at variance with one another and, in some cases, totally irreconcilable. Indeed, between 1835 and 1838, he leapt with such rapidity from one school of thought to another that it was almost impossible to keep track of his ideas. Yet this early period cannot lightly be dismissed for, during those years of restless searching and ceaseless questioning, he discovered a number of educational theories whose worth he was increasingly to esteem, the sharper his critical faculties grew.

It was in July 1835, at the age of thirty-one, that Dr. Kay severed his connection with medicine and embarked on a new career which soon involved him closely in questions concerning the educational and general welfare of children and teachers. In that month he was appointed Assistant Commissioner to the Central Poor Law Board and assigned to the counties of Norfolk and Suffolk. His duties were to superintend the activities of the newly created Boards of Guardians, to advise their officials and to form unions of parishes for the purpose of carrying into operation the Poor Law Amendment Act of 1834. On assuming his new position, however, he soon discovered that a lamentable result of the previous year's enactment had been to collect in the workhouses a heterogeneous mass of children and adults whose brutish behaviour defied description. It was not long, therefore, before his attention was directed specifically to the important task of separating the children from the adults and bestowing upon them an efficient training. Even at so early a date he saw clearly that the most powerful way of arresting pauperism— and especially hereditary pauperism—was to provide for the work-house children such an amount of moral, industrial, physical and intellectual training as would enable them to gain an independent livelihood without resorting to parochial relief.

His first practical move was to urge upon the Poor Law Com-missioners at Somerset House the necessity of creating four District Schools for the counties of Norfolk and Suffolk, each containing from 400 to 500 children. On enquiry, however, he found that the 1834 law was defective inasmuch as it made no provision for the separation of children into establishments distinct from those for the reception of adults, and accordingly he was compelled to seek other less expeditious means of reducing the incidence of pauperism. As he commented in one of his unpublished manuscripts:

Until the law enabled the Commissioners to form unions into groups each represented by a Board possessing powers to build and manage such District Schools, I had to make the best of adverse circumstances. (In Norfolk and Suffolk) there were 36 unions of 1,906 pauper children who were therefore distributed in groups of about 50 or 60 which were again subdivided into boys' and girls' schools. In the Houses of Industry whatever in-struction the children received had been given by paupers. All the evils of such an arrangement were not at once apparent to the new Boards of Guardians. The introduction of an efficient system of instruction could be resisted with some plausibility on the ground that it was not within the reach of the child of the inde-pendent labourer. *The idea that education was one of the most efficient antidotes to hereditary pauperism had to be implanted.* It was only step by step that even meagre salaries could be obtained for better teachers and a proper position provided for them in the work-houses. Moreover superior teachers generally shrank from an office the accessories of which were not attractive and the rewards of which were small. Under these circumstances slow progress was made in the organization of these small workhouse schools.[1]

This passage is worthy of note for it gives a compendious state-ment of the three main objectives Kay set himself to achieve in his capacity of Assistant Commissioner—to introduce an efficient system of instruction, to combat hereditary pauperism and to provide better trained teachers. Before assuming his duties, it is important to note, he had manifested no particular enthusiasm for such ideals. From 1836 onwards, however, he set himself patiently to learn all he could about schools, teaching, curricula and methods of instruction. His enquiries lasted many years; he travelled extensively both in Britain and abroad; he learnt German in order to familiarize himself with the best known pedagogical works of the day [2] and ultimately built up an educational philosophy to which he remained faithful until his death. Before examining the precise manner in which he did this, however, it is necessary to recall once again the wretchedness of the workhouse institutions of the 1830's and to turn to Kay's first journey in search of educational enlightenment.

In 1837, along with his friend and fellow Assistant Commissioner E. C. Tufnell, he set out for Scotland to discover as much as possible about the system of education and the means of training teachers which prevailed in that country.[3] Together they visited a large number of institutions and, in particular, became attracted by John

[1] This is an extract from the third of three notebooks which were partly written and partly dictated by Sir James towards the end of his life. Professor Frank Smith named them the '1877 MS.'—a title which has been used in the present work also

[2] There are several references to this fact in a diary which Kay kept during the months of May, June and July 1841: e.g. *Friday, July 9th*. Rode to Town at ½ past nine. German lesson from ten to eleven. *Tuesday, June 28th*. Meanwhile entered several people, and among them the Dean of Durham who brought me a list of several German works on education, which he had recently collected. Ordered them all at my booksellers'

[3] 'I take credit', wrote Tufnell, 'of having turned my friend's attention to this special point and of proposing to him to undertake a journey to Scotland in 1837, for the purpose of becoming acquainted with the system of education and of train-ing which in that country was, by general assent, very superior to the methods adopted in England.' (See article on 'Sir James Kay-Shuttleworth' by E. Carleton Tufnell in *The Journal of Education* (July 1877), pp. 307 and 308)

Wood's Sessional School in Edinburgh and David Stow's Normal Seminary in Glasgow—two well-known establishments of the day famous alike for their progressive outlook and interesting teaching methods.

The former dated from 1813 and had grown out of the parochial Sunday Schools, that were founded in Edinburgh during the previous year. Throughout the first decade of its existence it remained undistinguished and supplied instruction in Reading, Writing and Ciphering, as did hundreds of other primary institutions, in strict accordance with the monitorial method. Towards the end of that period, however, John Wood, an advocate of the Scottish bar, discovering the appalling ignorance of the majority of the pupils, set himself to remedy the defect. What he chiefly disliked was the mechanism, memorizing and drill of the mutual system and accordingly he strove to counteract those evils by substituting a more personal method of teaching. This, of course, necessitated a far larger staff and, in consequence, he enlisted a number of able assistants whom he trained with care not merely to concentrate on efficient methods of instruction but also, by a wise admixture of firmness and kindness, to win the boys' affection and stimulate their desire for learning. From that time forward, therefore, the school began to flourish. In 1824 new premises were constructed and by 1827 no less than five hundred pupils were in daily attendance.

The latter, which was likewise an offshoot of the parochial Sunday Schools, had originally been opened towards the end of 1816 by a young merchant named David Stow in order to rescue poor boys and girls from a life of vagabondage on the streets of Glasgow. By 1837, however, it had grown from modest beginnings into a co-educational school containing four departments and a thousand pupils. Its prime purpose, the Englishmen discovered, was to act as an instrument of social regeneration by stimulating a desire for self-improvement in the children and, as a result, it embraced more subjects in its curriculum than was usually the case in Scottish elementary schools. These included Natural History, Physical Science, Music and Art, in addition to Reading, Writing, Arithmetic and Scripture—most of which, it is interesting to discover, were so taught as to lead the pupils to worthy convictions and high ideals. This was in strict accordance with the founder's pedagogical theories, for one of his chief contentions was that true education should never be equated with instruction. It involved the development of correct physical, moral and intellectual habits, and was as intimately concerned with the growth of character as with the fostering of knowledge. Other notable tenets of his creed included a conviction that the training of children should begin at the age of two; an insistence that every minute of school life be regarded as valuable—even the time that was spent in the playground; a faith in the efficacy of the 'picturing-out' method by which pupils learnt to familiarize themselves with incidents from the Bible either by sketching them or by studying them in carefully selected illustrations and, finally, a belief that all children who showed promise of becoming efficient teachers should be afforded extra tuition and special incentives to study.[4]

As may be imagined, therefore, the English visitors were greatly impressed by what they discovered in Scotland—a fact that can readily be judged from Kay's remark to Tufnell at the end of their tour : 'How little we knew of this subject before our visit to Glasgow!' [5] Indeed so interested were they in what they saw that they determined forthwith to spare no effort to attract a number of trained teachers across the border to work in English schools. After some persuasion, then, Kay succeeded in enlisting the services of a few well-qualified assistants and in obtaining employment for them in the eastern counties. His purpose in so doing was to use them as organizing masters who would travel through Norfolk and Suffolk endeavouring to bring order, method and life into the workhouse schools. Yet his expectations in this respect were almost wholly defeated, for the majority of his recruits, unable to face such overwhelming difficulties, elected to return home. One of their number, however, named Horne, proved more resilient than the rest and, setting himself to implement Kay's instructions, soon achieved noteworthy results as the following description testifies: 'He commonly spent two or more months in one workhouse. He gave the masters instruction in the evening. In the day, having divided the scholars into classes, he surprisingly conducted the instruction of each class.

---

[4] See *Minutes of the Committee of Council on Education* (1842–43)—(Minute of a Meeting of the General Assembly's Education Committee, held 25th November, 1842, concerning Model and Normal Schools in Edinburgh and Glasgow), pp. 3–22

[5] See *The Journal of Education* (1877), page 308. Article on Sir James Kay-Shuttleworth by E. Carleton Tufnell.

Gradually both the pauper children and their teachers were awakened from their torpor.'[6]

The sentiments expressed in this extract clearly reveal the importance which Kay began to attach to the training of teachers. The visit to Scotland, in consequence, may be said to have marked a significant stage of his development, for it served to convince him of the hopeless inadequacy of the monitorial system[7] and of the necessity of 'going deeper into the question of education'. Indeed, after his return to England, it is obvious that he took an increased interest in the welfare of pauper children and that, thenceforward, he deliberately set himself to study any contemporary educational experiments which might throw light on the manner in which they should be trained. He was well aware, of course, that formidable difficulties confronted him and that, if he attempted to provide an education for the boys and girls of the workhouse schools which was superior to that given to the sons and daughters of the labouring classes, he would have perforce to brook intense hostility. Yet it seemed to him that such opposition was worth risking. He therefore urged yet again that the Commissioners in Somerset House give consideration to the creation of District Schools and, in the mean time, delved further into such subjects as teacher training and new methods of instruction.

It was at this time, significantly enough, that he began to visit Lady Noel Byron. Certainly, from December 1837 onwards, she was one of his most regular correspondents and her name figures largely both in his diaries and private notes.[8] Furthermore, in a

---

[6] 1877 MS.

[7] Though the Scottish visit would seem finally to have persuaded Kay of the insufficiency of the monitorial method there is evidence that he had been doubtful of its value for a number of years previously—e.g. in the 1877 MS. he expressly states that, whilst working in the slums of Manchester, he had not been 'an inattentive observer of its embarrassments and shortcomings'.

[8] The following extract from his 1841 diary furnishes abundant evidence of the high esteem in which Kay held Lady Byron:

'*Monday, July 5th:* After a long conversation with Mr. Harness, the late Lord B.'s friend, in which I earnestly requested him never to permit himself to utter one word in disparagement of Lady B. for whom my admiration and regard constantly increase. He listened to me with attention, and said he felt I must have strong reasons for admonishing him so earnestly, and that he should bear in mind what I said, yet he seemed incredulous when I told him that in my mind Lady B. was tender often to Lord B. now, and that Lord B. was singularly indebted to her exemplary patience and enduring attachment.

Rode home at ¼ to eight. My mother and sister went with me to a musical party

detailed report entitled *The Training of Pauper Children*, written in 1838 at Norwich, he gave unstinted praise to her educational venture. Indeed it seemed to him that Lady Byron had inaugurated an experiment which was destined to be of the greatest consequence to pauper children. In the first place she had shown how wayward boys could easily be habituated to patient industry by means of work on the land. Secondly she had proved that various kinds of industrial work could be of inestimable value to poor boys; and thirdly, by insisting that her pupils be taught to mend their own shoes and patch their own clothes, she had imbued them with a spirit of self-reliance which would last as long as they lived.

In giving more detailed consideration to what was required in his proposed District Schools, therefore, Kay came to the conclusion that they should 'be surrounded by a garden of six, eight or ten acres, in which the system of instruction in gardening adopted in Lady Byron's school at Ealing in conformity with the plans pursued in de Fellenberg's establishment at Hofwyl, ought to be pursued'.[9]

There, for the first time in an official document, we find a reference by Kay to a man whose contribution to educational theory and practice he came later to appreciate to a much fuller degree. Yet it would be unwise, because of this particular allusion, to suppose that he was unfamiliar with the name of de Fellenberg prior to visiting Ealing Grove. Indeed he could hardly have remained oblivious to the publicity which Hofwyl of late years had received in this country or to the fact that its founder had recently been elected an honorary member of the Central Society of Education. What is certain, however, is that, thanks largely to Lady Byron, de Fellenberg became a subject of interest to him and Switzerland the country which he was most anxious to visit. Why, then, one may wonder, at a time when he was giving particular attention to the needs of pauper children and the setting up of District Schools based on the Hofwyl model, did he suddenly decide to cross to Holland?

The problem is not easy of solution and no evidence is available to show what happened temporarily to divert Kay's attention from

at our neighbour's house—Sir Robt. C.'s. This was Mrs. Fitzherbert's house. Miss Murray there. Talked with her about Lady B. whom we agree in admiring and loving very much.

[9] See *The Training of Pauper Children* (p. 18), Norwich Report

Switzerland. All that one may conjecture is that the following incident was not unconnected with his change of plan.

In the early part of 1838 Horne was working in the eastern counties in his capacity of organizing master and achieving quite remarkable results in rousing both masters and pupils from the apathy into which they had sunk. It so happened, moreover, that he had lately quitted the Gressenhall Workhouse of the Mitford and Launditch Union of Norfolk when the master in charge there fell ill. This presented a grave problem to the chairman of the union, Frederick Walpole Keppel of Lexham, who immediately proceeded to the institution to see what aid could be furnished. On arrival, however, he discovered that the problem had been solved. A boy of fourteen named William Rush had installed himself as master in charge and was not only supervising the whole of the instruction but maintaining the school in perfect order. Without hesitation, therefore, Walpole Keppel approved the measure, confirmed Rush in his position and insisted that he continue at his work until the master was able to return to duty.

This incident, as Kay noted in his journal, lodged itself in his memory and gave him cause for much reflection.[10] He immediately asked himself whether, in this spontaneous action, there might not lie the solution to many of his difficulties with regard to the supply of teachers for workhouse schools. And he debated further whether, in the event of this measure proving successful, there might not be an admirable opportunity of giving orphans, who possessed a natural aptitude for teaching, a chance of ridding themselves of dependence on the poor-rate and earning a respectable livelihood. On maturer reflection, therefore, he determined that Rush should be allowed to continue at the Gressenhall School as an apprentice assistant even after the master returned to duty. No sooner had he made the decision, however, than several other workhouses declared their eagerness to inaugurate similar reforms. Kay, in consequence, openly stated his opinion that the guardians should be encouraged to retain the services of any scholars in their institutions who were desirous of becoming apprentice assistants and that the most successful among them should be called Pupil Teachers. Thus he inaugurated a new method of enlisting members of staff for primary schools which, as we shall see, he was later considerably to expand

[10] 1877 MS.

and, in 1846, to make an integral part of the English educational system.

It might easily be imagined, from the speed with which these events transpired, that Kay acted somewhat precipitately when he introduced this far-reaching reform into the poor-law institutions. Such, however, was far from being the case. His custom throughout life was ever to proceed with caution, and his decision, therefore, must have been the result of careful thought. Yet, once he had made it, there can be little doubt that he was beset with misgivings as to the precise manner in which it would benefit the workhouse schools. He knew, none better, the shortcomings of the monitorial system and was anxious lest its evils be further aggravated by pupil teachers. One thing, in consequence, he strove to make clear from the outset. If intelligent scholars were to be asked to offer their services as apprentice assistants they should not only be given 'some experience of life outside the workhouse walls' but also an adequate training which would transform their 'manners, habits and modes of thought'. Under no circumstances should they be launched on a career which, because of a lack of preparation, was bound to prove ineffectual and abortive.[11]

We may, therefore, appreciate the state of Kay's mind at the time when he decided to visit Holland. He was obviously anxious both to acquaint himself with the only country in Europe where pupil teachers were to be found and to learn something of a state system of education which was widely publicized. Accordingly he placed high hopes upon the outcome of his journey. And that he was in no way disappointed may be judged from the fact that, after a short interval, he resolved to pay a return visit—on this occasion accompanied by E. Carleton Tufnell.[12] Thus Kay was able to gain invaluable information concerning the selection and use of pupil teachers by a foreign power, to study the manner in which they were trained and, by means of his interpreter, de Raadt, to establish contact with many of them personally—an experience which, as he was careful to point out, confirmed his opinion of their value.[13]

[11] See pp. 50 and 51 of *The Life and Work of Sir James Kay-Shuttleworth* by Frank Smith where a lengthy extract from the 1877 MS. is given describing Kay's first reactions to the pupil-teacher system

[12] On his first journey to Holland Kay was accompanied by Nicholls, a Commissioner from Somerset House

[13] See *Four Periods of Public Education*, p. 289

That the Dutch journeys served to clarify Kay's ideas on the exact function and length of apprenticeship which pupil teachers ought to serve cannot be questioned. It is implicit in numerous passages in his private notes and official publications.[14] We do well, therefore, in contemplating the way in which the English system ultimately developed, to bear in mind such typical comments as the following: 'In Holland . . . by "pupil teacher" is meant a young teacher . . . whose attainments and skill are full of promise; and who, having consented to remain at a low rate of remuneration in the school, is further rewarded by being enabled to avail himself of the opportunities afforded him for attaining practical skill in the art of teaching, by daily practice in the school, and by the gratuitous superintendence of his reading and studies by the master, *from whom he receives lessons on technical subjects of school instruction every evening.* He commonly remains in the school in the rank of pupil teacher from the age of fourteen to that of seventeen . . . and then proceeds, by attendance at a Normal School, or by further proficiency attained by his own exertions, to qualify himself to act as an assistant master.' [15]

From this quotation it is possible to see the interest that Kay took, not only in the training of pupil teachers in Holland, but also in the goal towards which they were continually encouraged to strive—admission to a Government-sponsored Normal School. Previous to his experience abroad, the idea of Training Colleges was by no means prominent in his mind. Thereafter it became a subject of unusual interest to him. In investigating more closely the benefits that accrued from his Dutch visits, therefore, we begin to detect an increasing absorption in topics relative to such subjects as the desirability of small classes, the arrangement of desks and new methods of instruction, whilst his private correspondence admits of the necessity of travelling further into Europe and acquainting himself with the educational systems of Switzerland and Prussia, so as the better to be prepared to combat the evil of illiteracy.

Before discussing Kay's next tour of exploration, however, it is perhaps wise to pause in our investigations and note the rather confused state of his educational views after he had acted as Assistant

[14] See pp. 29 and 30 of *The Training of Pauper Children* (Norwich Report, 1838) and also pp. 58–61 of *Public Education*
[15] See pp. 52 and 53 of *Minutes of the Committee of Council on Education* (1839–40)

Commissioner for three years. Between 1835 and 1838, as has been shown, he spared no effort to acquaint himself with every kind of experiment that might be of use to him in bettering the lot of pauper children. In so doing, however, it is clear that he was often compelled to give earnest consideration to conflicting theories of education and that, as a result, his opinions tended to vacillate—a truth that becomes immediately apparent if we study his report on *The Training of Pauper Children* written at Norwich soon after his second journey to Holland. In it he views with concern the appalling state of instruction in the workhouse schools and proceeds to diagnose this condition as if it were a disease, prescribing suitable drugs and palliatives to lessen its virulency. But the more one studies this account the more curious it becomes, for, though it adumbrates the important truth that Kay's educational creed was to be a combination of all that he considered best in the theory and practice of various eminent teachers, it makes such strange recommendations as to lead one to suppose that he wrote it in great haste. Thus, in order to revitalize the methods of instruction in the pauper schools, he suggests that Horticulture be taught in accordance with the precept of Lady Byron, Physical Training as advocated by Stow of Glasgow, Reading and Scripture as recommended by Wood of Edinburgh, Writing and Drawing after the manner of Pestalozzi, and Mental Arithmetic, odd as it may seem, in conformity with the practice of Joseph Lancaster. More than this, he states, on one occasion, that 'the children in infant schools should learn the powers of letters in small words, and afterwards their names, according to the system invented by Labarre while a refugee in Holland' [16] and, on another, that 'while reading, the methods pursued in the Sessional School of the Church of Scotland, conducted by Mr. Wood in Edinburgh, should be adopted'.[17] It would appear, indeed, that Kay, at this stage of his development, was working too hard to catch up with interesting experiments in teaching and that, as yet, he had been unable to assimilate the vast amount of information he had amassed.

As a final summary of his thoughts in 1838, therefore, it would

[16] See p. 28 of *The Training of Pauper Children* (Norwich Report, 1838). The Labarre system was a modification of the Pestalozzian method of teaching Reading —a system introduced into a large number of Dutch schools by Prinsen, the friend of van den Ende   [17] Norwich Report, p. 32

seem safe to say that Kay's interest in the science of teaching was abundant, and that he was aware of the degree to which English primary schools lagged behind their Continental counterparts. But it would appear, too, that his knowledge of pedagogics was circumscribed, and his ideas on child-training inchoate. If, therefore, we are to discover the way in which he overcame these deficiencies we must follow his career to London, where he moved in July 1838, and study his efforts first as Assistant Commissioner of the Metropolitan District and later as Secretary of the Committee of Council on Education, not only to sort out his views on the formal training of pupils and teachers, but also to bring English education into closer contact with European thought and experience.

19

JAMES PHILLIPS KAY (JULY 1838 TO SEPTEMBER 1839) — A YEAR OF IMPORTANT EDUCATIONAL DISCOVERIES

> 'And for this reason, conversation with men is of very great use and travel into foreign countries; not to bring back (as most of our young monsieurs do) an account only of how many paces Santa Rotonda is in circuit; or of the richness of Signora Livia's petticoats; or, as some others, how much Nero's face, in a statue in such an old ruin, is longer or broader than that made for him on some medal; but to be able chiefly to give an account of the humours, manners, customs and laws of those nations where he has been, and that we may whet and sharpen our wits by rubbing them against those of others.'
>
> MONTAIGNE—*Of Education.* 1580

IN view of the fact that Kay's ideas on child welfare and teacher training were as yet fluid it is perhaps not surprising that his first education venture in London was an experiment. Indeed no sooner had he assumed the position of Assistant Commissioner of the Metropolitan District than he set himself the task of visiting every pauper school under his jurisdiction in the hope of finding one that would prove suitable for testing the new theories he was pondering. He soon discovered, however, that the poor-law institutions of Middlesex and Surrey differed considerably from those of Norfolk and Suffolk. In some of the unions, for example, pauper children were farmed out at so much per head—a practice which dated from the preceding century when Jonas Hanway, a notable humanitarian, decided that city workhouses were inimical to the nurture of correct social habits and that, in consequence, the boys and girls who frequented them should be set to work in country districts under the supervision of carefully chosen families. At first these measures were

effective and respectable citizens, who proved themselves capable of caring for one pauper child, were subsequently permitted, if they so desired, to employ two or more. But unfortunately, within a short time, far less worthy individuals came forward who were anxious to take six or a dozen, and so, step by step, the custom evolved of housing young people in contractors' establishments and hiring them out at fixed rates. In August 1838, moreover, when Kay was busy examining the Metropolitan District, he discovered that many such institutions were still in existence but that few, if any, were worthy of commendation. The truth of the matter was that they had long been unable to house the vast numbers of pauper children who sought admission at their gates, and were so hopelessly congested that their inmates were frequently forced to sleep three abed. Certainly in one of their number, the poor-law institute at Norwood, the horrors of overcrowding had reached such proportions as to cause Kay deep concern. Accordingly he selected it as well fitted for the purpose of testing his educational theories and, without delay, made approaches on the subject to its proprietor.

The latter, who was named Aubin, showed that he was fully prepared to accept Kay's direction of the establishment and to help in any way possible to improve the standard of learning of those committed to his charge. The greatest obstacle to progress, therefore, was easily surmounted. There remained, nevertheless, so many difficult problems to be solved that the task might well have daunted anyone with less determination than Kay. In the first place he found one half of the pupils being instructed according to the theories of education expounded by Bell and the other half on the system evolved by Lancaster, which meant that he had to contend with all the inadequacies of the monitorial method; secondly he discovered the school authorities had made little provision for industrial training and that such as existed consisted merely of 'sorting bristles and making hooks and eyes'; and thirdly, after but a cursory glance, he was able to discern that the physical, moral and intellectual education of the children was, in every instance, 'extremely defective'.[1] Little wonder, then, that he determined such an unsatisfactory state of affairs should not be allowed to continue and that measures were required to infuse new life into so repressive an institution.

[1] See p. 2 of report on *The Training of Pauper Children* by J. P. Kay, Esq., M.D. London, 1839

It is important fully to appreciate this situation if any under-standing of Kay's development is to be obtained, for at Norwood he was presented with an unique opportunity of starting his career afresh and of putting his pedagogical theories to the test. Every reform that he introduced, in consequence, may be taken as an indi-cation of the way in which his educational thought was progressing.

In the eastern counties, it will be recalled, though he had given earnest consideration to curricula and methods of instruction, he had not, so far as his official reports reveal, singled out any one subject as of greater importance than the rest. But at Norwood he early determined that particular emphasis be placed upon Religion. Accordingly his first reform was to appoint a chaplain, the Revd. Joseph Brown of Mill-hill, who was commissioned to perform Divine Service on Sundays and to superintend the teaching of Scripture throughout the week.[2] In addition he made special arrangements whereby licensed members of other denominations visited the school at certain fixed times in order to instruct the children of their par-ticular sects. Thus, after a brief period, he effected a considerable change both in the tone and prevailing character of the institute.

This interest in religious instruction may be taken as an indication of the way in which Kay's educational philosophy was developing. It was not, of course, new to him, for he had held a firm belief in Christian principles since the days of his boyhood, when he acted as a Sunday School teacher at Bamford.[3] The fact of the matter was, however, that he began to develop something more than this—a deeper insight into the value of moral training and a keener awareness of its connection with education. We see this clearly if we compare the two reports which he wrote on *The Training of Pauper Children*—the one at Norwich in 1838 and the other at London in 1839. In the former he was obviously anxious to stimulate a desire for learning in the workhouse schools, to describe the educational experiments he had seen on his tours and to furnish information on the way in which certain subjects should be taught. When, therefore, towards the end of the report, he came to deal with Scripture he confined himself to an account of the interesting Bible lessons he had witnessed in Scotland. He did not, however, afford any indication that he considered this subject the very cornerstone

[2] *Ibid.* p. 3
[3] See *The Life of Sir James Kay-Shuttleworth* by Frank Smith, pp. 3–8

on which the successful pauper school rested. But in the latter he emphasized the worth of moral training at the outset and, though he issued no detailed information as to the manner in which it should be taught, he manifested obvious concern that it should be at the heart of the school curriculum and that visiting clergy should be allowed to supervise it. Could it be, one wonders, that, in reflecting on the high moral tone and intellectual fervour of the Scottish and Dutch primary schools, he had come to the conclusion that those excellent qualities were in no small measure attributable to sound Christian doctrine?

Such a theory seems plausible, for so many of the thoughts that occupied Kay's mind at that time were clearly the result of his educational journeys. He was aware, for example, that there existed a connection between the inferior moral training of the Norwood pupils and the mutual method of instruction. He was conscious, too, that before he could improve the status of his institute he would have perforce to sever this connection. Accordingly, as on a previous occasion, he asked David Stow to provide him with a number of trained teachers. And the latter, in answer to his request, soon despatched a number of young men to London, prominent amongst whom was Walter Mcleod, a hardworking Scot, who later achieved distinction as a schoolmaster at Chelsea.[4] So it was that, by persistent endeavour, Kay was able not only to introduce the simultaneous method of teaching into Norwood but to do so with success.

Consequent upon this major change in the conduct and policy of the institute there followed a host of ancillary reforms which afford further evidence of his preoccupation with progressive educational experiments. Thus, to facilitate the working of the simultaneous method, two interesting improvements were adopted. First, the boys' and girls' schools, which together housed some eleven hundred pupils, were divided into special classes each containing approximately forty pupils; and secondly, every class was then separated from those adjacent by means either of sliding partitions or hanging curtains. In this way, and in strict accordance with what he had observed in Holland, Kay completely altered the internal organization of the establishment.[5]

A further amendment, and one which must also be viewed in the

---

[4] See *The History of St. John's College, Battersea* by Thomas Adkins, p. 110
[5] See report on *The Training of Pauper Children* (1839), p. 4

light of his Dutch experience, was to select the most promising pupils and make use of their services. Thus any boys or girls who reached the age of fourteen and were distinguished by their 'zeal, attainments and gentleness of disposition' were asked to stay on at Norwood in the capacity of assistant masters and mistresses. By way of recompense they were paid a small salary, provided with extra tuition in the evenings, clothed in special uniforms and granted the privilege of sleeping in separate cubicles. Many, we learn, responded to this request and so Kay was allowed to perpetuate the system of pupil-teaching that he had inaugurated in the eastern counties.[6]

A final reform was to draw up a new time-table—a time-table which, with almost uncanny precision, reflected the tenor of his educational thought. Thus one half of the day was devoted to the study of Reading, Writing, Arithmetic, History, Geography, Nature Study and Singing, whilst the other half was given to the 'acquisition of skill in handicrafts'—an obvious attempt at that fine adjustment between mental and physical training which was so successful at Ealing Grove. We see this clearly if we consult the 1839 report on *The Training of Pauper Children* which Kay wrote in part to justify his newly devised programme of studies. Significantly enough he was no longer concerned with Wood's theory of teaching Scripture or Lancaster's lessons on Mental Arithmetic. Instead he had become an advocate of the Pestalozzian method, which he described in wide terms as 'an effective means of leading children from the known to the unknown by gradual steps'. It was, so he averred, the most successful manner of instruction he knew because it 'invested the acquisition of knowledge with natural attractions' and 'helped to rear children in the practice of mutual forbearance and good will and in respect and love of their instructors'.[7] Furthermore it ensured that every pupil received at least some individual attention and that harmony subsisted in all parts of a school. For these and other reasons, therefore, he was anxious that it should prevail at Norwood. Yet the more one studies Kay's observations on this subject the more one is led to question how much of the Pestalozzian method he as yet understood, for, despite the fact that he had already paid two visits to Holland, he would seem to have viewed it as a relatively simple way of teaching which almost any instructor could pick up without undue preparation. Of that idea, however, he was quickly

[6] *Ibid.* p. 5   [7] *Ibid.* p. 6

to be disabused when he visited Germany and Switzerland. And meanwhile the significant fact remains that, by 1839, his imagination had been fired by the theory of the most influential member of the Nature School of educators.

The second characteristic of this time-table—its emphasis on industrial training—was likewise an indication of the way in which Kay's educational philosophy was developing. Indeed he insisted that manual pursuits were the most effective means of promoting physical and mental health, and that there was especial need of them at Norwood. Intent on introducing occupational training, therefore, he approached the Home Secretary, Lord John Russell, and explained the impossibility of doing anything to improve the lot of the pauper children at Norwood unless he obtained a grant-in-aid from the Government. The latter looked with some sympathy upon Kay's request and not only set aside £500 per annum for structural and educational improvements but undertook to visit the institute personally. In consequence a number of unusual reforms were adopted which would otherwise have proved impossible. Workshops, for example, were built and placed under the charge of skilled handicraftsmen so that the boys might be trained as tailors, shoemakers, blacksmiths and glaziers. In addition a small farm was rented and experienced gardeners engaged, to ensure that Agriculture and Horticulture took their proper places in the school curriculum.[8] And finally a ship's mast was obtained from Greenwich, two guns from the naval dockyard at Deptford and a gunner from H.M.S. *Excellent* at Portsmouth so that mariners' classes could be introduced.

The girls, too, it is interesting to note, soon benefited from this revised method of training. At first they practised such household duties as scouring floors, making beds and waiting upon their teachers; washing, mangling and ironing clothes; and knitting, sewing and marking linen. Afterwards they worked in the school kitchen where they were instructed in plain cooking, and later still in the sick-bay, where they were trained as nurses. Not all of them, however, were anxious constantly to be employed on domestic duties and so, for those who evinced a preference for different work, special

[8] See 1839 report on *The Training of Pauper Children*, p. 111. It was Kay's chief regret that the shortage of land at Norwood did not allow of more ambitious schemes for agricultural and horticultural training

classes were arranged on the farm where they were taught to milk, churn and make butter and so to prepare themselves for service as dairymaids.

In this manner both boys and girls were afforded a great degree of occupational training which not only stood them in good stead when they came to seek employment but also provided them with many hours of fruitful industry whilst they remained at school. In fact so marked was the influence which industrial and agricultural work had upon them that, within a few months, Kay was able to perceive a distinct alteration in their attitude of mind. 'The children now display evidence of happiness . . .' he commented. 'They have confidence in the kindness of all by whom they are surrounded.' [9]

From such information we are able to judge the great forethought and planning that went into the Norwood Institute. Indeed so anxious was Kay that it achieve creditable results that he spent three afternoons a week there, coping with any problems of internal organization that presented themselves and seeing that his carefully considered plans for industrial education were faithfully implemented. Small wonder then that, commenting on this phase of his career in the 1877 MS., he was able tersely to remark : 'After a few months the success of the Norwood School of Industry was clearly recognized.'

At this stage in his career, when he had successfully applied his educational theories for the first time and provided the Commissioners with an Industrial School which could bear comparison with that of Lady Byron, it might be imagined that Kay was reasonably satisfied with his achievements. But such was far from being the case. Instead he was beset with misgivings the effects of which were sufficient to convince him that as yet he had scarcely begun to understand the significance of pedagogical theory and that Norwood in no sense could be regarded as a solution to the problem of educating pauper children. In particular he was worried about the practice of sending young men there for a matter of weeks ostensibly to learn new methods of teaching—a practice which, because it was attended with much false publicity, led people to believe that the institute could produce results for which it was never intended. On maturer reflection, therefore, he decided that what was principally needed to act as a spur to educational reform was ot a poor-law

[9] *Ibid.* p. 12

establishment which entertained ambitious schemes of social amelioration but a college which would provide a regular supply of teachers. In the early weeks of 1839 this thought so possessed his mind, moreover, that he contemplated taking independent action and founding, at his own expense, a private Normal School for the training of teachers.

That Kay was not able immediately to realize his ambition was owing to a variety of reasons chief among which was an offer he received from Lord Lansdowne to become Secretary of a new Education Department which the Government intended to create —an offer that was tempting to him and one that, in view of his desire to improve the standard of English schools, he was anxious straightway to accept. Yet he demurred somewhat before making a decision and finally gave his consent only on the condition that, when he relinquished his duties as an administrator of poor relief in the Metropolitan District, he should be allowed to retain the superintendence of the schools for pauper children. This proviso was acceded to by the Government and so, in April 1839, he started a new career—a career which, strange as it may seem, was the first he had to be concerned exclusively with matters of education.

It is important to realize this fact if we are to understand Kay's next move, for everything that he did was invariably dictated by reason. His researches at Norwood had served to convince him of many points which were of great educational significance, such as the desirability of small classes, the necessity of occupational training and, above all, the value of religious teaching. At the same time he had begun to study Pestalozzi's theory and expressed a desire to intrepret it in a Training College of his own. Was it not logical, therefore, that, before proceeding further, he should wish to undertake an examination of the educational experiments which were most renowned in Europe at that time, so as the fuller to appreciate their significance and the better to prepare himself for the new assignment Lord Lansdowne had given him? Such, at any rate, was the conclusion Kay himself reached and, in consequence, soon after his appointment as Secretary to the Committee of Council on Education, he embarked, in company with E. C. Tufnell, on a three months' tour through Europe.

Together they visited Holland, France, Prussia and Switzerland —the four countries which, by 1839, had established state systems of education. As a companion during the early stages of their tour, moreover, they took with them Walter Mcleod, the head of the industrial department at Norwood, who was anxious to avail himself of the opportunity of meeting Dutch pupil teachers. After seeing him safely settled in the Netherlands, however, Kay and Tufnell did not linger but proceeded forthwith to France where they established contact with Cousin and Villemain. One would love to know something of their reactions to this famous French couple whose knowledge of European education was immense and whose joint endeavours some six years previously had provided France with an extensive network of primary schools and an inspectorate. Indeed it could hardly have been fortuitous that the two Englishmen, who were later to lay the foundations of our own state system of education, straightway sought them out. Yet of their interview not one word has been recorded. Perhaps the reason for this was primarily religious, for, though Kay was prepared always to befriend Roman Catholics and frequently to commend their educational endeavours, his heart never warmed to them in the way it did to Protestants. In fact it was his firm conviction that those countries which had thrown off the yoke of Rome at the time of the Reformation had done most to check the incidence of illiteracy and that, as a result, their educational systems were worthiest of imitation by England. The point need not be unnecessarily laboured but it is instinct in too many passages of his reports wholly to be ignored.[10]

The two Englishmen, nevertheless, spent a profitable time in France. They visited Normal Schools at Dijon and Versailles, primary institutions in various parts of the country and the Maison Mère and Noviciate of the Brothers of the Christian Doctrine in Paris. In each, moreover, they contrived to learn something of value. Thus, both at Dijon and Versailles, they were immediately impressed by the extraordinary amount of time which the students devoted to drawing. It was, so Kay asserted, a healthy reminder to Englishmen of the value of aesthetic training and, at the same time, a delightful manifestation of the French genius—a genius which demanded that even the teachers of poor children should become proficient in painting and drawing. Yet what fascinated him even more than the artistic ability of the students was the manner in

[10] See 'First Report on the Training School at Battersea' reprinted in *Four Periods of Public Education*, pp. 303 and 359

which they were trained. This, he discovered, followed a method of art instruction invented by Alexandre Dupuis, professor at the Académie des Beaux-Arts, who, in 1831, having tired of seeing his students do little save copy famous masterpieces, reached the conclusion that what they principally needed was not so much practice in faithful reproduction as in perspective drawing. Accordingly he devised an elaborate instrument to which various objects were attached by means of a wire—an instrument that could be raised or lowered at will. Some of the objects were well known to the students (e.g. circles and triangles); others, perhaps less common, but clearly recognizable (e.g. rhomboids and hexagons); and others still of such strange proportions as to be thoroughly unfamiliar. In the initial stages Dupuis insisted that the objects be drawn either singly or in twos. Then, by raising or lowering the instrument, he contrived various combinations or patterns of the said objects so that greater skill was required to sketch them. Next he devised even more elaborate patterns and so on until, after sixteen adjustments of the instrument, he eventually covered all the points concerning perspective drawing with which he hoped to familiarize his students.

This unusual method of instruction immediately commended itself to Kay because, by means of it, a pupil was enabled 'to proceed by gradual steps through a series of combinations until he was able to draw faithfully any object, however complex'.[11] In other words he saw in it the same educative principle that had been enunciated in *How Gertrude Teaches Her Children*—the gradual building up of knowledge in easy stages. As far as one can tell, however, he was mistaken for there is no evidence to suggest that Dupuis was in any way indebted to Pestalozzi. Indeed the idea would seem to have been present in Kay's mind that the latter's influence on France was more powerful than was actually the case. He saw proof of it also in the 'fixed doh' system of teaching Singing devised by Wilhem —a system which, as we have already noted, was discovered and enunciated solely through its originator's contact with the mutual school at Saint-Jean-de-Beauvais.[12]

As may be appreciated, then, Kay found much to stimulate him

[11] See p. 354 of 'First Report on the Training School at Battersea' reprinted in *Four Periods of Public Education*

[12] See p. 750 of Vol. I (article on Alexandre Dupuis) and pp. 2992 and 2993 of Vol. II (article on the mutual school at Saint-Jean-de-Beauvais) of *Dictionnaire de Pédagogie et d'Instruction Primaire*

in France. In fact wherever he went he was made aware of fresh ideas, new methods of teaching and a different educational perspective. He did not, however, offer unstinted praise to all he saw or fail to censure what he considered inferior. Occasionally he found the schools ill-equipped, badly ventilated, overcrowded and lacking in moral purpose. If that were so, however, he did not elaborate on the imperfections. He usually stated them briefly at the outset of his comments and then proceeded to a more lengthy assessment of what he found commendable. We see this clearly if we consider his account of the schools of the Brothers of the Christian Doctrine. At first he thought them deficient in 'the niceties of organization' and in 'exact methods of instruction'.[13] Later, however, he came to prize them for what he described as their 'harmonious atmosphere' —an atmosphere which he attributed to the example of Christian zeal set by the Brothers themselves. 'Their manners are simple, affectionate and sincere', he stated; 'and the children are singularly attached to them. . . . No one can enter the schools of the Brothers of the Christian Doctrine without feeling instinctively that he is witnessing a remarkable example of the development of Christian charity.' [14] In addition he commended the thoroughness of the training that the novices received; the diligence with which the Superior singled out those pupils who possessed unusual talents and saw to it that their gifts were used to the greater glory of God; and, most important of all, the incredible industry of the entire Order which literally ensured that miracles were performed among the very poorest element of society. 'With such motives', he added, 'should the teachers of elementary schools and especially those who are called upon to the arduous duties of training pauper children go forth to their work.' [15]

If, as has been shown, France served to convince Kay of the interesting possibilities of the Pestalozzian method with regard to the teaching of Art and Singing, and if, as a result of his contact with the 'Frères Ignorantins', he learnt a valuable lesson in the Christian virtue of self-sacrifice, there can be little doubt that his experiences in Germany and Switzerland served even more to broaden his knowledge and enrich his ideals. For there he came within the full

[13] See p. 388 of *Four Periods of Public Education*
[14] *Ibid*. p. 357. 'First Report on the Training School at Battersea'
[15] *Ibid*. p. 358

orbit of Pestalozzi's influence and, thanks largely to Sir John Boileau who acted as his guide, established contact with teachers who had devoted many years of their lives to the study of pedagogical theory. That he enjoyed this experience, moreover, cannot be questioned. It is apparent alike in the two reports that he wrote at the time and in the journal he kept towards the end of his life— so long did the savour of it linger in his memory. We do well, therefore, to pay the strictest attention to his comments on this phase of the tour if we are to understand the benefit he reaped from it and the use he ultimately made of the information he acquired.

In the first place it is important to note that, though Kay visited a large number of educational establishments in Germany and Switzerland, he was obviously not intent on examining the precise rôles they filled in their respective state systems of education. If that had been the case he would undoubtedly have undertaken a detailed examination of the innumerable laws and regulations governing public instruction which were in force in both countries—an examination which, of necessity, would have had to give some consideration to the many outstanding differences between the German and Swiss attitudes towards educational legislation. As it was, however, he chose to ignore all points of divergence and to concentrate rather on the way in which they jointly strove to promote Pestalozzi's ideals —an interesting point of view which again illustrates his absorption in the pedagogical theory of the most important member of the Nature School of educators. Indeed the most significant result of the entire tour was undoubtedly the way in which, thanks largely to first-hand acquaintance with progressive educational experiments, Kay gradually sorted out his ideas and came to realize why Pestalozzi had exerted so profound an influence.

We may see an illustration of this point if we consider the careful study which he gave to the German and Swiss Normal Schools. Thus, during the course of his journey, he contrived to visit no less than ten of them in such widely separated parts as Eisleben (Prussia), Schluchten (Hesse Cassel), Esslingen (Würtemberg), Dresden, Carlsruhe, Kreuzlingen (Canton de Vaud), Lausanne, Lucerne, Berne and Zurich. The lessons he learnt there, moreover, served to convince him of two things—that a prolonged period of study was necessary if a master were to be thoroughly trained (e.g. in the Fletcher Normal Seminary at Dresden the duration of the course was four years), and that much detailed exposition was essential if Pestalozzi's theories were fully to be understood (e.g. in the Normal Schools at Eisleben and Lausanne one hour daily was devoted to this subject for a period of two years). Yet that so careful a preparation ultimately justified itself was readily apparent. Raw students, who had little knowledge either of schools or teaching, were soon transformed into responsible human beings anxious both to combat illiteracy and to do so amongst the poorest people. This alone was sufficient testimony to the worth of their training—a training which, whilst stressing the necessity of Mathematics, History, Geography, Music, Art, Singing, French, German and Pedagogics, did not remain unmindful of the benefits that accrued from outdoor activity. And in this connection Kay noted with approval that almost all the Normal Schools not only included agriculture and horticulture in their curricula but also insisted that their students take frequent excursions into the country 'to read the great truths of Nature left on record in the features of the landscape'.[16] In fact he began to appreciate the value of those pedagogical ideals which had emanated from the famous colleges at Burgdorf and Yverdun—to educate the heart and the feelings as well as the intellect and to teach the importance of a life stripped of artificiality and pretence.

The extent to which Kay's attitude was modified by this experience was impressive. He had embarked on the tour fully convinced that if he were effectively to combat the evils of ignorance and illiteracy he would have some day to establish a Training College and give earnest consideration to progressive methods of instruction including those of Pestalozzi. But he had not, as far as his writings reveal, reached any definite conclusions as to the precise manner in which he was going to fulfil his intentions. After visiting the seminaries at Eisleben, Dresden, Berne and Zurich, however, he would appear not only to have gained additional insight into the problems that confronted him but also to have realized—and this to a degree which he had never done previously—that those establishments which were seeking faithfully to interpret Pestalozzi's doctrines were as intimately concerned with the discipline and moral development of their pupils as with their instruction. That this revelation struck

[16] See 'First Report on the Training School at Battersea' reprinted in *Four Periods of Public Education*, p. 319

him as important, moreover, may be judged from the following
quotation:

> Those Normal Schools which have paid the deference due to
> the lessons of Pestalozzi are remarkable for the gentleness and
> simplicity of the intercourse between the scholar and his master.
> The formation of character is always kept in mind as the great
> aim of education. The intelligence is enlightened in order that it
> may inform the conscience and that the conscience, looking forth
> through this intelligence, may behold a wider sphere of duty and
> have at its command a greater capacity for action.[17]

It is perhaps hardly surprising, then, that the last important
mission Kay undertook before returning to London was to establish
contact with a number of eminent thinkers and teachers who likewise set great store by moral training and were anxious that it
should receive due recognition in the Swiss primary schools. Thus,
as an interesting climax to his tour, he contrived to call on such
eminent figures as Father Girard, de Fellenberg and Wehrli. Unfortunately, however, his interviews with them, save one, were so
tantalizingly brief that we learn little either of the subjects discussed
or the personalities involved. They are, nevertheless, worth record-
ing if only for the obvious pleasure Kay took in conversing with some
of the men whose vision and enterprise had made Switzerland outstanding in Europe for its educational thought and practice.

It was at Fribourg in the convent of the Capuchin friars that he
saw Father Girard who was busy officiating at a religious festival.
During his sojourn abroad Kay had, of course, frequently heard of
this humble priest who devoted his life to the welfare of poor boys.
Once the service was over, therefore, he begged to be introduced
and soon found himself involved in a lengthy discussion with the
'venerable Franciscan' that ranged over a variety of topics from
current methods of instruction to the scarcity of reading manuals
for young children. In fact he learnt with satisfaction that Father
Girard was so perturbed about the general shortage of text books
that he had decided to write a series himself—a series whose publication, incidentally, Kay was still anticipating some two years
later.[18] By far the most important result of this brief encounter,
however, was an invitation the Englishman received to inspect the

---

[17] See *Four Periods of Public Education*, p. 298   [18] *Ibid.* p. 301

Fribourg schools. Thus he was able to judge for himself the 'pious labours' of his distinguished contemporary and to pass judgment as follows:

> The Père Girard has a European reputation among those who have laboured to raise the elementary instruction of the poorer classes . . . and the success of his schools appeared chiefly attributable—first to the skill and assiduity with which the monitors had been instructed in the evening by the Father and his assistants, by which they had been raised to the level of the pupil teachers of Holland; and secondly to the skilful manner in which he and his assistants had infused a moral lesson into every incident of the instruction, and had bent the whole force of their minds to the formation of the character of the children.[19]

The next interview was with de Fellenberg—an interview which must surely have been among the most interesting Kay had if only for the reason that both parties were friends of Lady Byron and, thanks to her kindness, had already interchanged letters.[20] Yet of their encounter very little has been recorded. Indeed Kay would seem to have been under the impression that the work of de Fellenberg was sufficiently well known to require no further elaboration by him, as may be judged from a brief entry in his journal to the effect that all who were interested in Hofwyl should consult the detailed accounts of it which had been written by the 'late lamented Mr. Duppa'.[21] That he regarded the occasion of their meeting as important, however, is evident from the following passage:

> Near Berne we spent much time in conversation with M. de Fellenberg. . . . What we learned from the conversation of this patriotic and high-minded man we cannot find space here to say. His words are better read in the establishment which he has founded and which he superintends, and in the influence which his example and his precepts have had on the rest of Switzerland and on other parts of Europe.[22]

[19] See 'First Report on the Training School at Battersea' reprinted in *Four Periods of Public Education*, p. 301
[20] See p. 52 of *The Life and Work of Sir James Kay-Shuttleworth* by Frank Smith
[21] 1877 MS.
[22] See 'First Report on the Training School at Battersea' reprinted in *Four Periods of Public Education*, p. 302

From Berne, at de Fellenberg's suggestion, Kay next proceeded to the shores of Lake Constance to see the famous Kreuzlingen Normal School—the last important event of his tour and undoubtedly the one which lingered longest in his memory. There he met ninety young men, varying in age between eighteen and twenty-six, and Wehrli, the former head of the Hofwyl Poor School, who welcomed him with unfeigned frankness and sincerity. 'I am a peasant's son,' said he; 'I wish to be no other than I am, the teacher of the sons of the peasantry. You are welcome to my meal; it is coarse and homely but it is offered cordially.' [23]

These simple words would seem immediately to have indicated to the English visitor the very character of the Normal School and its director. Indeed so impressed was he with the degree to which the establishment reflected Wehrli's personality that he decided to spend two days there studying in detail both the students' hour to hour activities and the manner in which they were trained. He observed them working in the garden, sawing logs of wood, gathering vegetables, preparing meals and doing household chores. He attended their lessons on Mathematics, Elementary Science, Drawing, History, Geography, Grammar, Pedagogics and Scripture. And he listened with wonder to the words of counsel by which Wehrli strove to impress upon his charges the thought that poverty rightly understood was no misfortune.

We are peasants' sons [he would repeat]; we would not be ignorant of our duties; but God forbid that knowledge should make us despise the simplicity of our lives. The earth is our mother, and we gather our food from her breast, but while we peasants labour for our daily food we may learn lessons from our mother earth. There is no knowledge in books like an immediate converse with nature, and those that dig the soil have nearest communion with her. Believe me, or believe me not, this is the thought that can make a peasant's life sweet and his toil a luxury. I know it; for see, my hands are horny with toil. The lot of men is very equal, and wisdom consists in the discovery of the truth that what is *without* is not the source of sorrow but that which is within. A peasant may be happier than a prince if his conscience be pure

[23] See 'First Report on the Training School at Battersea' reprinted in *Four Periods of Public Education*, p. 304

before God and he learn not only contentment but joy in the life of labour, which is to prepare him for the life of heaven.[24]

As may be imagined such sentiments made a deep impression upon Kay. He had travelled far in search of information and had found much to interest and stimulate him but never previously had he seen an institution which combined such intellectual endeavour with such simplicity of life. Indeed it seemed to him that there by the shores of Lake Constance he had discovered an answer to many of his problems—an establishment expressly designed for future teachers of the poor that not merely recognized the importance of moral training, but also, through the prodigious efforts of its director, enshrined the highest ideals of Pestalozzi and de Fellenberg.

The extent to which this discovery served to clarify Kay's ideas, moreover, cannot be questioned. It was not merely that he became aware of the truth that men similarly trained would be best fitted to reclaim the pauper youth of England, nor yet that he saw in the Kreuzlingen Normal School a model for the Training College he intended to found. It was rather that he finally discovered the yard-stick by which his own educational efforts could be measured.

As a final comment on this all-important phase of the 1839 tour, therefore, it is perhaps permissible to quote the following description that Kay wrote of an episode at Kreuzlingen that afforded him particular pleasure—an episode which should be compared with Rengger's experience at the Hofwyl Poor School in 1813.[25]

> As we returned from the garden with the pupils on the evening of the first day, we stood for a few minutes with Wehrli in the court-yard by the shore of the lake. The pupils had ascended into the classrooms, and the evening being tranquil and warm, the windows were thrown up, and we shortly afterwards heard them sing in excellent harmony. As soon as this song had ceased, we sent a message to request another, with which we had become familiar in our visits to the Swiss schools; and thus, in succession, we called for song after song, imagining that we were only directing them at their usual hour of instruction in vocal music. When

[24] *Ibid* p. 307
[25] See *Translation of the Reports of M. e Comte de Capo d'Istria and M. Rengger, upon the Principles and Progress of the Establishment of M. de Fellenberg at Hofwyl, Switzerland* by John Attersoll, p. 30

we had listened nearly an hour Wehrli invited us to ascend into
the room where the pupils were assembled. We followed him,
and on entering the apartment great was our surprise to discover
the whole school, during the period we had listened, had been
cheering with songs their evening employment of peeling potatoes,
and cutting the stalks from the green vegetables and beans which
they had gathered in the garden. As we stood there they renewed
their choruses till prayers were announced. Supper had been
previously taken. After prayers, Wehrli, walking about the apartment, conversed with them familiarly on the occurrences of the
day, mingling with his conversation such friendly admonition as
sprang from the incidents, and then, lifting his hands, he recommended them to the protection of heaven and dismissed them to
rest.[26]

Such passages are rare in Kay's writing for he usually expressed
his sentiments in stilted and turgid prose. Occasionally, however,
under the impact of some vital experience he would drop his official
demeanour and speak in simple terms of what he had seen. We may
remember in this connection his vivid account of the way in which
the cholera plague swept through the slums of Manchester when he
was a physician at the Knot Mill Hospital [27] or, in quite a different
vein, the descriptions of Pennine scenery he included in his novels.
Indeed it was probably these rare outbursts of poetic feeling that
prompted Charlotte Brontë to remark—'Nine points out of ten in
him are utilitarian—the tenth is artistic. This tithe of his nature
seems to me at war with all the rest.' Yet her judgment cannot surely
be accepted as final, for to argue that the man who took such
pleasure in listening to a group of youths singing the traditional airs
of the Bernese Oberland was at variance with the Assistant Commissioner who worked so hard to reorganize the pauper schools of
the Metropolitan district is obviously absurd. Rather would one say
that the part of Kay which was essentially idealistic provided the
impetus for his major educational reforms and that, as a result, the
two sides of his nature were essentially complementary. And if
proof of this be needed we have only to turn to his next major

[26] See 'First Report on the Training School at Battersea' reprinted in *Four
Periods of Public Education*, pp. 306 and 307
[27] See *The Life and Work of Sir James Kay-Shuttleworth* by Frank Smith, pp. 21–23

undertaking—the founding of the Battersea Normal School—and note the patient way in which he strove to promote among his students both a love of art and music and a healthy respect for manual labour.

20

THE BATTERSEA EXPERIMENT—
THE FIRST ENGLISH NORMAL SCHOOL

'A good schoolmaster ought to be a man who knows much more than
he is called upon to teach, that he may teach with intelligence and
taste; who is to live in a humble sphere, and yet to have a noble and
elevated mind, that he may preserve that dignity of sentiment and
deportment without which he will never obtain the respect and confidence of families; who possesses a rare mixture of gentleness and
firmness for, inferior though he be in station to many individuals in
the parish, he ought to be the obsequious servant of none; a man not
ignorant of his rights, but thinking much more of his duties; showing
to all a good example, and serving to all as a counsellor; not given to
change his condition, but satisfied with his situation because it gives
him the power of doing good; and who has made up his mind to live
and die in the service of primary instruction, which to him is the
service of God and his fellow-creatures. To rear masters approaching
to such a model is a difficult task; and yet we must succeed in it, or
else we have done nothing for elementary instruction.'

> FRANÇOIS GUIZOT, Minister of Public Instruction in
> France, 11th October, 1832–10th
> November, 1834; 18th Novem-
> ber, 1834–22nd January, 1836;
> and 6th September, 1836–15th
> April, 1839

IT is a question of some nicety to decide how much benefit Kay
derived from his foreign travels for he was never prompted to supply
detailed information on the subject himself and, as a result, such
proof of it as exists has to be pieced together from various passages in
his notes and reports. Broadly speaking, however, it would seem safe
to assert that, from October 1839, he became increasingly appreci-
ative of Continental theories with regard to child welfare and
teacher training and more anxious than ever to start a Normal
School of his own where he could interpret them to the best advantage. An important result of this, moreover, was to turn him into a
keen student of comparative education—an aspect of his develop-

ment which, for the most part, has been overlooked. Indeed it is commonly held that the pioneer work in this relatively new field of enquiry began, as far as this country is concerned, during the second half of the nineteenth century and was heralded by the important researches of Matthew Arnold. Such, however, was not entirely the case as may be judged from the second report in *Four Periods of Public Education* which Kay wrote soon after his return from the Continent.

In it he advanced his usual argument that, by 1839, popular instruction was spreading apace throughout Europe and achieving the most noteworthy results amongst those peoples who embraced the cause of Protestantism. To substantiate his thesis, moreover, he supplied the following statistics:

PROPORTION OF SCHOLARS IN ELEMENTARY SCHOOLS TO WHOLE
POPULATION [1]

	Pupil		Inhabitants
Thurgovia, Switzerland (1832)	1	in	4·8
Zurich, Switzerland (1832)	1	in	5
Argovia, Switzerland (1832)	1	in	5·3
Bohemia (1833)	1	in	5·7
Würtemberg	1	in	6
Prussia (1838)	1	in	6
Baden (1830)	1	in	6
Drenthe, Province of, Holland (1835)	1	in	6
Saxony	1	in	6
Province of Overyssel (1835)	1	in	6·2
Canton of Neuchâtel (1832)	1	in	6·4
Frise (1833)	1	in	6·8
Norway (1834)	1	in	7
Denmark (1834)	1	in	7
Bavaria (1831)	1	in	8
Austria (1832)	1	in	10
Scotland (1834)	1	in	10·4
Belgium	1	in	11·5
England	1	in	11·5
Lombardy (1832)	1	in	12·6
France	1	in	17·6
Ireland	1	in	18
Roman States	1	in	50
Lucca	1	in	53
Tuscany	1	in	66
Portugal	1	in	88
Russia	1	in	367

[1] See *Four Periods of Public Education*, p. 220

From such information, Kay asserted, it was possible to see not only the great impetus that the Reformation had given to primary instruction [2] but also the degree to which England alone had failed to interpret its spirit. In giving more careful consideration to what was required to bring his country into closer contact with other Protestant states, therefore, he undertook a brief survey of the educational progress achieved throughout the preceding half century by Scotland, Denmark, Sweden, Prussia, Switzerland and Holland. Thus he commended his Scottish fellow-subjects for having devised a system of parochial education that was peculiarly adapted to their national genius, approved the wisdom of the Danish parliament which had shown an ever-increasing awareness of the need of public instruction, and praised the efforts of the Swedish reformers who of late years had recaptured the visionary enthusiasm of Gustavus Vasa and invented an effective remedy for the formidable evils of corrupt feudalism. As might be imagined, however, he was more particularly concerned with those countries that he had recently visited and so the greater part of his account was devoted to the comprehensive educational programmes undertaken by Prussia, Switzerland and Holland.

Of these he dealt first with Prussia and instanced her remarkable foresight in deciding, even during the dark days of the early nineteenth century, that particular care should be given to primary instruction. This policy, he pointed out, had gradually borne fruit until, by 1838, with a population of 14,000,000 she possessed some 22,910 elementary schools in which 2,717,745 boys and girls were receiving instruction from 27,575 trained members of staff. In addition she could boast 45 well-equipped Normal Schools housing no less than 2,583 students. [3] Small wonder, then, that, with such carefully conceived plans, Prussia had made astounding progress. She far outstripped England in this direction. Yet, when he contemplated the highly rigid system she had devised, Kay, even as Cousin before him, was of the opinion that many alterations would have to be made if it were successfully to be copied by other nations.

As far as Switzerland was concerned Kay confined his attention to the Protestant cantons and spoke enthusiastically of the consider-

---

[2] See also *Public Education*, chapter 1, p. 33
[3] See *Four Periods of Public Education*, p. 210

able improvements they had effected during the past sixteen years. He regretted, however, that no account had yet been published in English of what was undoubtedly their chief contribution to educational progress—the building, staffing and equipping of a large number of Normal Schools. This was truly remarkable when one bore in mind the size of the country where they were to be found and showed with what fidelity the Swiss nation had interpreted the wishes of Pestalozzi and de Fellenberg. That such expensive measures were producing satisfactory results, moreover, could not be doubted. It was evident both in the Normal Schools themselves and in the primary institutions of even the most remote country districts. In fact Kay gave it as his opinion that particular attention should be paid to the Protestant cantons of Switzerland, for their educational programmes were undoubtedly among the most advanced in Europe.

After dealing with Prussia and Switzerland Kay turned next to Holland. He recalled the pioneer efforts of such men as van den Ende, Prinsen and Baron Falk and commended their wisdom in founding Normal Schools which, from their very inception, had striven to interpret Pestalozzi's doctrines. Then, after a brief description of the Dutch educational system, he laid stress on two of its characteristics which struck him as particularly noteworthy. The first was the method of school inspection which was 'so devised as to be in perfect harmony with the municipal institutions of the country and the character and feeling of the inhabitants'. 'The Dutch inspectors', he reported, 'form the medium of communication between the Government, the municipal councils, the provincial authorities and the committees and directors of schools. It is their duty to foster the exertions of the local communities and to direct them to useful objects. The inspection of schools; the examination of teachers, and their special authorization; together with the diffusion of information concerning the best methods of teaching, the proper apparatus and most useful books, are among the inspectors' duties.' And the second characteristic was, as might be expected, the extended use of pupil teachers. 'It is a part of the discipline of the Dutch schools', he remarked, 'to select and train the most promising pupils, first as assistants in the more mechanical arrangements of the school, and then as apprentices in every department. At the same time they receive such instruction as may fit them, when they arrive at maturity, successfully to perform the duties of teachers in primary schools.' [4] For these and other reasons, therefore, Kay was prepared to place Holland alongside Prussia and Switzerland as one of the best instructed nations in Europe.

From this brief review of the educational progress achieved by Scotland, Denmark, Sweden, Prussia, Switzerland and Holland, Kay hoped to demonstrate how manfully the Protestant states had striven to overthrow illiteracy. Indeed he argued that the measure of their success could best be gauged by the readiness of Catholic countries to imitate their methods. Thus Ireland, Belgium and France were all struggling under adverse circumstances to introduce far-reaching educational reforms. Indeed it seemed to him that over a large part of Europe the powers of darkness were finally beginning to disperse and a brighter future was dawning for many thousands of poor children.

There remained, nevertheless, one outstanding and wholly unwarrantable exception to all this. How came it, Kay questioned, that England with a comparatively serene political atmosphere, abundant wealth and vast territorial possessions should be so neglectful of the means whereby the civilization of her people could be produced? The problem apparently defied solution. Yet it was obviously shameless to protest that this country could ill afford the expenditure which educational reform would involve, for her commercial cities and manufacturing towns contained middle classes whose wealth, enterprise and intelligence had no successful rivals in Europe. Nor could it be argued that she was totally unaware of the extent to which she lagged behind other countries, for Cousin's reports on Holland and Prussia had been translated into English and read with avidity in many parts of the country. The truth of the matter was that England could produce 'no excuse' for her laziness. Indeed it was scarcely credible that with endowments to the extent of half a million pounds per annum her primary education should be in 'utter ruins'. Furthermore, if such a policy were allowed to continue unabated, sooner or later she would awaken to the unpleasant truth that 'the ignorance—nay, the barbarism—of large portions of her countrymen' had been cultivated at too great a cost. [5]

These were among the strongest words Kay ever used. To study the concluding passages of his report, therefore, is to realize the

---

[4] See *Four Periods of Public Education* p. 217   [5] *Ibid.* p. 228

depth of his concern. He was obviously ashamed of English insensibility towards educational reform and, at the same time, determined to do everything in his power to challenge it. Accordingly, believing that shocks often furnish the first approach to reform, he spared neither bluntness nor acerbity to rouse his fellow-subjects from their apathy and to convince them that their attitude, under whatever guise they might attempt to camouflage it, was nothing short of a national calamity.

Having denounced his compatriots, however, Kay was not prepared to sit back and await further developments. He knew that if England were to take her rightful place alongside Continental countries as a champion of learning her elementary schools would have perforce to be staffed with adequately trained teachers.[6] Accordingly he determined to implement his long-cherished plan and to open, in company with Tufnell, a private Normal School based on the Swiss model. Indeed, as Tufnell took care to point out some thirty-five years later : 'the effect of our journey through Holland, France, Germany and Switzerland was to produce a perfect conviction in our minds that the methods of training teachers then in practice in England were utterly unsound and accordingly, on our return, we devised the Battersea Training College. The principles on which it was founded were those we had learnt from inspecting the institutions set on foot by Pestalozzi and de Fellenberg.' [7]

Battersea was selected, we understand, for two reasons—first because of its vicar, the Honourable and Reverend Robert Eden,[8] who declared his willingness not only to supervise the religious instruction of the students but also to allow them to do their practice-teaching in the village schools, and secondly because of its manor house, situated in five acres of ground, which provided a suitable site for a Training College. In February 1840, therefore, after the building had undergone structural alterations, Kay was ready to embark on his project and to welcome the first pupils—eight orphan boys of thirteen years of age who formerly had been in attendance at the Norwood School of Industry. As might be expected, moreover, from one who was invariably the acme of competence, he had already

---

[6] See *The Life of Sir James Kay-Shuttleworth*, p. 93. Letter from Kay to Sir John Shaw Lefevre

[7] See *The Journal of Education*, July 1877, p. 308. Article on 'Sir James Kay-Shuttleworth' by E. Carleton Tufnell

[8] Subsequently Lord Auckland, Bishop of Bath and Wells

mapped out their course of training in great detail. On arrival they were all given 'a plain, dark dress of rifle green and a working dress of fustian cord', told that their course of study would last three years during two of which they would receive training as pupil teachers for three hours daily in the village schools, and charged to pay particular attention to their studies as, once the course was completed, they would be expected to take an examination on the results of which their future would depend. Those who passed would be granted certificates and allowed to seek employment as assistant masters in pauper schools. Those who failed, on the other hand, would have to remain for a further period of study and take the examination again.

So cheerless a welcome, it would seem, might well have daunted many of the poor orphans but apparently such was not the case, for they quickly settled in their new surroundings and soon improved in health as a result of the regular hours of work and sleep Kay prescribed. After a few weeks, moreover, so securely were they established that the directors decided to accept sixteen more, though beyond that number they would not proceed for, remembering the secret of Wehrli's success at Hofwyl, they thought it wiser in the initial stages to tread with caution.

The twenty-four pupil teachers did not, however, constitute the entire personnel. In addition there were nine young men, ranging in age between twenty and thirty, who were admitted on the recommendation of intimate friends of Dr. Kay for a period of study lasting approximately one year. Thus the portion of Battersea which ultimately won renown as a training department first saw the light of day; and among those who enrolled students there were Leonard Horner, Lady Byron and Lord Chichester—three prominent social reformers whose activities have already been noted.

Such were the earnest beginnings of what was undoubtedly one of the most important educational establishments to be founded in England during the first half of the nineteenth century. The story of its early days has been told so often, however, both by its founders and those who have commented on their work, that there would seem to be little point in repeating it here.[9] Yet what is perhaps of

[9] See *Reports on the Training School at Battersea* by J. P. Kay-Shuttleworth and E. C. Tufnell; *The Life of Sir James Kay-Shuttleworth* by Frank Smith, chapter 4; and *The History of St. John's College, Battersea* by Thomas Atkins

interest to note is the way in which, during the two years Kay acted as its director, the new college came to reflect the tenor of his educational thought and to demonstrate how much he owed to foreign experiment. For Battersea, odd as it may seem, became one of the most curious amalgams of pedagogical ideals that has ever existed and could never have been devised, let alone made to function, by anyone save an arch-conciliator and a native of Great Britain.

So contentious a statement cannot, of course, be made lightly or without sufficient corroboratory evidence. If, therefore, we are to appreciate its exact significance, it is perhaps wise to bear in mind three major reforms which Kay devised at the outset of his undertaking and which he introduced with the obvious intention of bringing his establishment into line with Continental practice. In the first place he chose to live on the premises, taking charge of all administrative duties and holding himself responsible for everything that happened there, as was the custom in Continental Normal Schools. Thus, from the start, he strove to demonstrate the truth of the Prussian maxim 'As is the master, so is the school'—a saying to which both he and Tufnell were addicted.[10] Secondly he selected as his personal assistants three men who had been trained by Stow of Glasgow and whose worth he already knew—Tate, whom he placed in charge of the senior students, Horne, whom he made answerable for the pupil teachers, and Mcleod to whom he entrusted the village school. And thirdly he himself assumed responsibility both for the curriculum and methods of teaching—two subjects to which he devoted such care that the entire establishment became, as it were, a cogent manifesto of the educational truths by which he set greatest store.

Bearing in mind these three important factors, then, we may examine more closely the host of ancillary reforms that were likewise introduced and that, almost without exception, traced their origin to foreign educational experiment.

Thus the domestic arrangements at Battersea were kept as simple as possible. Indulgences were frowned upon, the household chores were undertaken by the students themselves, and no servants permitted save an aged matron who acted as cook. In addition the

---

[10] See p. 19 of report from Carelton Tufnell, Esq., on *The Education of Pauper Children* (1839). See also p. 7 of report on *The Training of Pauper Children* by J. P. Kay

dormitories, living and recreation rooms were furnished with the barest essentials and even the meals were 'as frugal as was consistent with constant activity of mind'. All this was quite deliberate, moreover, for, by emphasizing the necessity of retrenchment and plain living, Kay hoped to impress upon all concerned that the life of a schoolmaster was invariably one of toil and self-denial—a truth which, it will be recalled, had been impressed upon him by Wehrli.[11]

As time progressed a small experimental farm was started which comprised two cows, three pigs and three goats. These animals were fed and tended by the students themselves because 'such occupations were deemed important as giving them, by actual experience, some knowledge of a peasant's life and truer and closer sympathy with his lot'. Extensive gardens were also laid out, and four hours daily devoted to the study of horticulture. A connection between academic training and a life closely associated with the soil was thereby early established—a point of educational doctrine stressed repeatedly by Pestalozzi, de Fellenberg, Wehrli and Kay's intimate friend— Lady Byron. Indeed, if we consider a typical day in the Battersea College, we are instantly reminded of such establishments as the Hofwyl Poor School, the Kreuzlingen College and Ealing Grove.

The whole school [Kay reported] rose at half-past five. The household work occupied the pupil teachers altogether, and the students partially, till a quarter to seven o'clock. At that time they marched into the garden and worked till a quarter to eight, when they were summoned to prayers. Then they marched to the tool-house, deposited their implements, washed and assembled at prayers at eight o'clock. At half-past eight they breakfasted. From nine to twelve they were in school. They worked at the garden from twelve to one, when they dined. They resumed their labour in the garden at two and returned to their classes at three, where they were engaged till five, when they worked another hour in the garden. At six they supped and spent from seven to nine in their classes. At nine, evening prayers were read, and immediately afterwards they retired to rest.[12]

In order that the daily routine should not become too monotonous both pupil teachers and students were often taken for long walks in

---

[11] See *First Report on the Training School at Battersea*, p. 312
[12] *Ibid.* pp. 314 and 315

the country. And, on these excursions, 'their habits of observation were cultivated, their attention was directed to what was most remarkable, and to such facts and objects as might have escaped observation from their comparative obscurity'. Such tours, it will be remembered, had frequently been undertaken by Pestalozzi and de Fellenberg and were common to all the Normal Schools of Switzerland because they furnished excellent opportunities for the students to get to know one another and, while so doing, to study 'the great truths of Nature left on record in the features of the landscape'.[13] In the early stages of his experiment, therefore, Kay rarely lost sight of any occasion which would help to weld his college more closely together. Thus, besides the activities already mentioned, he insisted that both pupil teachers and students unite to say prayers at least twice daily and attend church regularly on Sundays. And this was done so that they should think and act as if they were members of one body and not an ill-assorted collection of individuals assembled haphazardly from a variety of regions—again a typically Pestalozzian sentiment.[14]

Another reform which was quickly introduced and which clearly bore testimony to Kay's early training as a doctor was an attempt to improve the physical condition of the students. With this end in view, therefore, a gymnastic frame and parallel bars were purchased and 'marching exercises' and 'extension movements' practised with great regularity so that every youth should acquire both muscular vigour and a good deportment. A slouching gait, Kay maintained, was 'a sign of vulgarity' and should be corrected as soon as possible for 'by giving a child an erect and manly bearing, a firm and regular step, precision and rapidity in his movements, promptitude in obedience to commands and neatness in apparel and person, a teacher was insensibly laying the foundations of correct moral habits'. He added further that the importance of this truth had long been recognized in Germany and Switzerland, and that he himself had been made increasingly aware of it when visiting a Normal School in the Canton de Vaud, whence he had copied both the methods of physical training and the apparatus subsequently brought into use at Battersea.[15]

As may be seen, then, the gymnastic exercises of the pupil teachers

---

[13] See *First Report on the Training School at Battersea*, p. 319
[14] *Ibid.* pp. 323 and 324   [15] *Ibid.* p. 318

and students had not reference solely to health. They were considered an important element of the discipline and moral tone of the college. And so it was with regard to the actual conduct of the classes. Kay constantly emphasized the necessity of peace and quiet when lessons were in progress, because these two qualities gave more direct help to students than any precepts inculcated by word of mouth. 'In some of our English schools,' he complained, 'a notion is prevalent that a considerable noise is unavoidable, and some teachers are understood to regard the noise as so favourable a sign of the activity of the school as even to assert that the greater the noise, the greater the intellectual progress of the scholars.' Such a theory, however, was not held on the Continent. Indeed in Holland the absence of shouting and unnecessary movement was particularly noteworthy and yet the intellectual activity of her boys and girls far exceeded that of our own.

Having traced the debt which Battersea owed to Continental practice in its domestic arrangements, outdoor activities, gymnastic exercises and internal discipline we may turn to its academic training and note the extent to which that, too, was subject to foreign influence. Indeed in no other aspect of the college life was the result of Kay's persistent enquiries abroad more readily apparent. Reading, for example, was taught according to the 'laut or phonic method' which had been invented in Germany by a disciple of Pestalozzi named Lautier and was introduced into Battersea because so many of the students spoke with 'broad provincial accents'; Writing followed the method devised by Mülhauser, another student of Pestalozzi, because it enabled a pupil 'to learn the simplest elements of knowledge first, and then to proceed in a regularly graduated series to those combinations which, if presented in the first instance, would occasion him much difficulty and consequent discouragement'; and Arithmetic in accordance with the system of Pestalozzi himself because it, too, guided a beginner's steps from the easier to the more difficult parts of a subject with immense care and helped, whilst so doing, to fortify his intelligence.

Thus the real afflatus as far as the three basic subjects of the curriculum were concerned was Pestalozzi. And what was true of them was no less true of Geography, History, Nature Study, Mechanics, Algebra and Religion—all of which were so taught as to give 'constant exercise to the students' reasoning powers'. To study Kay's two reports on the Training School at Battersea, consequently, is to realize the importance he attached to the educational theory which had emanated from Yverdun and revolutionized the methods of instruction prevalent in Switzerland, Germany and Holland. Perhaps this was scarcely to be wondered at for, even in the early days at Norwood, he had shown a marked predilection for what he described as 'the synthetical method of teaching'. The fact remains, nevertheless, that nowhere did he give more unstinted praise to Pestalozzi than in these two reports or show a livelier appreciation of his pedagogical theories.

And, at this juncture, having traced Kay's career in some detail from 1835 onwards, we do well to take stock of the situation and note the enormous strides he had made in his understanding of educational theory and practice. From his first tentative gropings after a satisfactory educational creed he now emerged as an ardent champion of the greatest teacher of the Nature School—so ardent a champion, indeed, that occasionally he was prompted to see evidence of Pestalozzi's influence where none existed. And in this connection reference need only be made to Drawing and Singing. Both these subjects were duly emphasized at Battersea and both were taught, on Kay's own admission, according to 'the synthetical method'.[16] But, in point of fact, neither was so taught. Art, for example, was undertaken by Butler-Williams who had been sent to Dupuis for special instruction and arrived back at Battersea complete with the elaborate apparatus which has been described in the preceding chapter. And Music was in the capable hands of John Pyke Hullah who, at Kay's request, went to Paris expressly to study under Wilhem and subsequently returned to this country full of enthusiasm for the 'fixed doh' method of teaching Singing. But neither Dupuis nor Wilhem, as has already been shown, had any known connection with Pestalozzi or his theory.

The significant fact emerges, notwithstanding, that, both in Art and Music, Battersea was deeply influenced by foreign thinkers. And, as regards the latter subject, the benefit to English education was immense, for not only did Hullah win great acclaim for the college itself but likewise popularized his methods of instruction in many parts of the country. Thus, on 26th December, 1840, a notable assembly of schoolmasters, including Dr. Hawtrey, the headmaster

[16] See *First Report on the Training School at Battersea*, pp. 352 and 354

of Eton, arrived at Battersea in order to hear an account of the 'fixed doh' system—a visit which ultimately led to its adoption by such famous public schools as Eton, Winchester, Charterhouse and Merchant Taylors'.[17] On 4th February, 1841, moreover, the Battersea choir, under Hullah's direction, gave a recital of songs in Exeter Hall in the presence of Queen Adelaide, the Duke of Wellington and the Marquis of Lansdowne which attracted nation-wide publicity. And, in the course of 1842, many notable figures decided to visit the college expressly to hear its famous choir, prominent amongst whom were Prince Albert, the Duchess of Sutherland and M. François Guizot, French Ambassador to the Court of St. James and former Director of Public Instruction in Paris. In fact so unprecedented was the interest created that, in answer to popular demand, Hullah decided, during the summer of 1843, to visit various parts of the country with a select group of Battersea boys giving recitals in public halls. Some idea of the reception accorded him, moreover, may be judged from the following entry in a journal kept by Caroline Davenport [18] of Capesthorne, Cheshire:

June 11th, 1843: We expected Mr. and Mrs. Hullah to arrive at half-past ten. We stayed reading and talking till nearly twelve and they did not arrive, but just as we got into bed they came, and Mr. Kay-Shuttleworth with them. They gave a most interesting account next morning of the meeting at Manchester. Mr. Hullah says it is by far the most gratifying thing he has witnessed as a result of his system—1,500 work people from the towns round and 5,000 spectators in the great hall at Manchester. They say that at the station whilst waiting for the train afterwards they stood in groups singing and also sang as they went along standing up in open carriages. In one instance their clergyman had come with them. An address of thanks to Mr. Hullah for having placed this means of amusement within their reach was presented to him. He says they were extremely well conducted.

Such was the tremendous enthusiasm aroused by a choral concert

[17] See chapter 6 of *The History of St. John's College, Battersea*

[18] Caroline Anne Davenport (*née* Hurt), born 1814, died 1897. Married (1) Edward Davenport of Capesthorne, Cheshire, and (2) Edward John Walhouse Littleton, 1st Baron Hatherton of Teddesley. She was first cousin to Janet Shuttleworth of Gawthorpe Hall, Burnley, Lancashire, whom Dr. Kay married in 1842 assuming, under the royal licence, the name and arms of his wife and becoming known thenceforward as James Phillips Kay-Shuttleworth

in Manchester on 11th June, 1843. As we read of it we are instantly reminded of the vast assemblies that thronged the Halle-aux-Draps in Paris during the 1830's to learn singing under the inspired conductorship of Wilhem and Hubert. And the same recollection must have occurred to another who was present in Manchester on that occasion—James Kay-Shuttleworth—to whom the honour was due not merely of having discovered Hullah but of having sent him to Paris to be trained.

With such a thought in mind we may reflect on the brief history of Battersea College up to that date and note how, from the moment of its inception in the mind of Kay until the time when it won nation-wide acclaim through the efforts of Hullah, it was consciously and constantly influenced by foreign educational thought and practice. In fact so many ideas from so many men and nations went into its making that the miracle was it worked at all—ideas culled, it will be recalled, from such widely differing sources as Pestalozzi, de Fellenberg, Wehrli, Lady Noel Byron, Stow, Dupuis and Wilhem as well as from the state systems of Holland and Prussia. Reflecting on the resultant amalgam, therefore, one is driven to the conclusion that no one save a native of Britain and a remarkable conciliator could have either conceived it or made it work. To Kay-Shuttleworth, however, who eventually effected an even greater reconciliation by securing the benefits of national education without a breach between Church and State, the adjustment of conflicting opinions was the spice of life. He truly believed, in the words of Lord Morley, that there was a sharp distinction between legitimate and illegitimate compromise, and that the man who allied himself to the former 'shortened the duration of the empire of prejudice and hastened the arrival of improvement'.[19] As far as educational theory was concerned, moreover, he did so for certain definite reasons. His own investigations had convinced him that too strict an adherence to a highly inflexible system, as manifested for example in Prussia, was alien to the very nature of the English people. What was needed was something more pliable which could grow and be modified in the light of experience. And so he turned Battersea into an exemplar of all the points of educational doctrine he had learnt most to admire on his journeys through Europe.

In the last resort, however, it has to be borne in mind that he did

---

[19] See *On Compromise* by John Viscount Morley, p. 172

all this not merely because he was enamoured of foreign experiment but because he was anxious to provide England with a body of trained teachers, who would cheerfully devote their lives to instructing outcast and indigent children 'born in the worst purlieus of a great city or in the most wretched hovels on the parish waste'.[20]

[20] See p. 297 of *First Report on the Training School at Battersea*

21

THE RESULTS OF BATTERSEA AND OF OTHER REFORMATORY MEASURES DEVISED BY KAY-SHUTTLEWORTH TO IMPROVE THE STANDARD OF PRIMARY INSTRUCTION IN BRITAIN

'Among those whose labours have lifted England physically, intellectually and morally during the last forty years Kay-Shuttleworth will be held, I doubt not, by all competent judges, to have done a giant's work.'

DR. MONTAGU BUTLER, Headmaster of Harrow. 1878

IT was in February 1842, on the occasion of his marriage, that Kay-Shuttleworth decided to quit Battersea and devote his energies more specifically to the task of building up a national system of education. After acting as principal for two years he felt, with a certain amount of justice, that he had discharged his main obligations and that the time was ripe for him to hand over the reigns of responsibility to another. He insisted also that he and Tufnell could not be expected indefinitely either to maintain their co-directorship or to defray all expenses from their private purses. That there was nothing inconsistent in this attitude, moreover, may be judged from the repeated assurances which the two founders gave that they did not intend to remain permanently at Battersea. They simply hoped that, once they had effectively demonstrated the value of trained teachers, the Government would step in of its own volition and secure the future of their venture by means of adequate grants. In this, however, they were disappointed and the story of their protracted negotiations with Sir Robert Peel, Lord John Russell and Lord Lansdowne makes sorry reading.[1] The upshot was, therefore, that, in December 1843,

[1] See pp. 115–122 of *The Life and Work of Sir James Kay-Shuttleworth* by Frank Smith

they handed over Battersea to the Committee of the National Society and allowed it to continue its existence as a Church of England Training College.

There is little point in discussing here the prolonged controversies which resulted in this move for they have no bearing either on Kay-Shuttleworth's educational philosophy or his debt to foreign thinkers. What is of importance to note, however, is that, under its new principal, the Revd. Thomas Jackson, Battersea continued the wise policy formulated by its founders. Thus the ties that bound it to Europe remained unbroken for Jackson, we discover, 'spared no pains to make himself thoroughly acquainted with the best educational thought of all lands and usually passed his vacations on the Continent, visiting great masters and enquiring into their methods, just as his predecessors had done'. [2]

This connection with European thought and experience was likewise maintained by a number of other institutions that sprang into life from 1841 onwards. Such well-known colleges as Chester, St. Mark's, Whitelands, Norwich and Lincoln all developed during this period and all, to a greater or lesser extent, owed something to Battersea. Thus tangible results of Kay-Shuttleworth's and Tufnell's voyages of exploration began to manifest themselves. Indeed it was with obvious delight that in 1875 the latter remarked:

> The point of my past career which I look back upon with the greatest pride and satisfaction is the part I took in the foundation of the first training college in England—the training college at Battersea. . . . I was ashamed of my own country, and in conjunction with Lord Auckland [the Hon. and Revd. Robert Eden] and Sir James Kay-Shuttleworth [Dr. Kay], we founded the Battersea Normal School. We were poohpoohed, then abused, then imitated. The last was the only thing I cared for; and now I have the satisfaction of seeing the establishment of forty training colleges all founded upon the principles first exemplified at Battersea. [3]

From such statements we are able to discern not only the tremendous impetus which Battersea gave to educational reform but also the degree to which it influenced the curricula and methods of

[2] See p. 109 of *The History of St. John's College, Battersea* by Thomas Adkins
[3] *Ibid* p. 106

instruction adopted by other Training Colleges. In other words, thanks largely to Kay-Shuttleworth's researches, hundreds of teachers came to hear of 'the synthetical method of instruction' and to demonstrate its importance even in the most remote villages. Thus the effects of his composite educational philosophy, built up with immense difficulty between 1835 and 1839, gradually made themselves felt.

It was not alone by means of Battersea, however, that Kay-Shuttleworth helped to revitalize teaching. Indeed the founding of this pioneer college was in some respects incidental to his main work for, in 1839, he was appointed Secretary to the Committee of Privy Council on Education. During a number of years, in consequence, he discharged two wholly separate functions and spent his waking hours rushing backwards and forwards between Battersea and Whitehall. That he achieved remarkable success in both spheres of activity, moreover, cannot be questioned, though how he did so will ever be a cause of wonderment. His energy must have been prodigious. Yet the truth remains that, by sheer industry, not only did he watch over the destiny of his college until 1843 but likewise, between 1839 and 1849, served as Britain's first Permanent Secretary of Education and laid the ground plan of a national system of schools.

In view of Kay-Shuttleworth's dual rôle, therefore, it is only too easy to lose sight of the main track of his educational thought and become engrossed in the disputes that dogged his life from the moment of his appointment as first Secretary—disputes in which almost every eminent ecclesiastic and politician of the land took part and in which the Church and civil powers argued vehemently as to whether the one or the other should be in control of schools. But such controversies, vital though they are to an understanding of Kay-Shuttleworth's career, have little relevance when assessing his pedagogical beliefs, for they tend to obscure the fact that the founder of the Battersea Normal School and the Secretary of the Committee of Council were one and the same person and that many of the ideas and ideals which revolutionized primary instruction in Switzerland, Holland and Prussia were identical with those which modified educational policy in Great Britain.

Brief mention, nevertheless, must be made of the Concordat of 1840 [4] by means of which a compromise was reached between the

---

[4] See *Minutes of the Committee of Council on Education* (1839–40), p. 21

Church and the civil powers with regard to the inspection of schools
—a compromise essentially British in nature which determined that,
whilst the former should be allowed to nominate inspectors, the
latter should actually appoint them. In other words the Archbishops
were empowered to vet all would-be inspectors and issue directives
on the manner in which religious instruction should be given, whereas the Committee of Council was made fully responsible for secular
instruction. As may be seen, then, a golden opportunity was suddenly presented to Kay-Shuttleworth (Dr. Kay) to promote his
carefully conceived plans for formal education—an opportunity
which, needless to say, he exploited to the full.

Before examining the precise manner in which he did this, however, it is perhaps wise to remind ourselves of the appalling state of
primary instruction in England and Wales at the time—nowhere
more graphically depicted than in the *Minutes of the Committee of
Council on Education*. Indeed it is only by studying the detailed reports
they contain that we can form any idea of the task which confronted
Kay-Shuttleworth. In South Wales, for instance,

> the schools were, for the most part, dirty and ill-ventilated. A
> rudely constructed desk for the master occupied one corner; forms
> and desks for the children were ranged along the walls, and from
> side to side. . . . A pile of detached covers, and leaves too black
> for further use, often occupied another corner, betokening the
> result of long struggles with unmeaning rows of spelling, with con-
> finement and constrained positions, and the other adversities of
> elementary learning. In many, silence was only maintained for a
> few minutes at a time by loud exclamations and threats. In some,
> the room was also appropriated to the domestic purposes of the
> household. And in one, a deserted chapel, half the space was
> occupied with hay piled up to the roof.[5]

What was true of South Wales, moreover, was equally true of
Durham, Northumberland, Birmingham and Liverpool—all of
which were replete with sordid dame schools, classrooms of un-
speakable filth and distressingly ignorant teachers.[6]

This overwhelming evidence of neglect, supplied to Kay-Shuttleworth in the reports of the inspectors, convinced him that no matter,

[5] See *Minutes of the Committee of Council on Education* (1839–40), p. 179
[6] See *Minutes*, 1840–41, appendix III

however seemingly trivial, that touched on the betterment of schools or the welfare of children, could afford to be neglected. Accordingly one of his earliest moves was to take stock of existing conditions and suggest ways in which they might be improved. He dealt, for example, with such vexed problems as bad ventilation and unhealthy sanitary conditions, offering his expert medical advice on what he termed 'the adoption of more scientific methods of hygiene'. He also gave detailed consideration to the actual lay-out of school buildings and classrooms, the size and disposition of desks and benches, and the area that should be occupied by gardens and recreation grounds.[7] All this he did, moreover, in the hope that the school would become not merely an institution where poor children were educated but also a centre of community life where social clubs could hold regular meetings and where the working classes could spend profitable hours of study instead of resorting to the local tavern.

As may be seen, then, Kay-Shuttleworth's mind ranged far and wide over the field of education touching on a host of problems which theretofore had received but scant consideration. And the significant fact was that, even when drawing up detailed suggestions to enhance the value of schools, he once again demonstrated his indebtedness to Continental precedent. Thus the source whence he derived the bulk of his information was Holland and, in particular, Wijnbeck, the Dutch Inspector-General.[8] Indeed Kay-Shuttleworth recommended that particular attention be paid to the large primary schools which had grown up under the latter's aegis in The Hague, Haarlem, Amsterdam and Utrecht because all of them catered for upwards of a thousand children and yet, thanks largely to careful planning, promoted highly individual methods of teaching. He added further that the excellent discipline and perfect obedience of Dutch children were unrivalled, and that those estimable qualities could in no small measure be attributed to the fact that every school and every department within that school had been designed with scrupulous care.

We do well to emphasize the great importance Kay-Shuttleworth attached to Holland for there can be no doubt that he copied her in more ways than is generally suspected. Evidence has already been supplied of his enthusiasm for the tidiness, order and method that prevailed in Dutch schools and of the efforts he made to promote the

---

[7] See *Minutes*, 1839–40, appendix I   [8] *Ibid.* pp. 67–71

same characteristics in our own primary institutions. What has not been noted, however, is his admiration of the Dutch inspectorate and his attempts to embody its prevailing spirit of toleration in the British system. Indeed, if any real understanding is to be obtained of the way in which a system of school inspection took root in this country, it is essential to keep in mind not merely the Dutch Education Act of 1806 but also the pioneer efforts of such men as van der Palm and van den Ende. The latter, in particular, is worthy of note for he it was who stressed that those who were given the difficult assignment of watching over the work of others should invariably be courteous and tactful. From 1808 onwards, moreover, he insisted that those responsible for supervising school activities in the Netherlands—particularly those who worked in remote country districts—should remember that their prime responsibility was to help and to advise. Thereby he ensured that the inspectors became the friends and counsellors of pupils and teachers and not, as in Prussia, petty despots empowered to evict Jewish children from state schools or to cause the arrest of negligent parents who refused to have their sons and daughters educated.

That this policy had a profound effect upon Kay-Shuttleworth cannot be questioned, for his unpublished papers and private notes contain a number of references to what he invariably called 'Holland's wise inspectorate'. Perhaps the most cogent exposition of his views, however, was prepared for the *Minutes of the Committee of Council on Education* where, under the heading 'Instructions', he emphasized the fact that school inspectors, though intimately concerned with the discipline, management and academic training of schools, should not confine their attention solely to those ends but 'embrace a more comprehensive sphere of duty' and encourage any and every local effort that led to 'the improvement and extension of elementary education'. Furthermore, as early as 1839, he demonstrated how completely he subscribed to van den Ende's theory that school inspectors should be friendly advisers rather than carping critics—a point of view which he impressed upon such early pioneers as Allen, Gibson and Tremenheere with great earnestness.

When a system of inspection of schools aided by public grants is for the first time brought into operation [he informed them], it is of the utmost consequence you should bear in mind that this inspection is not intended as a means of exercising control, but of affording assistance; that it is not to be regarded as operating for the restraint of local efforts, but for their encouragement; and that its chief objects will not be attained without the co-operation of the school committees—the Inspector having no power to interfere and not being instructed to offer any advice or information excepting where it is invited.[9]

It was not alone by such counsels as these, however, that Kay-Shuttleworth piloted the steps of the first inspectors. In addition he supplied them with copies of recently published text books and, perhaps most significant of all, drew up 174 questions for their guidance —questions covering a wide variety of topics connected with school life from the manner in which classrooms were arranged to the way in which registers were kept. Thereby he hoped to convince them of the magnitude of their task—a fact that is readily discernible if we consult such typical questions as the following:

No. 32   Are the school-rooms sufficiently ventilated and heated?

No. 34   Is an exercise-ground provided? If so, at what distance from the school?

No. 48   Do the teachers keep up any intercourse with the parents or confine their attention to the children during the hours they are in school?

No. 64   Are corporal punishments employed? If so, what is their nature, and what are the offences to correct which they are used?

No. 86   Is any library connected with the school? If so, of what books and of what number of volumes does it consist? [10]

These questions are revealing, for they indicate the minute care with which Kay-Shuttleworth tackled any and every subject connected with school life. Indeed, during the ten years he acted as Secretary to the Committee of Council on Education, he obviously made a determined effort both to mould the inspectors' pedagogical theories in conformity with his own and to spread a new gospel of enlightenment through the land. Thus, in addition to preparing his detailed list of questions on schools, he took pains to inform the inspectors of current methods of teaching Reading, Writing and Vocal

<hr>

[9] See *Minutes*, 1839–40, pp. 22 and 23   [10] *Ibid.* pp. 33–45

Music on the Continent, describing with care the educational theories of Pestalozzi, Mülhauser and Wilhem.[11] He also outlined for their use suitable methods of teaching Grammar, Composition, Geography, History and Arithmetic, supplying them with a further list of questions especially designed to help rural schoolmasters. And the effect of this, needless to say, was momentous, for not only did it ensure that the inspectorate developed a certain uniformity of outlook but also that primary schools in many parts of the country became animated by the same stimulus and learned to place increasing reliance on enlightened pedagogical theory.[12]

It must not be imagined, however, that great educational changes were wrought throughout the country from the moment when the inspectors began their work. Such was far from being the case as any glance at the Minutes of 1843 and 1844 will testify. In fact, in many primary schools, the monitorial system still remained triumphant and incompetent teachers continued to expound the three R's in unsanitary and overcrowded rooms. Nevertheless, as time passed, people began to tire of such outmoded methods of instruction and to demand reform. 'What is necessary to make education in England as efficient as it is in Holland and Prussia?' demanded Dr. Hook, the vicar of Leeds,[13] and Kay-Shuttleworth, taking up the challenge, suggested more schools and better teachers. With a view to remedying the latter deficiency, moreover, he devised, in 1846, the famous *Minutes of the Committee of Council on Education* which ultimately ensured a regular supply of apprentice assistants for British schools.

Mention has already been made of Kay-Shuttleworth's early patronage of William Rush, of his journeys to Holland in search of information about 'a well-tried and efficient system of pupil teachers' and of the various attempts he made at Battersea to turn a number of poor orphans into efficient assistants ready for service in rural schools. It was as no mere tyro, therefore, that he framed the Minutes of 1846 which laid the ground plan of a system of pupil teachers for this country. In his scheme he announced that certain schools which had received the commendation of the inspectors,

---

[11] *Minutes*, 1840–41, pp. 33–51

[12] See article 'James Kay-Shuttleworth—Pioneer of National Education' by Professor A. V. Judges printed in *Pioneers of English Education*, 1952, p. 119

[13] See p. 175 of *The Life of Sir James Kay-Shuttleworth* by Frank Smith

should be recognized as training establishments and that young people, who were desirous of becoming teachers, should be allowed to enter them at the age of thirteen for a period of training lasting five years. He also gave notice that pecuniary benefits should attend the venture—that the pupil teachers themselves should be given a salary of £10 per annum rising by annual increments of £2 10s. to £20, and that the headmasters of the schools where they were undergoing training should receive a supplement to their salaries of £5 for one apprentice assistant, £9 for two, and £3 for every additional one. Thus he inaugurated a scheme which proved reasonably attractive to all concerned. It remains to be noted, however, that, in order to merit the annual increases of salary, the pupil teachers had to fulfil certain requirements. Throughout their period of apprenticeship they were compelled to receive at least one and a half hours' instruction daily from their headmasters, to take charge of a class of twenty-five pupils and to pass a written examination at the end of each academic year. Once their training was completed, moreover, they had to present themselves for the Queen's Scholarships on the results of which their future depended. Those who were successful received exhibitions to the value of £20 or £25 per annum for further study at a Normal School, whilst those who failed were given minor appointments in the Government revenue departments.

Such were the main provisions of the Minutes of 1846 as regards pupil teachers—minutes which had a profound effect on the educational destiny of this country. Indeed so marked was their influence that it is virtually impossible to consider primary instruction in Great Britain between 1846 and 1923 without referring to them in one guise or another. Yet their origins, odd as it may appear, were not indigenous. They lay in Holland and, in particular, in the Dutch Education Act of 1806. That important decree, it will be recalled, determined that certain children possessed of more than average ability should be coached in the evenings by their headmasters with a view to becoming assistant teachers.[14] As time progressed, moreover, it further decided, by means of supplementary clauses, that special classes should be formed in all large towns for the purpose of preparing young apprentices for the qualifying examination to the 'Rijks Kweekschool voor Schoolonderwijzers' at Haarlem. Thus, when fully implemented, the 1806 Act ensured that Dutch pupil

[14] See Horner's translation of the Cousin Report of 1836, p. 24

teachers remained under the control of their headmasters during the period of their apprenticeship and eventually rounded off their education at a Normal School—the same two conditions which, it will be noted, were insisted upon by the Minutes of 1846.

As may readily be seen, therefore, in creating a system of apprentice assistants for British schools, Kay-Shuttleworth was deeply obligated to his experience abroad. Indeed the more one studies his carefully laid plans the clearer this debt becomes, for he gave proof of it not only in the general regulations governing his scheme but also in the programme of studies he devised for the benefit of his pupil teachers—a programme which, as might be expected, clearly reflected his educational philosophy. Thus he stipulated every subject these young people should learn during their five years' apprenticeship and even went so far as to indicate at what precise stage of their training they should begin to study Decimal Arithmetic, Algebra, Geometry, etc. He sketched out the curriculum so minutely, in fact, that one cannot help wondering how rigidly it was required to be interpreted and whether, for instance, an intelligent boy with a ready grasp of Mathematics was invariably compelled to postpone the study of Algebra until his fifth year. Nevertheless one can clearly discern the purpose in Kay-Shuttleworth's mind. He was obviously attempting to lead the students from the known to the unknown in a series of graduated steps and, at the same time, to make them aware of the contribution which such teachers as Pestalozzi, Wilhem and Dupuis had given to educational thought and practice.

The 1846 Minutes, in consequence, must be reckoned as a major achievement for elementary education in this country—an achievement as great in its way as was that of the founding of Battersea or the creation of an Inspectorate. In truth, to obtain any clear idea of 'the humble origins of a state system of schools in Great Britain', these three pioneer ventures must be considered together, for they were all initiated by the same man and all designed with one purpose in view. On closer scrutiny, moreover, we may see that they were all guided and animated by the same philosophy.

To discover the central point of this philosophy may well be difficult for it is obvious that Kay-Shuttleworth, unlike Pestalozzi, built up his pedagogical beliefs by a laborious mental process rather than by intuition. The indisputable fact emerges, notwithstanding, that, by intense study both at home and abroad, he eventually determined those educational truths which he deemed to be of the greatest value and, having formed his conclusions, never changed them.

As a final comment, therefore, it is perhaps not too fanciful to compare him with Tennyson who, in reply to a question as to what his political beliefs were, once remarked: 'I am of the same politics as Shakespeare, Bacon and every sane man.' In like manner, if questioned as to the nature of his pedagogical beliefs, one feels that Kay-Shuttleworth might well have responded : 'I am of the same educational philosophy as Pestalozzi, de Fellenberg, Wehrli, Father Girard, van den Ende, Wilhem and Dupuis' and that despite the obvious absurdity of juxtaposing names which are commonly, and to some extent justifiably, taken to represent totally divergent schools of thought. In other words he viewed education steadily and viewed it whole, resolutely refusing to wander in the blind alleys of dogmatism and dispute that so frequently marred its progress, and clinging with singular tenacity to what he believed to be the best in all systems of belief. He did so, moreover, with one clear purpose in mind—to make Great Britain take her rightful place alongside Switzerland, Holland and Prussia as a champion of educational reform.

22

SUMMARY AND CONCLUSION

'To the critic all periods, types, schools of taste are in themselves
equal. In all ages there have been some excellent workmen and some
excellent work done. The question then is: In whom did the stir, the
genius, the sentiment of the period find itself? Where was the recep-
tacle of its refinement, its elevation, its taste?'

WALTER PATER—*The Renaissance*

IT is hoped that the preceding chapters, if they have served no other
purpose, have at least made clear that the year 1789 was a turning
point in the history of European civilization. Indeed it may well be
said that, from that time forward, percipient people on the Continent felt themselves to be living in a vastly different and highly
stimulating age. A fresh spirit was abroad, advanced ideas were
being hotly discussed, and the modern world with its faith in individual rights and social progress was slowly emerging. Certainly in
Switzerland, Holland and Prussia many thinkers, and among them
educationists of importance, not only recognized the changing times
but sought means of founding their work on principles faithful to the
new spirit of enquiry. And of their number special reference may be
made to Pestalozzi, de Fellenberg, Wehrli, Father Girard, van der
Palm, van den Ende, Nicolovius and Süvern—all of whom strove to
inaugurate a new era of mental and moral training for children and
all of whom subscribed to the theory, initially propounded by
Rousseau, that Nature was a better guide than precedent.

It is also hoped that, in the second half of this work, some impression has been given of the way in which Great Britain differed
from her Continental neighbours during these critical years. In 1789,
it will be recalled, though to some extent isolationist in her views because of her geographical position, she could nevertheless claim a
number of prominent subjects who were convinced that, by throw-
ing aside the Ancien Régime, France had set the rest of the world

a great example. Wordsworth, Coleridge and Fox, for instance, all reacted with great enthusiasm to French initiative at this time. Yet, within a few years, each had changed his mind and was openly contemptuous of the revolutionary doctrines. Nor was this wholly to be wondered at, for, once Napoleon came to power, few in this land were able to maintain that aloofness to the turn of events abroad which was demonstrated, for example, by Jane Austen. Indeed the majority, spurred on by a hatred of despotism, became united as they never had been before in their determination to preserve their native soil from alien occupation. And this naturally fostered among them a detestation of France and her satellites—so much so, in fact, that, when the 'grande armée' was finally routed, there existed in these islands so formidable a barrier of hostility towards ideas of Continental origin that it took the better part of thirty years to break it down.

Granted this situation, there is perhaps a particular interest in studying the efforts of a few remarkable reformers who, in the years succeeding Waterloo, pitted themselves against the tide of national insularity and strove not only to acquaint themselves with the work of prominent educationists abroad but also to persuade their compatriots how retrogressive were their ideas on schools and child-training in comparison with those entertained by the Swiss, the Dutch and the Prussians. Indeed, as chapters 12 to 21 have endeavoured to illustrate, it was largely owing to such individuals that Britain awoke to the peril of her educational position and eventually made an effort to lever herself out of the slough of intellectual inertia into which she had sunk. Their importance, then, cannot be questioned. Yet, so far in this investigation, though great emphasis has been placed both on their tours abroad and subsequent work at home, no effort has been made either to correlate their activities or to show how they themselves, quite naturally, created three spheres of influence. And, at this stage, such a task would seem to be worth attempting if only to explain the significance of Kay-Shuttleworth's educational endeavours—for he, it must be realized, more than any other man of his time, succeeded in unifying and perpetuating the ideals of a large number of those who, during the first half of the nineteenth century, sought educational inspiration abroad.

First and foremost, then, special mention must be made of such men as Synge, Greaves and Mayo—all of whom visited Switzerland, conceived a liking for Pestalozzi and, after returning to this country, either published accounts of what they had seen or started educational establishments of their own in direct imitation of the Yverdun model. Thus it was that, by 1836, the United Kingdom could boast at least two Pestalozzian schools (one at Ham and another at Cheam), a training department for nursery and primary teachers (in the Gray's Inn Road, London), and such valuable additions to her pedagogical literature as *A Biographical Sketch of the Struggles of Pestalozzi to establish his System*, *A Sketch of Pestalozzi's Intuitive System of Calculation*, *Letters on Early Education*, *Lessons on Objects* and *Lessons on Shells*. Indeed there can be little doubt that, by virtue of their endeavours, Synge, Greaves and Mayo not only presented a formidable challenge to those—and there were many such —who believed that the Bell-Lancaster system of instruction by means of monitors was the most effective method yet discovered of checking the incidence of illiteracy but also supplied evidence of new and highly individualistic ways of teaching that had long enjoyed popularity on the Continent.

What was true of them, moreover, was no less true of another band of pioneers who likewise turned to Switzerland for guidance but whose imagination was particularly fired by the work of de Fellenberg. He, it will be recalled, though immensely indebted to the pedagogical truths enunciated by Pestalozzi, nevertheless gave an original contribution to educational progress by insisting that all members of society, be they aristocrats or peasants, rich or poor, could learn to live together in harmony and good-will provided their daily occupations were closely connected with the cultivation of the land—a theory which, when translated into practice on his property at Hofwyl, made his name famous throughout Europe. Small wonder, then, that Robert Owen, after visiting Switzerland in 1818, boldly asserted that Hofwyl was 'two or three steps in advance of anything of the kind either in England or on the Continent'. And the same sentiments were echoed on several occasions between 1818 and 1835 by Henry Brougham—another ardent champion of educational reform. Nor was this all, for, in 1834, Lady Noel Byron, after a prolonged sojourn in Berne, started an experimental school for vagrant boys at Ealing Grove which was modelled on the famous 'Wehrlischule'. So successful did this venture prove and so speedily did it transform the characters of those who attended it that, within a short

time, it was copied by other reformers who were likewise anxious to
see if a life closely associated with the soil would help the offspring of
the poor—by Lord Chichester at Brighton, for example, by Lord
Lovelace at Oakham and by James Cropper at Warrington. Thus,
between 1835 and 1840, there grew up in various parts of England
a number of agricultural establishments—all of which were inspired
by the Hofwyl Poor School and all of which bore testimony to the
efficacy of de Fellenberg's pedagogical theories. In investigating
more closely the benefits that Britain derived from foreign educational experiments during the first half of the nineteenth century,
then it is obvious that, thanks to the efforts of those in this country
who were familiar with the scope of Hofwyl, a large number of
people came to realize both that de Fellenberg and Wehrli were
bold innovators and that a life associated with Nature was a powerful means of helping those whom fewest cared to help—the ignorant
and neglected offspring of the masses.

The disciples of Pestalozzi and de Fellenberg were by no means
the only people, however, to appreciate the importance of foreign
educational experiments at that time. In addition there was a small
group of enthusiasts who, having travelled abroad, became anxious
that this country, in accordance with Continental precedent, should
establish a nation-wide network of primary institutions. And of their
number special reference must be made to Sarah Austin who, in
1834, published an able translation of Cousin's *Report on the State of
Public Instruction in Prussia* and, in her preface, argued persuasively in
favour of a state system of schools. Much the same theme was stressed
by Leonard Horner when, in 1838, he published his translation of
Cuvier's *On the Establishments for Public Instruction in the Netherlands*
and of Cousin's *Narrative of my journey in Holland*. In fact, exactly as
Mrs. Austin had done, he argued that the United Kingdom would
never succeed in stamping out illiteracy unless it took steps to secure
a Ministry of Public Instruction. Unlike her, however, he drew
inspiration from the immensely tolerant state system of schools inaugurated by the Dutch in 1806. Nor were Prussia and Holland the
only countries to be held up as worthy of Britain's imitation at that
time. In 1833 J. A. Roebuck, when moving that 'the House proceed
to devise a means for the universal education of the people', gave
great praise to the Code of Popular Instruction recently promulgated by the French; and, in 1835 and 1837, both in his 'Address on

the Education of the People' and in his 'Speech on Moving the First Reading of Bills on Education', Lord Brougham emphasized the fact that nothing but good would result if teachers and administrators from this country were sent to study in Switzerland. Indeed it is perfectly clear that a variety of influences from at least four nations in Western Europe served to foster in this country an increased awareness of the advantages to be gained from a widespread extension of educational privilege.

As may be seen, then, there were, roughly speaking, three main groups of individuals who, during the first half of the nineteenth century, strove to widen the frontiers of educational experience in the United Kingdom by importing ideas from abroad. Yet, interesting though each of them was, it is clear that they would never have exercised any appreciable influence had they not, at least to some extent, become fused. And that is why considerable importance must be attached to the work of the Central Society of Education. For this important body of thinkers accepted as its guiding principles the three aims which each of the groups attempted to sponsor individually. In other words it strove to replace the mutual method by a more personal method of teaching—the ideal which inspired the educational efforts of Synge, Greaves and Mayo; to demonstrate the value of a life closely associated with the soil as did the founders of the Agricultural Schools; and to impress upon the nation the necessity of creating a state system of education—the object pursued by Mrs. Austin and Horner. Nor was this all, for it numbered among its members such reformers as de Fellenberg, Lady Noel Byron, Lord Chichester and E. Carleton Tufnell—all of whom were intent on forging a closer cultural link between Britain and the Continent. And lastly, by virtue of its annual publications, it did much to propagate foreign pedagogical discoveries in this country. There can be little doubt, therefore, that, thanks to the efforts of its secretary, B. F. Duppa, the Central Society of Education served in more ways than is generally recognized not only to cure Britain of its attitude of excessive insularity but also to prepare the ground for an administrator of rare genius who, above all things, was to bring this country into harmony with educational developments on the Continent.

And this important person, needless to say, was Dr. J. P. Kay (later Sir James Kay-Shuttleworth, Bart.) whose educational career, in some respects, may be regarded as a logical outcome of the ideas originally propounded by members of the three groups and of the Central Society of Education. Thus, even in the days when he was an Assistant Poor Law Commissioner in Norwich, he showed definite interest in the Pestalozzian method of instruction. And, at Norwood, he further extended his knowledge of foreign educational thought and practice by studying the work of de Fellenberg. In fact so interested did he become in any and every scheme that would promote the welfare of poor children and so carefully did he investigate the pedagogical ideas of such pioneers as Mrs. Austin, Leonard Horner, Lady Noel Byron, Lord Chichester and B. F. Duppa that soon he developed a clear idea of the major reforms that were required to put this country on an equal educational footing with Holland, Prussia and Switzerland. Then, by means of further research and tours to foreign parts—usually undertaken in company with his friend E. Carleton Tufnell—he acquired such familiarity with contemporary educational developments on the Continent that he became quite capable of discussing detailed questions concerning the training of teachers, curricula and methods of instruction with such acknowledged experts as van Wijnbeck, Father Girard, de Fellenberg, Wehrli, Cousin, Villemain and the Brothers of the Christian Doctrine. Nor was this all for, ever conscious of the idea that this country had much to learn from abroad, he not only gathered information wherever he went but later used it to advantage in Britain. And the upshot of this was that England could soon boast a Normal School, an inspectorate and a system of pupil teachers—all of which were deeply influenced by pedagogical theories engendered abroad. In other words, by 1846, this country had completely revised its hostile attitude towards educational ideas of foreign origin and, thanks largely to Kay-Shuttleworth's initiative, was prepared to give sympathetic consideration to methods of teaching singing and drawing imported from Paris, a system of physical training originating in the Canton de Vaud, a Training College closely modelled on that in existence at Kreuzlingen, and an inspectorate and pupil-teacher system remarkably similar to those then functioning in Amsterdam.

At this juncture, having traced the history of those pioneers of popular enlightenment in the United Kingdom who, during the first half of the nineteenth century, found a repository of educational wisdom on the Continent, it is perhaps wise to pause in our investigations and note three major results of their work.

In the first place it is obvious that, from their joint endeavours, Great Britain acquired both a healthier attitude towards social reform and an increased awareness of her responsibilities towards poor children. This does not mean that, by the mid-century, such institutions as she could boast for the benefit of the rising generation were invariably efficient. Such was far from being the case. But what it does indicate is that the inadequacies of the dame schools and common day schools were beginning to disappear, that pupil teachers were supplanting monitors, and that the training of pupil teachers was looked upon, certainly in official quarters, as essential. As evidence of this, it is necessary only to consult the *Minutes of the Committee of Council on Education* (1839–49) which manifest a lively concern that Britain, following the examples of Switzerland, Holland and Prussia, should do everything possible to give education a greater efficiency and an enhanced vitality.

Secondly there can be no doubt that, consequent upon their labours, much greater attention was paid to improved methods of tuition. In other words, as the mutual method waned in its influence, more and more people came to realize that teaching should develop the pupil as a whole, guide and stimulate self-activity, foster the growth of knowledge through the training of the senses and observe a right gradation and progression in development. And this was perhaps only to be expected for the influence of Pestalozzi made itself felt not only through direct propagandists such as Synge, Greaves and the Mayos but also through those who admired the work of de Fellenberg and those who, like Sarah Austin and Leonard Horner, were convinced that this country had much to learn from the state systems of schools then in operation in Prussia and Holland. In fact it is perfectly clear that influences from a variety of sources served to foster in this land a greater appreciation of the pedagogical truths embodied in such a work as *How Gertrude Teaches Her Children*.

And thirdly it is clear that, thanks to all these reformers, Great Britain developed a wider educational perspective and, with it, a juster appreciation of foreign pedagogical theory. Indeed it may well be argued that their efforts to familiarize themselves with all that was best in contemporary educational philosophy and to break down the insularity of their compatriots alone rendered possible such investigations of foreign systems as were undertaken by Matthew Arnold in the 1860's. And it may also be argued that their attempts to see the world with a new vision and to interpret its movements so changed the outlook of this country that thereafter it never hesitated to transplant ideas from alien soil and nourish them in its own. Thus, during the second half of the nineteenth century, we get the impact of Froebel and Herbart upon educational life in this land, and, later still, that of Madame Montessori.

As may be appreciated, then, among the reformers who, directly and indirectly, did so much to fashion the modern English educational system, special mention must be made of the handful of men and women who, during the years succeeding Waterloo, ventured from these shores to gain inspiration abroad. Yet it is all too easy, in a brief summary of this nature, to convey the im· .ession that their work was achieved without difficulty and that they themselves, conscious of their high purpose, were usually optimistic as to the outcome of their endeavours. Such, however was far from being the case, as any glance at their writings will testify. For to their contemporaries they represented mischief and the march of new ideas. Furthermore they were one and all committed to the task of forcing Britain to think along new lines—a service for which she is not apt to be over-appreciative. Indeed to study their publications is to realize not only the obstinacy, ignorance and insularity which impeded their every move, but also the feelings of exhaustion, loneliness and utter frustration which, at some time or other, each of them had to overcome. As proof of this we need only cite the following passage, written by Kay-Shuttleworth in 1853, in which, surely, he speaks as much for his predecessors as for himself. 'The obstacles to the introduction of a more efficient system of education [into this country] were so numerous as, at first, to appear almost insurmountable. The names of Bell and Lancaster had become the watchwords of party, and for a time their great exertions and success in establishing Day Schools had rendered every part of their system sacred. So great was the dread of introducing from the Continent either the rationalism or the mysticism of Germany, the democratic principles of Switzerland, or from France the sneering infidelity of Voltaire, or the natural religion of Rousseau; and especially, so strong was the national antipathy to that system of centralization which the military conquests and genius of Napoleon had spread over the

Continent that every improvement having a Continental origin was denounced as the offspring of one of these objects of dread.' [1]

Despite these difficulties, however, it may be said that such pioneers as Synge, Greaves, the Mayos, Sarah Austin, Horner, Lord Brougham, Lady Byron, Lord Chichester, Tufnell and Kay-Shuttleworth succeeded more effectively than any other reformers of their generation both in challenging the apathy of their fellow-countrymen towards educational reform and in demonstrating the superiority of foreign pedagogical discoveries. And that they were able to do so was, in a very real sense, an indication of their greatness. For neither hostility nor criticism could deflect them from their goal. They sensed aright that their creed was feared and mistrusted simply because it was new. And to this creed they clung with intensity and sometimes with irrationality.

By way of conclusion, then, we have to emphasize both their wisdom and unity of purpose. All were distressed by the ignorance of their fellow-countrymen; all felt the need of a new gospel of enlightenment which would revolutionize current methods of teaching and learning; all used foreign pedagogical theory as a basis for individual experiment at home; all strove to secure an extension of the frontiers of educational imagination; and all were intent on fostering closer cultural relationships between Britain and the Continent. Indeed without them, and particularly without Kay-Shuttleworth, it is obvious that the very foundation of our national system of primary education would have been a poorer thing. And for this reason our debt to them cannot be overestimated.

[1] See p. 60 of *Public Education as Affected by the Minutes of the Committee of Privy Council from 1846 to 1852 with suggestions as to future policy* by Sir James Kay-Shuttleworth, Bart. (1853)

BIBLIOGRAPHY

CHAPTER 1

1. *Travels in France during the years 1787, 1788 and 1789* by Arthur Young. Edited by Constantia Maxwell. Cambridge University Press. 1929
2. *De La Salle—A Pioneer of Modern Education* by W. J. Battersby. Longmans, Green. 1949
3. *The Conduct of the Schools of Jean-Baptiste de la Salle.* Translation and Introduction by F. de la Fontainerie. McGraw-Hill, New York. 1935
4. *Memoirs of Jean Frederic Oberlin* by Mrs. Francis Cunningham. Holdsworth and Ball, London. 1831
5. *Dictionnaire de Pédagogie et d'Instruction Primaire.* Edited by F. Buisson. Articles on 'Frères des Ecoles Chrétiennes', 'France' and 'Ecolâtre'. Hachette, Paris. 1887.
6. *Zur Biographie Pestalozzis—Ein Beitrag zur Geschichte der Volkserziehung* by H. Morf. Winterthur. 1869

CHAPTER 2

1. *Adventures of Ideas* by Professor A. N. Whitehead. Cambridge University Press. 1933
2. *Emile* by Jean-Jacques Rousseau. Translated by Barbara Foxley. Everyman's Library, Dent, London. 1911
3. *Rousseau on Education* by R. L. Archer. Edward Arnold, London. 1928
4. *The Living Thoughts of Rousseau* by Romain Rolland. Cassell, London. 1939
5. *The Meaning of Rousseau* by Ernest Hunter Wright. Oxford University Press. 1929
6. *Romanticism and the Modern Ego* by Jacques Barzun. Little, Brown, Boston. 1944

7. *La Réforme de l'Education au dix-huitième siècle. Basedow et le Philanthropinisme* by A. Pinloche. Armand Collin, Paris. 1889

8. *J. B. Basedows Elementarwerk.* Edited by Theodor Fritzen. Ernst Wiegandt, Leipzig. 1909

9. *Levana or the Doctrine of Education* by J. P. Richter. Longman, Brown, Green and Longmans, London. 1848

10. *Critical and Miscellaneous Essays, Volume II,* by Thomas Carlyle. Chapman and Hall, London. 1899

11. Articles on Salzmann and Richter in *Dictionnaire de Pédagogie et d'Instruction Primaire.* Edited by F. Buisson. Hachette, Paris. 1887

12. Article entitled 'Education' in *Encyclopaedia Britannica*, 9th Edition, Volume VII. Adam and Charles Black, Edinburgh. 1877

CHAPTER 3

1. *Pestalozzis sämmtliche Werke.* Edited by L. W. Seyffarth. 18 Volumes. Adolf Müller, Brandenburg

2. *J. H. Pestalozzis Ausgewählte Werke.* Edited by Friedrich Mann. 4 Volumes. Hermann Byer and Sons. Langensalze. 1902

3. *Pestalozzi and His Times.* Introduction by Professor Hans Stettbacher. Buchdruckerei Berichthaus, Zürich. 1928

4. *Pestalozzi, His Life and Work* by Roger de Guimps. Swan Sonnenschein, London. 1890

5. *Pestalozzi's Educational Writings* by J. A. Green. Edward Arnold, London. 1912

6. *How Gertrude Teaches Her Children* by J. H. Pestalozzi. Translated by Lucy E. Holland and Francis C. Turner. Edited with Introduction and Notes by Ebenezer Cooke. Swan Sonnenschein, London. 1907

7. *Begegnungen mit Pestalozzi*, with a Foreword by Willibald Klinke. Benno Schwabe, Klosterberg, Basel. 1945

8. *Pestalozzi—His Life, Work and Influence* by Hermann Krüsi. Eclectic Press, Cincinnati. 1875

9. *The Educational Ideas of Pestalozzi* by Henry Barnard. C. W. Bardeen, Syracuse, N.Y. 1881

10. *Dictionnaire de Pédagogie et d'Instruction Primaire.* Edited by F. Buisson. Article on Pestalozzi. Hachette, Paris. 1887

11. *The Education of Man.* Introduction by William H. Kilpatrick. Philosophical Library, New York. 1951

12. *Philosophy*, Volume XI, No. 43, dated July 1936. Article by Professor J. L. Stocks on 'Reason and Intuition'. Macmillan, London

CHAPTER 4

1. *Monumenta Germaniae Paedagogica*, Volume 25. Weidmannsche Buchhandlung, Berlin. 1910

2. *The Education of the Peasantry in England: what it is and what it ought to be. With a somewhat detailed account of the Establishment of M. de Fellenberg, at Hofwyl, Switzerland* by Baldwin Francis Duppa. Charles Knight, London. 1834

3. *Translation of the Reports of M. le Comte de Capo d'Istria and M. Rengger upon the Principles and Progress of the Establishment of M. de Fellenberg at Hofwyl, Switzerland* by John Attersoll, Esqre. Printed for Gossling and Redshaw, Charles Street, Soho Square, London. 1820

4. Article on de Fellenberg in *Dictionnaire de Pédagogie et d'Instruction Primaire.* Edited by F. Buisson. Hachette, Paris. 1887

5. *Vor Skole* by Hans Kyrre. Jul. Gjellerup, Copenhagen. 1933

6. *Central Society of Education—First and Second Publications.* First Publication 1837. Second Publication 1838. Printed for Taylor and Walton, Booksellers and Publishers to the Society. Upper Gower Street, London

CHAPTER 5

1. *The Establishments of M. Emanuel de Fellenberg at Hofwyl considered with reference to their claim upon the attention of men in public stations, by the Count Louis de Ville Vielle.* Longman, Hurst, Orme and Brown, London. 1820

2. *Translation of the Reports of M. le Comte de Capo d'Istria and M. Rengger upon the Principles and Progress of the Establishment of M. de Fellenberg at Hofwyl, Switzerland* by John Attersoll. Esqre. Printed for Gossling and Redshaw, Charles Street, Soho Square, London. 1820

3. *Reports on European Education* ('A Year in Europe' by John Griscom). Edited by Edgar W. Knight. McGraw-Hill, New York. 1930

4. 'Wehrlis Lebensgang und Pädagogische Bedeutung' by Philipp Hartleb in *Encyclopädisches Handbuch der Pädagogik*, Volume X. Hermann Beyer und Söhne, Langensalza. 1910

5. *The Education of the Peasantry in England; what it is and what it ought to be* by Baldwin Francis Duppa. Charles Knight, London. 1834

6. *Central Society of Education—Second Publication*. (Letter of de Fellenberg to B. F. Duppa.) Printed by Taylor and Walton, Booksellers, Upper Gower Street, London. 1838.

7. *Four Periods of Public Education* by Sir James Kay-Shuttleworth. Longmans, Green, Longmans and Roberts. 1862

8. Article on Wehrli in *Dictionnaire de Pédagogie et d'Instruction Primaire*. Edited by F. Buisson. Hachette, Paris. 1887.

CHAPTER 6

1. *L'Instruction Publique en France pendant la Révolution*. Discours et Rapports de Mirabeau, Talleyrand, Condorcet etc. C. Hippeau. Paris. 1881

2. *Essay on National Education or Plan of Studies for the Young* by Louis de La Chalotais. Translated from the French with an Historical Introduction by H. R. Clark. Edward Arnold, London. 1934

3. *Encyclopédie ou Dictionnaire raisonné des Sciences, des Arts et des Métiers par une société de gens de lettres*. 1751–65. A Genève, chez Cramer l'aîné et compagnie. 1772

4. Articles on La Chalotais, Rolland d'Erceville, Turgot and Helvétius in *Dictionnaire de Pédagogie et d'Instruction Primaire*. Edited by F. Buisson. Hachette, Paris. 1887

5. *Correspondance de Voltaire* by L. Foulet. Hachette, Paris. 1913

6. *Voltaire* by R. L. Graeme Ritchie. Nelson. 1927

7. P. L. van Eck Jr., *Pestalozziana, Bibliografiese bijdrage tot de kennis van Pestalozzi's invloed op de Nederlandse Pedagogiek* (serie: 'Losse Paedagogische Studiën') by J. B. Wolters. Groningen, Den Haag. 1927

8. *Oxford Companion to English Literature*. (Summary concerning Ephraim Chambers). Compiled and edited by Sir Paul Harvey. Oxford University Press. 1932

CHAPTER 7

1. *On the State of Education in Holland as regards Schools for the Working Classes and for the Poor* by M. Victor Cousin. Translated by Leonard Horner. John Murray, London. 1838
2. *De l'instruction publique en Hollande* by Victor Cousin. Paris. 1837
3. *Rapport sur les établissements d'instruction publique en Hollande.* Paris. 1811
4. *Geschiedkundig Overzigt van het Lager Onderwijs in Nederland, uitgegeven door de Maatschappij tot Nut van t'Algemeen.* D. du Mortier, Leyden. 1849
5. *Publicatie van Hun Hoogmogende vertegenwoordigende het Bataafsche gemeenebest, aangaande het Lager Schoolwezen en Onderwijs in de Bataafsche Republiek.* Ter Staatsdrukkerije, The Hague. 1806
6. *Paedagogische Studien, 27e jaargang, afl. 4, April 1950*
7. P. L. van Eck Jr., *Pestalozziana, Bibliografiese bijdrage tot de kennis van Pestalozzi's invloed op de Nederlandse Pedagogiek* (serie: 'Losse Paedagogische Studien') by J. B. Wolters. Groningen, Den Haag. 1927

CHAPTER 8

1. *German Education Past and Present* by Friedrich Paulsen. T. Fisher Unwin, London. 1908
2. *Addresses to the German Nation.* Translated by R. F. Jones and G. H. Turnbull. Open Court Publishing Co., Chicago and London. 1922
3. *The Educational Theory of J. G. Fichte* by G. H. Turnbull. The University of Liverpool Press. 1926
4. *Report on the State of Public Instruction in Prussia* by M. Victor Cousin. Translated by Sarah Austin. Effingham Wilson, Royal Exchange, London. 1834
5. *Reports on European Education* by John Griscom, Victor Cousin, Calvin E. Stowe. Edited by Edgar W. Knight. McGraw-Hill, New York. 1930
6. *Dictionnaire de Pédagogie et d'Instruction Primaire.* Edited by F. Buisson. Article on Prussia. Hachette, Paris. 1887
7. *Publications of the Central Society of Education. Volumes I and II.* Taylor and Walton, London. 1837 and 1838

8. *The Charity School Movement in the XVIIIth Century* by M. G. Jones. Cambridge University Press. 1938

9. *Geschichte der Erziehung vom Anfang an bis auf unsere Zeit*, Volume 5, by J. A. Schmid. J. G. Coltalsche, Stuttgart. 1901

10. *Geschichte des Gelehrten Unterrichts auf den deutschen Schulen und Universitäten vom Ausgang des Mittelalters bis zur Gegenwart*, Volume II, by Dr. Friedrich Paulsen. Leipzig. 1897

CHAPTER 9

1. Articles on 'Enseignement Mutuel', la Rochefoucauld-Liancourt, de Lasteyrie, de Laborde, Jomard, de Géranod, the Abbé Gaultier and Wilhem. Also on Spain, France, Italy, Modern Greece, Denmark, Sweden and Norway in *Dictionnaire de Pédagogie et d'Instruction Primaire*. Edited by F. Buisson. Hachette, Paris. 1887

2. *Den Danske Landsbyskoles Historie til 1848* by L. Koch. G. E. C. Gad, Copenhagen. 1882

3. *Salmonsens Konversationsleksikon*. J. H. Schultz, Copenhagen. 1915

4. *Vor Skole* by Hans Kyrre. Jul. Gjellerup, Copenhagen, 1933

5. *Pestalozzi—An Account of His Life and Work* by H. Holman. Longmans Green, London. 1908

6. *A Cyclopedia of Education* by P. Munroe. New York. 1911.

7. *The Practical Parts of Lancaster's 'Improvements' and Bell's 'Experiment.'* Edited by David Salmon. Cambridge University Press. 1932

8. *Landmarks in the History of Education* by T. L. Jarman. Cresset Press, London. 1951

9. *How to read music and understand it* by John Curwen. Edited by J. Spencer Curwen. London. 1881

CHAPTER 10

1. *Notice Biographique sur le Père Girard de Fribourg* by Ernest Naville. Joël Cherbuliez, Geneva. 1850

2. *Reports on European Education* by John Griscom, Victor Cousin, Calvin E. Stowe. Edited by Edgar W. Knight, Professor of Education University of North Carolina. McGraw-Hill, New York. 1930

3. *Dictionnaire de Pédagogie et d'Instruction Primaire.* Edited by F. Buisson. Article on 'Le Père Girard'. Hachette, Paris. 1887

4. *Pestalozzis sämmtliche Werke.* Edited by L. W. Seyffarth. 18 Volumes. Adolf Müller, Brandenburg

CHAPTER 12

1. *Publications of the Central Society of Education, Volume I.* Taylor and Walton, London. 1837

2. *The History of St. John's College, Battersea* by Thomas Adkins· National Society's Depository, London. 1906

3. *The Charity School Movement in the XVIII Century* by M. G. Jones. Cambridge University Press. 1938

4. *History of Elementary Education in England and Wales from 1800 to the Present Day* by C. Birchenough. University Tutorial Press, London. 1925

5. *Manchester and the Movement for National Elementary Education 1800–1870* by S. E. Maltby. Manchester University Press. 1918

6. *The Life and Work of Sir James Kay-Shuttleworth* by Frank Smith. John Murray, London. 1923

7. *Commentaries on the Laws of England* (Book 1) by Sir William Blackstone, Knt., one of the Justices of His Majesty's Court of Common Pleas. Tenth Edition. London. 1886

8. *An Inquiry into the Nature and Causes of the Wealth of Nations* by Adam Smith. Edited by James E. Thorold Rogers. Clarendon Press, Oxford. 1880

9. *Rights of Man—Being an Answer to Mr. Burke's Attack on the French Revolution* by Thomas Paine, Secretary for Foreign Affairs to Congress in the American War. Printed by James Cary, No. 83, North Second Street, Philadelphia. 1797

10. *An Essay on the Principles of Population, or, a View of its Past and Present Effects on Human Happiness with an Inquiry into our Prospects respecting the Future Removal or Mitigating of the Evils which it*

occasions by T. R. Malthus. Book IV. 5th Edition. John Murray, London. 1817

11. *The Works of Jeremy Bentham,* published under the Superintendence of his Executor, John Bowring. Volume I. William Tait, Edinburgh. 1859

12. *The State of the Poor; or, an history of the Labouring Classes in England, from the Conquest to the Present Day,* Volume 3, by Sir Frederic Morton Eden, Bart. Printed by J. Davis, London. 1797

13. *A History of English Literature* by Emile Legouis and Louis Cazamian. Dent, London and Toronto. 1934

14. *The Complete Poetical Works of William Wordsworth.* Macmillan. 1930

15. *Dictionnaire de Pédagogie et d'Instruction Primaire.* Edited by F. Buisson. Article on Turgot. Hachette, Paris. 1887

16. *Turgot* by G. Schelle. Felix Alcan, Paris. 1909

17. *State Intervention in English Education* by J. E. G. de Montmorency. Cambridge University Press. 1902

18. *The Old Public Schools of England* by John Rogers. Batsford, London. 1938

CHAPTER 13

1. *The Life of the Revd. Andrew Bell* by Robert Southey. In Three Volumes. John Murray, London. 1844

2. *The Practical Parts of Lancaster's 'Improvements' and Bell's 'Experiment.'.* Edited by David Salmon. Cambridge University Press. 1932

3. *The Life of Robert Owen, written by Himself. With selections from his writings and correspondences,* Volume I. Effingham Wilson, Royal Exchange, London. 1857

4. *Robert Owen, A Biography* by Frank Podmore, Volume I. Hutchinson, London. 1906

5. *Robert Owen* by G. D. H. Cole. Benn, London. 1925

6. *Robert Owen of New Lanark* (1771–1858) by Margaret Cole. Batchworth Press, London. 1953

7. *Threading My Way. Twenty-Seven Years of Autobiography* by Robert Dale Owen. Trübner, London. 1874.

8. *Memoirs of John Frederic Oberlin, Pastor of Waldbach in the Ban-de-la-Roche.* Third Edition. Holdsworth and Ball, London. 1831

CHAPTER 14

1. *Speeches of Henry Lord Brougham, upon questions relating to Public Rights, Duties and Interests; with Historical Introductions and a Critical Dissertation upon the Eloquence of the Ancients.* In Four Volumes. Edinburgh: Adam and Charles Black; Longman, Orme, Brown, Green and Longmans; Ridway and Sons; and Charles Knight and Co., London. 1838

2. 'The Speech of Mr. Henry Brougham, in the House of Commons, on Wednesday, June 28th, 1820, on the Education of the Poor.' Reprinted as Appendix 3 to *State Intervention in English Education* by J. E. G. de Montmorency. Cambridge University Press. 1902

3. *Reports from Committees: Education of the Lower Orders* by Henry Brougham. Session 27 January–10 June, 1818. Ordered by the House of Commons to be Printed, 17th March, 1818

4. *The Edinburgh Review, or Critical Journal* (December 1818–March 1819, Volume XXXI). Printed by David Wilson, Edinburgh. 1819

5. *Lord Brougham* by G. R. Garratt. Macmillan, London. 1935

6. *The Correspondence of William Wilberforce.* Edited by his sons, Robert Isaac Wilberforce and Samuel Wilberforce. In Two Volumes. John Murray, London, 1740

7. *The Creevey Papers—A Selection from the Correspondence and Diaries of the late Thomas Creevey, M.P.* Edited by the Rt. Hon. Sir Herbert Maxwell, Bart. In Two Volumes. John Murray, London. 1904

8. Hansard. *The Parliamentary Debates from the Year 1803 to the Present Time.* Volume XXXIV. From 26th Day of April to the Second Day of July, 1816. Edited by Hansard, Peterborough Court, Fleet Street, London. 1816

9. *An Outline of English Education* (1760–1902) by J. W. Adamson. Cambridge University Press. 1925

10. *A History of English Elementary Education* (1760–1902) by Frank Smith. University of London Press. 1931

CHAPTER 15

1. *A Biographical Sketch of the Struggles of Pestalozzi to establish his system; compiled and translated chiefly from his own works by an Irish traveller.* Printed by William Folds, 38 Great Strand Street, and sold by Martin Keene, College-Green, and Thomas Bowes, 69 Lower Gardiner Street, Booksellers, Dublin. 1815

2. *A Sketch of Pestalozzi's Intuitive System of Calculation, compiled and translated by an Irish traveller.* Printed by William Folds, 38 Great Strand Street, Gardiner Street, Dublin. 1815

3. *The Relations and Descriptions of Forms, according to the Principles of Pestalozzi.* Sold by Martin Keene, Booksellers, College-Green, Thomas Bowes, 67, Lower Gardiner Street, and at the Committee House for Charitable Societies, 16 Upper Sackville Street. Dublin. 1817. Printed by George P. Bull, Printer, Roundwood, Wicklow

4. *Reports from Committees: Education of the Lower Orders* by Henry Brougham. Session 27 January–10 June, 1818. Ordered by the House of Commons to be Printed, 17th March, 1818

5. *The Quarterly Educational Magazine and Record of the Home and Colonial School Society.* Volume I. Sampson Low, London. 1948.

6. *Pestalozzi and his Educational System* by Henry Barnard. C. W. Bardeen, Syracuse, N.Y. 1881

7. *Pestalozzi* by Albert Ansmann. H. Zipperlen, Stuttgart. 1946

8. *How Gertrude Teaches Her Children* by J. H. Pestalozzi. Translated by Lucy E. Holland and Francis C. Turner. Edited with Introduction and Notes by Ebenezer Cooke. Swan Sonnenschein, London. 1907

9. Articles on Greaves and Pestalozzi in *Dictionnaire de Pédagogie et d'Instruction Primaire.* Edited by F. Buisson. Hachette, Paris. 1887

10. Articles on Greaves, Charles Mayo and Elizabeth Mayo in *Dictionary of National Biography.* Edited by Leslie Stephen and Sidney Lee. Smith, Elder, London. 1908

11. *Letters on Early Education addressed to J. P. Greaves, Esq. by Pestalozzi.* Sherwood, Gilbert and Piper, Paternoster Row, London. 1827

12. *Lessons on Objects* and *Lessons on Shells* by Elizabeth Mayo. R. B. Seeley and W. Burnside, London. 1832

13. *Lessons on the Miracles of our Blessed Lord* by Elizabeth Mayo. Seeley, Burnside and Seeley, London. 1845
14. *Religious Instruction in a Graduated Series of Lessons for Young Children* by Elizabeth Mayo. Seeley, Burnside and Seeley, London. 1845
15. *Model Lessons for Infant School Teachers and Nursery Governesses* by Elizabeth Mayo. R. B. Seeley and W. Burnside, and sold by L. and G. Seeley, London. 1838
16. *Observations on the Establishment and Direction of Infants' Schools; being the substance of a lecture delivered at the Royal Institution, May 1826,* by the Rev. Charles Mayo, LL.D., Fellow of St. John's College, Oxford. L. B. Seeley and Sons, London. 1827
17. *History of Elementary Education in England and Wales* by Charles Birchenough. University Tutorial Press, London. 1925

CHAPTER 16

1. *On the State of Education in Holland as regards Schools for the Working Classes and for the Poor* by M. Victor Cousin. Translated, with Preliminary Observations on the necessity of legislative measures, to extend and improve education among the working classes and the poor in Great Britain; and on the course most advisable to pursue at the present time; by Leonard Horner, Esqre., F.R.S. John Murray, London. 1838
2. *Report on the State of Public Instruction in Prussia; addressed to the Count of Montalivet* by M. Victor Cousin. Translated by Sarah Austin. Effingham Wilson, London. 1834
3. *Publications of the Central Society of Education*—1837 and 1838. Printed for Taylor and Walton, Booksellers and Publishers to the Society, Upper Gower Street, London. 1837
4. *The Edinburgh Review, or Critical Journal* from January to July 1833, Volume LVII. Printed by Ballantyne, Edinburgh. 1833

CHAPTER 17

1. *The Life and Work of Sir James Kay-Shuttleworth* by Frank Smith. John Murray, London. 1923

2. The private papers of Sir James Kay-Shuttleworth, Bart.

3. *Report on the Training of Pauper Children* by J. Phillips Kay, Esqre., M.D. (Norwich Report). Her Majesty's Stationery Office. 1839

4. *The Edinburgh Review, or Critical Journal*, December 1818–March 1819, Volume XXXI. Printed by David Wilson, Edinburgh. 1819

5. *The Life and Letters of Anne Isabella, Lady Noel Byron, from unpublished papers in the possession of the late Ralph, Earl of Lovelace* by Ethel Colburn Mayne. Appendix IV—'History of Industrial Schools' by Lady Noel Byron. Constable and Co., Ltd., London. 1929

6. *What de Fellenberg Has Done for Education* by Lady Noel Byron. Saunders and Otley, London. 1839

7. *Minutes of the Committee of Council on Education: with Appendices* (1842–3). Her Majesty's Stationery Office. 1843

8. *The Education of the Peasantry in England: what it is and what it ought to be* by Baldwin Francis Duppa. Charles Knight, London. 1834

9. *Publications of the Central Society of Education, Volume I.* (Article by B. F. Duppa entitled 'Industrial Schools for the Peasantry'.) Printed for Taylor and Walton, Upper Gower Street, London. 1837

10. *Translation of the Reports of M. le Comte de Capo d'Istria and M. Rengger upon the Principles and Progress of the Establishment of M. de Fellenberg at Hofwyl, Switzerland* by John Attersoll, Esqre. Printed for Gossling, London. 1820

11. *Inciclopedia Italiana di Scienze, Lettere ed Arti.* Edited by Giovanni Treccani. Roma. 1936

CHAPTERS 18–21

1. *The Life and Work of Sir James Kay-Shuttleworth* by Frank Smith. John Murray, London. 1923

2. *The History of St. John's College, Battersea* by Thomas Adkins. National Society's Depository, London. 1906

3. *The Moral and Physical Condition of the Working Classes employed in the Cotton Manufacture in Manchester* by Dr. J. P. Kay. Ridgway, London. 1832

4. *Recent Measures for the Promotion of Education in England* by J. P. Kay. Ridgway, London. 1839

5. *Minutes of the Committee of Council on Education* (1839–49)

6. *Public Education* by Sir James Kay-Shuttleworth, Bart. Longman, Brown, Green and Longmans. 1853

7. *Four Periods of Public Education* by Sir James Kay-Shuttleworth, Bart. Longmans, Green, Longman and Roberts. 1862

8. *The Training of Pauper Children* by James Phillips Kay, Esqre., M.D. 1838 and 1839

9. *The Journal of Education*, July 1877. Article on 'Sir James Kay-Shuttleworth' by E. Carleton Tufnell. (New Series—No. 19)

10. Private papers of Sir James Kay-Shuttleworth including the 1877 MS., part of a diary kept in July 1841, and Caroline Davenport's Journal

11. *Dictionnaire de Pédagogie et d'Instruction Primaire.* Edited by F. Buisson. Articles on 'Wilhem' and 'Dupuis'. Hachette, Paris. 1888

12. *Translation of the Reports of M. le Comte de Capo d'Istria and M. Rengger upon the Principles and Progress of the Establishment of M. de Fellenberg at Hofwyl, Switzerland* by John Attersoll, Esqre. Printed for Gossling, London. 1820

13. *On Compromise* by John Viscount Morley. Macmillan, London. 1928

14. *Pioneers of English Education.* Edited by A. V. Judges. Article on Kay-Shuttleworth by Professor Judges. Faber, London. 1952

INDEX

Abrahamson, Captain Josef Nicolai, 109, 130
Alembert, J. le R. d', 65, 66, 143
Arnold, Matthew, 247, 279
Austin, Sarah, 190–3

Basedow, 17, 20
Battersea Training College, 246, 251–6, 259
Bell, Andrew, 101, 102, 109, 110, 128, 147–51
Bentham, Jeremy, 141
Birkbeck, Dr., 168
Blackstone, Sir William, 140
Bodmer, 24
Borough Road Society, 167, 171
Breitinger, J. J., 24
Brontë, Charlotte, 244
Brothers of the Christian Schools, *see* Christian Schools
Brougham, Lord, 158–72, 201
Buffon, Comte de, 65
Burgdorf, 31–4, 100, 113
Butler, Dr. Montagu, 261
Byron, Lady Noel, 202–8, 220, 252

Campbell, Thomas, 169
Catherine, Empress of Russia, 67
Central Society of Education, 198–200
Chalotais, La, 67
Charity Schools, English, 137
— French, 5, 6
Chateaubriand, Vicomte de, 13
Chichester, Earl of, 210, 211, 252
Chimay, Prince de, 52, 200
Christian Schools, Brothers of the, 6–9, 125, 126, 128, 237
Cleoboulos, George, 108

Clindy, 177
Committee of Council on Education 1846, Minutes of, 268–70
Condorcet, Marquis de, 68, 69, 70, 130, 143
Cousin, Victor, 79–84, 90, 98, 99, 159, 235
Cropper, James, 209, 210
Cuvier, G. L., 77

Dame Schools, 136
Dessau, 17, 18, 20, 66
Diderot, 12, 65, 66, 67, 143

Ealing Grove, 204–8
Ende, van den, 77, 82, 83, 128, 266

Fearnhead, 209
Fellenberg, P. E. de, his greatness insufficiently recognized, 42; his early life, 43; his purchase of Hofwyl, 44; his aims and methods, 45–9; his boarding school at Hofwyl, 49–51; his influence, 52; mention of, 130, 155, 156, 200, 240
Fichte, J. G., 40, 85, 88
Frederick William III, 86
Frères Ignorantins, *see* Christian Schools, Brothers of the
Fribourg, 114–24, 150, 153, 241
Froebel, Friedrich, 40

Garde, Count Jacob de la, 109
Gaultier, Abbé, 103, 130
Gauthier, J., 3